GLOBAL INEQUALITY

GLOBAL INEQUALITY

A New Approach for the Age of Globalization

BRANKO MILANOVIC

THE BELKNAP PRESS
OF HARVARD UNIVERSITY PRESS

Cambridge, Massachusetts
London, England
2016

First printing

Library of Congress Cataloging-in-Publication Data

Names: Milanović, Branko, author.
Title: Global inequality : a new approach for the age of globalization / Branko Milanovic.
Description: Cambridge, Massachusetts : The Belknap Press of Harvard University
  Press, 2016. | Includes bibliographical references and index.
Identifiers: LCCN 2015043601 | ISBN 9780674737136 (alk. paper)
Subjects: LCSH: Equality. | Income distribution. | Globalization—Social aspects. |
  Globalization—Economic aspects.
Classification: LCC HM821 .M555 2016 | DDC 305—dc23 LC record available at
  http://lccn.loc.gov/2015043601

Contents

Acknowledgments

This book is the product of years of work on income inequality in general and, more specifically, on global income inequality. Thanking everyone from whom I learned over such a long period is impossible, so I will focus more narrowly on the writing of this book. As everyone knows, the most difficult part is figuring out the structure of a book. Once I decided to begin with the greatest reshuffling of personal incomes in the past two centuries, that is, with the effects of globalization on the distribution of incomes in the world, the rest of the chapters, as in a jigsaw puzzle, quickly fell into place.

The second most difficult problem in writing a book is starting it. The dread of the first sentence. On the advice of my friend Niels Planel, who is himself a writer of nonfiction, I decided to jump-start the book by going for a week to Bocas del Toro in Panama. It was an excellent decision. After a week almost fully dedicated to the book (with a few dips in the Caribbean in between), a good part of the text was done.

It was a pleasure to learn early on from Ian Malcolm of Harvard University Press that the press was interested in publishing the book. There was also, as is often the case in such situations, an element of serendipity: I happened to be in London then, and we agreed on all the details over a coffee (or was it a tea?). Ian made significant contributions as an editor. He went through the text with great care and curiosity, all the while keeping in mind the author's best interests and suggesting revisions with precision and tact. His suggestions improved the book, and some structural modifications that he proposed made it more focused and easier to read.

Louise Robbins did a fabulous job in editing the text. I was very happy that we quickly agreed on a workable approach—where the voice of the writer would be left unaltered, but mistakes would be corrected and inconsistencies highlighted and ultimately fixed. I am very grateful to Louise for making the book better. It was a real pleasure working with her.

Others at Harvard University Press whose assistance I appreciate include Anne McGuire, who carefully checked the references, and Stephanie Vyce, who was most helpful in doing the review of the sources and quotes I used in the book.

Parts of the chapters that deal with global income distribution have been presented in various talks and conferences, and I am thankful for the feedback I received. For the material in Chapter 2, where I redefine the Kuznets hypothesis and introduce the concept of Kuznets waves, I am grateful for the excellent written comments I received from (in alphabetical order) Guido Alfani, Bob Allen, Christoph Lakner, Peter Lindert, Leandro Prados de la Escosura, and Walter Scheidel, and also for the comments that I received at seminars and conferences where I presented that part of the book: from Steve Broadberry, Ljubomir Madžar, and Filip Novokmet in Belgrade; Leandro Prados de la Escosura, Francisco Goerlich, Facundo Alvaredo, Roy van der Weide, and Peter Lanjouw in Valencia; John Bonin at

Wesleyan University; Walter Scheidel, Peter Turchin, and Peer Vries in Vienna; and Joe Stiglitz and Suresh Naidu in New York City. Carla Yumatle was very helpful with her comments and discussion of Frantz Fanon's work.

I am grateful to friends who generously shared their data with me and answered my many questions: Leandro Prados de la Escosura and Carlos Álvarez Nogal, Peter Lindert and Jeffrey Williamson, Giovanni Vecchi and Andrea Brandolini, Jonathan Cribb, Guido Alfani, Walter Ryckbosch, Javier Rodríguez Weber, Christoph Lakner and Tony Atkinson, Luis Bértola, Jan Luiten van Zanden, Wenjie Zhang, Larry Mishel, Michael Clemens, and Çağlar Özden. I would especially like to thank Ann Harrison and Peter Nolan, who were first-rate reviewers and whose many suggestions I took very seriously and tried to incorporate into the text. Janet Gornick of the Graduate Center of the City University of New York and Luxembourg Income Study, where I was based during the entire period of the writing and production of this book, was extraordinarily understanding and encouraged me to press on, even during times when I had some doubts.

My wife, Michele de Nevers, and our sons, Nikola and Georgie, were happy to see me write another book. It provided entertainment for me, and gave more free time to them. I am grateful to Michele for gracefully accepting our commuting lifestyle between New York and Washington, DC.

GLOBAL INEQUALITY

Introduction

This is a book about global inequality. Throughout the book, I look at both income inequality and political issues related to inequality from a global perspective. Because the world is not united under a single government, however, we cannot dispense with the need to look at individual nation-states. On the contrary, many global issues are played out politically at the level of the nation-state. Thus, greater openness (commercial interchange between individuals from different countries) will have political consequences not at some imaginary worldwide level but within actual countries where the people who are affected by trade live. As a consequence of globalization, for example, Chinese workers might ask for free trade union rights from their government, and US workers might ask for protective duties from their government.

Although individual nation-state economies are important, and almost all political action takes place at this level, globalization is an ever stronger force affecting everything from our income levels, our employment prospects, and the extent of our knowledge and information, to the costs of the goods we buy daily and the availability of fresh fruit in the middle of winter. Globalization also introduces new rules of the game through the nascent process of global governance, whether through the World Trade Organization, limits on CO_2 emissions, or crackdowns on international tax evasion.

It is therefore time to look at income inequality not as a national phenomenon only, as has been done for the past century, but as a global one. One reason to do so is simply out of curiosity (a trait much appreciated by Adam Smith)—our abiding interest in how other people, outside our own country, live. But in addition to "mere" curiosity, information about the lives and incomes of others may also serve more pragmatic purposes: it may help us in evaluating what to buy or sell and where, in learning ways to do things better and more efficiently, in making decisions about where to migrate. Or we may use the knowledge acquired from how things are done elsewhere in the world to renegotiate our salary with the boss, to complain about too much cigarette smoke, or to ask the waiter for a doggy bag (a custom that has spread from one country to another).

A second reason to focus on global inequality is that we now have the ability to do so: in the past decade or so, the data required to assess and compare income levels of all individuals in the world have become available for the first time in human history.

But the most important reason, as I believe the reader of this book will appreciate, is that a study of global inequality over the past two centuries, and especially during the past twenty-five years, allows us to see how the world has changed, often in fundamental ways. Shifts in global inequality reflect the economic (and frequently political) rise, stagnation, and decline of countries, changes in inequality levels within countries, and transitions from one social system or political regime to another. The rise of western Europe and North America following the Industrial Revolution has left its imprint on global inequality, driving it up. More recently, the fast growth of several Asian countries has had an equally significant impact, pushing global inequality back down. And national inequality levels, whether increasing in England during the early industrial period or increasing in China and the United States during recent decades, have also had global implications. Reading about global inequality is nothing less than reading about the economic history of the world.

This book opens with the description and analysis of the most significant changes in income distributions that have occurred globally since 1988, using data from household surveys. The year 1988 is a convenient starting point because it coincides almost exactly with the fall of the Berlin Wall and reintegration of the then-communist economies into the world economic system. This event was preceded, just a few years earlier, by a similar reintegration of China. These two political changes are not unrelated to the increased availability of household surveys, which are the key source from which we can glean information about changes in global inequality. Chapter 1 documents in particular (1) the rise of what may be called the "global middle class," most of whom are located in China and other countries in "resurgent Asia," (2) the stagnation of the groups in the rich world that are globally well-off but nationally middle- or lower-middle class, and (3) the emergence of a global plutocracy. These three salient phenomena of the past quarter century open up several important political questions about the future of democracy, which I address in Chapter 4. But before thinking about the future, we return to the past to understand how global inequality has evolved in the long run.

Global inequality, that is, income inequality among the citizens of the world, can be formally considered as the sum of all national inequalities plus the sum of all gaps in mean incomes among countries. The first component deals with inequality in incomes between rich and poor Americans, rich and poor Mexicans, and so on. The second component deals with income gaps between the United States and

Mexico, Spain and Morocco, and so on for all countries in the world. In Chapter 2 we consider within-nation inequalities, and in Chapter 3, among-nation inequalities.

In Chapter 2, I use long-term historical data on income inequality, going back in some cases to the Middle Ages, to reformulate the Kuznets hypothesis, the workhorse of inequality economics. This hypothesis, formulated by Nobel Prize–winning economist Simon Kuznets in the 1950s, states that as countries industrialize and average incomes grow, inequality will at first increase and then decrease, resulting in an inverted-U-shaped curve when one plots inequality level against income. The Kuznets hypothesis has recently been found wanting because of its inability to explain a new phenomenon in the United States and other rich countries: income inequality, which had been decreasing through much of the twentieth century, has recently been on an upswing. This is difficult to reconcile with the Kuznets hypothesis as originally defined: the increase of inequality in the rich world should not have happened.

To explain this recent upswing in inequality, as well as shifts in inequality in the past, going back to the period before the Industrial Revolution, I introduce the concept of Kuznets waves or cycles. Kuznets waves can not only satisfactorily explain the most recent spell of increasing inequality but can also be used to predict inequality's future course in rich countries like the United States or in middle-income countries like China and Brazil. I distinguish between Kuznets cycles as they apply to countries with stagnant incomes (before the Industrial Revolution) and as they apply to countries with steadily rising mean incomes (the modern era). I distinguish between two kinds of forces that drive inequality down: "malign" forces (wars, natural catastrophes, epidemics) and "benign" forces (more widely accessible education, increased social transfers, progressive taxation). I also emphasize the role of wars, which in some instances may be caused by high domestic inequality, insufficient aggregate demand,

and search for new sources of profits that require control of other countries. Wars can lead to declines in inequality but also, unfortunately, and more importantly, to declines in mean incomes.

In Chapter 3, the focus is on the differences in mean incomes among countries. Here we face the interesting situation that now, for the first time since the Industrial Revolution two centuries ago, global inequality is not being driven by rising gaps among countries. With the increases of mean incomes in Asian countries, the gaps between countries have actually been narrowing. If this trend of economic convergence continues, not only will it lead to shrinking global inequality but it will, indirectly, also give relatively greater salience to inequalities within nations. In fifty years or so, we might return to the situation that existed in the early nineteenth century, when most of global inequality was due to income differences between rich and poor Britons, rich and poor Russians, or rich and poor Chinese, and not so much to the fact that mean incomes in the West were greater than mean incomes in Asia. Such a world would be very familiar to any reader of Karl Marx, and indeed to any reader of the canonic European literature from the nineteenth century. But we are not there yet. Our world today is still a world in which the place where we were born or where we live matters enormously, determining perhaps as much as two-thirds of our lifetime income. The advantage that people born in wealthier countries possess is what I call "citizenship rent." I discuss at the end of Chapter 3 its significance, its political philosophy implications, and its direct consequence: pressure to migrate from one country to another in search of higher income.

After having looked at the separate components of global inequality, we can return to considering it as a whole. In Chapter 4, I discuss the likely evolution of global inequality in this century and the next. I avoid the seemingly exact projections of global inequality, because in reality they are treacherous: we know that even much more elementary projections of countries' GDPs per capita are most of the time not worth the paper they are written on. It is better, I believe, to try to isolate the key forces (income convergence and Kuznets waves) that are driving nations' and individuals' incomes today and to see where they might lead us in the future. We must remember, though, that in making these predictions, we are often on speculative ground.

While writing Chapter 4, I went back to some of the popular books of the 1970s and 1980s that were trying to predict the future by extrapolating from current trends. I was struck by how time-bound they were, as if imprisoned not only in their space (the place or country where they were written) but even more so in their time.

At the end of *À la recherche du temps perdu*, Proust marvels at how old people seem to touch, in their own personas, very different epochs through which they have lived. Or as Nirad Chaudhuri writes in the second volume of his beautiful autobiography (*Thy Hand, Great Anarch!*), it is not impossible to have seen, in one's lifetime, both the peak and the nadir of a civilization—Roman glory at the time of Marcus Aurelius, and the moment when the Forum was abandoned to grass-grazing sheep. Perhaps with age we acquire some wisdom and the ability to compare different epochs that might allow us to better see the future. Yet that wisdom was not evident to me in the writings of the important authors from thirty or forty years ago. It seemed to me that some authors who wrote a century or more ago were more prescient of our dilemmas today than those who were much closer to us in time. Was it because the world dramatically changed in the late 1980s with the rise of China (which nobody writing in the 1970s foresaw) and the end of communism (which similarly was never envisaged)? Can we rule out similarly unexpected events in the next several decades? I do not think so. Yet I hope, though I am far from being certain, that this wisdom of which Proust and Chaudhuri speak and which is acquired with age may be more in evidence to the reader of this book thirty or forty years hence.

I end Chapter 4 with a discussion of three important political dilemmas that face us today: (1) How will China deal with the rising participatory and democratic expectations of its population? (2) How will rich countries manage perhaps several decades of no growth among their middle classes? and (3) Will the rise of the top one-percenters nationally and globally lead to political regimes of plutocracy or, in an attempt to placate the "losers" of globalization, populism?

In the last chapter, I review the main points of the book, distilling its key lessons and making proposals that I believe will be crucial for reducing domestic and global inequalities in this century and the next. For within-national inequalities, I argue for a much greater focus on equalizing endowments (ownership of capital and level of education) rather than on taxation of current income. For global inequality, I argue in favor of faster growth of poorer countries (a rather uncontroversial position) and in favor of lower obstacles to migration (somewhat more controversially). The chapter is divided into ten reflections on globalization and inequality that are more speculative and, unlike the rest of the book, draw more on my opinions than on specific data.

Perhaps the best way to understand the organization of the book and appreciate its symmetry is by means of a schematic chart of its major chapters (Figure I.1).

As the reader can easily see (if she holds a print copy of the book, or if she looks at the total number of words in an electronic copy), this is a relatively short book. It has quite a few graphs, but I hope that they are easy to understand and will help the reader visualize the main points. It is a book that, I believe, can be read with equal appreciation and ease by specialists and by members of the general public, whether well-informed or less-well-informed (even if it is doubtful that anyone would place himself or herself into that last category).

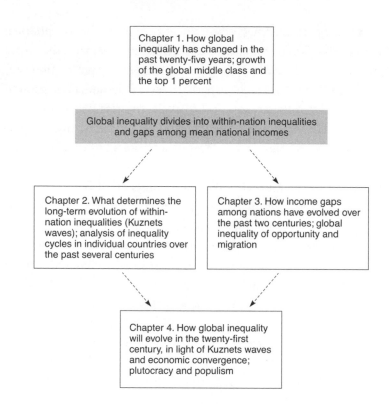

FIGURE I.1. Schematic outline of *Global Inequality*

I owe the reader an explanation about the use of pronouns in the book. I switch quite a lot between the plural *we* and the singular *I*. In general, I use *we* as the usual writer's plural—whenever I think that I am articulating a view that is shared by a significant percentage of economists, social scientists, readers of magazines, or whatever the case may be. Clearly, not everyone whom I embrace under a particular "we" may really hold that opinion. I am aware both of my ascription of opinions to large groups of people and of the fluid nature of the groups themselves. But I try to distinguish this *we* from the *I* that I use when I want to emphasize that some opinions, decisions, ideas, or terms are my own. Thus, to give an example, "we" (that is, economists working on inequality) might think that the Kuznets hypothesis has been discredited by its inability to forecast the recent rise of income inequality in rich countries, but "I" have attempted to redefine it and reformulate it here in such a way that, in the future, "we" may change our opinion about the usefulness of the hypothesis. Yet there is a long way to go before this "I" becomes a "we."

I offer now to the reader the duty—or the pleasure—of taking the first step on the road to the study of global inequality, and perhaps ultimately to global governance, and *the world as one.*

1

The Rise of the Global Middle Class and Global Plutocrats

> Intercourse between nations spans the whole globe to such an extent that one may almost say all the world is but a single city in which a permanent fair comprising all commodities is held, so that by means of money all the things produced by the land, animals and human industry can be acquired and enjoyed by any person in his own home.
>
> —GEMINIANO MONTANARI (1683)

Who Has Gained from Globalization?

The gains from globalization are not evenly distributed.

Figure 1.1 shows this phenomenon in a stark way. By plotting percentage gain in income against the original income, we can see which income groups have gained the most in the past few decades. The horizontal axis shows the percentiles of the global income distribution, ranging from the poorest people in the world on the left to the richest (the "global top 1 percent") on the extreme right. (People are ranked by after-tax household per capita income expressed in dollars of equal purchasing power; for details of how income compari-

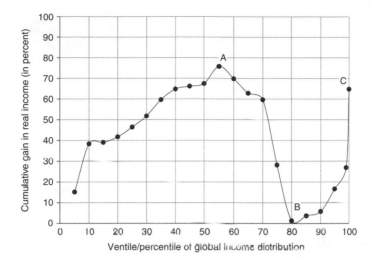

FIGURE 1.1. Relative gain in real per capita income by global income level, 1988–2008

This graph shows relative (percentage) gain in real household per capita income (measured in 2005 international dollars) between 1988 and 2008 at different points of the global income distribution (ranging from the poorest global ventile, at 5, to the richest global percentile, at 100). Real income gains were greatest among people around the 50th percentile of the global income distribution (the median; at point A) and among the richest (the top 1%; at point C). They were lowest among people who were around the 80th percentile globally (point B), most of whom are in the lower middle class of the rich world. Data source: Lakner and Milanovic (2015).

sons between countries are made, see Excursus 1.1.)[1] The vertical axis shows the cumulative growth in real income (income adjusted for inflation and differences in price levels between the countries) between 1988 and 2008. This twenty-year period coincides almost exactly with the years from the fall of the Berlin Wall to the global financial crisis. It covers the period that may be called "high globalization," an era that has brought into the ambit of the interdependent world economy first China, with a population of more than one

EXCURSUS 1.1. Where Do the Data for Global Income Distributions Come From?

There is no global household survey of individual incomes in the world. The only way to create a global income distribution is to combine as many national household surveys as possible. Such household surveys select a random sample of households and ask a number of questions on demographics (age, gender, and other characteristics of respondents) and location (where the household lives, including what province, whether in a rural or urban area, and so on), and, for our purposes the most important, questions about the sources and amounts of household income and consumption. Income data include wages, self-employment income, income from ownership of assets (interest, dividends, rental of property), income from production for the household's own consumption (very common in poorer and less monetized economies where households produce their own food), social transfers (government-provided pensions, unemployment benefits), and income deductions such as direct taxes. Consumption data cover money spent on everything from food and housing to entertainment and restaurant services.

Household surveys are the only source of such individualized, detailed information on incomes and expenditures that cover the entire distribution, from the very poor to the very rich. By contrast, data from fiscal sources, such as tax records, generally include only the households of better-off people, that is, those paying income taxes. There are many such households in the United States, but very few in India. Thus, fiscal data cannot be used to generate a worldwide distribution of income.

The size of household surveys varies. Some are large because the country is large: the Indian National Sample Survey includes more than 100,000 households, or more than half a million individuals; the US

Current Population Survey includes more than 200,000 individuals. Many surveys are small, with about 10,000–15,000 people. Such survey data, while never easily available, have recently become more accessible to researchers. For example, in the 1970s and 1980s, not only did relatively few countries conduct surveys, but it was very rare that researchers could get access to "microdata" (that is, individual household data, anonymized to preserve confidentiality). Income distributions were estimated using the government-published fractiles of income recipients (e.g., so many households with incomes between $x and $y). More recently, with greater openness of statistical offices and improvements in the processing of large data sets, almost all data, with the notable exception of China, are available at the micro level. This presents significant advantages to researchers: they can redefine income or consumption so as to be comparable across countries or produce inequality measures that are based on households, individuals, or what are called "equivalent units" (adjusting for the fact that larger households enjoy some economies of scale; that is, they do not need a proportional increase in income to be as well-off as smaller households). None of these adjustments is possible without access to the microdata.

The main sources of such microdata are the Luxembourg Income Study (LIS), which includes harmonized survey data (i.e., definitions of income variables that are made as comparable as possible between the countries), mostly from rich countries; the World Bank, which has extensive country coverage and makes some surveys available to outside researchers while other data are available only to World Bank staff; the Social and Economic Database for Latin America and the Caribbean (SEDLAC), located at Universidad de la Plata in Buenos Aires; and the Economic and Research Forum (ERF), located in Cairo, which includes surveys from the Middle East. All of these sources can be easily found on the Internet, but often access to the microdata is restricted to noncommercial uses and "bona fide" researchers, or access is difficult because of the need to know how to download massive databases and apply statistical programs. In addition, for a number of countries (e.g., India, Indonesia, and Thailand), although the data can be accessed directly from statistical offices, that process requires clearance and long waiting periods. So while access to data is becoming much better, it is still not easy. It is also important to realize that even if all the data were suddenly to become easily accessible, factors such as the sheer size of the files, complicated definitions of the variables, and comparability issues mean that income distribution data would never be as simple to use as much more aggregated statistics like Gross National Product.

Now, if each country were to conduct such surveys annually, we could, by collating them, obtain annual estimates of global income distribution. Only rich and middle-income countries have regular annual surveys, however, and even among these countries, annual surveys are something of a novelty. And in many poor countries, especially in Africa, household surveys are done at irregular intervals, on average every three or four years. There are also numerous countries that do surveys only at very long intervals, either because they have no money or technical expertise to field them or because they are at war, civil or foreign. This is the reason why global data can be put together only at approximately five-year intervals (as in this chapter) and are centered around one year, called the "benchmark year," which includes surveys from that year and one or two surrounding years.

National household surveys represent the first building block for determining the global income distribution. The second building block is conversion of such income or consumption data from local currencies into a global currency that should in principle have the same purchasing power everywhere. Why is this important? Because to assess people's incomes and make them comparable, we have to allow for the fact that price levels differ between countries. Thus, to express the real standard of living of people who live in very different environments (countries), not only do we need to convert their incomes into a single currency, but we also have to account for the fact that poorer countries generally have lower price levels. Put in simpler terms, it is less costly to attain a given standard of living in a poorer than in a richer country: ten dollars will buy more food in India than in Norway. This second building block relies on an exercise called the International Comparison Project (ICP) that is conducted at irregular intervals (the last three rounds were done in 1993, 2005, and 2011) and whose objective is to collect price data in all countries of the world and to use these data to calculate countries' price levels.

The ICP is the single most massive empirical exercise ever conducted in economics. Its final products are the so-called PPP (purchasing power parity) exchange rates. The PPP exchange rate is the exchange rate between, say, the US dollar and the Indian rupee, such that at that exchange rate a person could buy the same amount of goods and services in India as in the United States. To give an example, consider the results for 2011. The market exchange rate was 46 Indian rupees for 1 US dollar. But the estimated PPP exchange rate was 15 rupees per dollar. In other words, if you lived in India, you needed only 15 rupees to buy the same amount of goods and services as a person living in the United States could have bought with 1 dollar. The reason why you needed only 15 rupees (and not 46) is because the price level in India was lower; we can say that it was about one-third (15/46) of the US price level.

It is by applying these PPP exchange rates to the incomes from national household surveys that incomes are converted into PPP (or international) dollars and made comparable across countries. This conversion then enables us to calculate global income distribution. We can see, then, that global income distribution is impossible to calculate without two enormous empirical exercises: hundreds of national household surveys, and individual price data that are aggregated into national price indexes.

However, such massive exercises have their own problems. For household surveys, the most important problem is the imperfect inclusion of people at both ends of the income distribution: the very poor and the very rich. The very poor are omitted because household surveys choose households randomly based on place of residence. Homeless people and institutionalized populations (soldiers, prisoners, and students or workers who live in dormitories) are thus not included, and these people are generally poor. At the other end of the spectrum, the rich tend to underreport their incomes (especially their income from property) and, more alarmingly for researchers analyzing income data, sometimes refuse to participate in surveys altogether. The effect of such refusals on income distribution is difficult to prove directly (because one obviously does not know the income of a household that has refused to be interviewed) but can be estimated from where those who refuse to participate live. It has been estimated that US income inequality might be underestimated by as much as 10 percent because of such nonparticipation (Mistiaen and Ravallion 2006).

These problems are similar or even more serious in other countries and are reflected in two discrepancies between household surveys and macrodata: first, income and consumption reported from household surveys do not fully match household private income and consumption calculated from national accounts (that is, from GDP calculations), and second, statistical discrepancies (called errors and omissions) occur in balance of payments data because of, among other things, money transferred to tax havens (see Zucman 2013, 2015), which, for obvious reasons, is unlikely to be reported in surveys. It is therefore safe to say that household surveys underestimate the number of people who are poor (whatever the definition of poverty) and the number of people who are rich, and their incomes. Lakner and Milanovic (2013) try to adjust globally for the latter, but any such adjustment, while useful, contains a very large degree of arbitrariness due to the simple fact that we know next to nothing about people who refuse to participate in surveys.

The International Comparison Project also suffers from several problems. The most well-known, to which there is no theoretical solution, is the trade-off between (a) the "sameness" of the baskets of goods and services that are used to measure prices in different countries, and (b) the representativeness of such baskets. To measure differences in price levels, we would ideally like to include the same goods in the "baskets" in all countries. But if we make the baskets exactly the same, we lose representativeness because the staple goods are not the same in all countries. We could achieve identity of baskets by comparing the prices of wine, bread, and beef in all countries, for example, but such a comparison would have little meaning for countries where these items are not widely consumed (e.g., where people consume beer, rice, and fish instead).

It is difficult to find the best solution for this problem, and the ICP at times seems to err in one direction only to then overcompensate by erring in the opposite direction. This produces too much variability in the estimated price levels (see the excellent discussion by Deaton [2005] and Deaton and Aten [2014]). This variability was especially evident for the Asian countries in the last two ICP exercises, in 2005 and 2011. When Chinese or Indian price levels compared to the US price level vary by 20 to 30 percentage points between different rounds of ICP, this produces either much higher or much lower PPP incomes for those countries and thus large swings in the estimates of global inequality. Fortunately for our purposes here, such volatility affects estimated levels of global inequality much more than it affects changes in inequality (up or down) over time.

The data used in this chapter come from more than 600 household surveys covering about 120 countries and more than 90 percent of the world's population over the period 1988–2011. (Most of the data are available on my website: https://www.gc.cuny.edu/Page -Elements /Academics-Research-Centers-Initiatives/Centers-and -Institutes/Luxembourg-Income-Study-Center/Branko-Milanovic, -Senior-Scholar/Datasets.) In the more recent period, after the year 2000, all household survey data are available at the micro level (the billion people, and then the centrally planned economies of the Soviet Union and Eastern Europe, with about half a billion people. Even India can be included, since, with the reforms in the early 1990s, its economy has become more closely integrated with the rest of the world. This period also saw the communications revolution, which allowed firms to relocate factories to distant countries where they could take advantage of cheap labor without relinquishing control. There was thus a double coincidence of "peripheral" markets opening up and core countries being able to hire labor from these peripheral countries *in situ*. In many respects, the years just before the financial crisis were the most globalized years in human history.[2]

But the gains, perhaps not unexpectedly in a process of such complexity, were unequally distributed, with some people seeing no gain at all. We focus in Figure 1.1 on three points of interest, where income growth was either the highest or the lowest. They are denoted A, B, and C. Point A is around the median of the global income distribution (the median divides the distribution into two equal parts, each containing 50 percent of the population; one half better-off, the other half worse-off than the people at the median income). People at point A had the highest real income growth: some 80 percent during the twenty-year period. Growth was high, however, not just for those near the median but for a broad swath of people, ranging from those around the 40th global percentile to those around the 60th. This is, of course, one-fifth of the world population.

Who are the people in this group, the obvious beneficiaries of globalization? In nine out of ten cases, they are people from the emerging Asian economies, predominantly China, but also India, Thailand, Vietnam, and Indonesia. They are not the richest people in these countries, because the rich are placed higher in the global income distribution (that is, more to the right in the graph). They are the people around the middle of the distributions in their own countries, and, as we have just seen, in the world, too. Here are some examples of the remarkable cumulative growth experienced by these middle-income groups. The two median deciles (fifth and sixth) in urban China and rural China had their real per capita income multiplied by 3 and about 2.2, respectively, between 1988 and 2008. For Indonesia, median urban incomes almost doubled, and rural incomes increased by 80 percent.[3] In Vietnam and Thailand (where the population is not split into rural and urban), real incomes around the medians more than doubled.[4] These groups were the main "winners" of globalization between 1988 and 2008. For convenience, we call them the "emerging global middle class"—although, as I shall explain later, because they are still relatively poor compared with the Western middle classes, one should not assign to the term the same middle-class status (in terms of income and education) that we tend to associate with the middle classes in rich countries.

Let us move now to point B. The first thing to notice is that it is to the right of point A, meaning that people at point B are richer than people at point A. But we also notice that the value on the vertical axis at point B is nearly zero, indicating the absence of any growth in real income over twenty years. Who are the people in this group? They are almost all from the rich economies of the OECD (Organization for Economic Cooperation and Development).[5] If we disregard those among them who are from the relatively recent OECD members (several Eastern European countries, Chile, and Mexico), about three-quarters of the people in this group are citizens of the "old-rich" countries of Western Europe, North America, Oceania (the three areas are sometimes represented by the acronym WENAO), and Japan. In the same way that China dominates at point A, so do the United States, Japan, and Germany dominate at point B. People at point B generally belong to the lower halves of their countries' income distributions. They are from the bottom five deciles in Germany, which from 1988 to 2008 managed cumulative growth of only between 0 and 7 percent; from the lower half of the US income distribution, which experienced real growth of between 21 and 23 percent; and from the lower deciles in Japan, which saw either a decline of real income or overall growth of 3 to 4 percent. For simplicity, these people may be called the "lower middle class of the rich world." And they are certainly not the winners of globalization.

It is simply by contrasting the groups at these two points that we have established empirically something that has been felt by many people and widely discussed in economic literature as well as in public fora. We have also highlighted one of the key issues of the current globalization process: the diverging economic trajectories of people in the old rich world versus those in resurgent Asia. In short: the great winners have been the Asian poor and middle classes; the great losers, the lower middle classes of the rich world.

Such a bald statement may not surprise many people today, but it would certainly have been surprising to many if it had been made in the late 1980s. Politicians in the West who pushed for greater reliance on markets in their own economies and the world after the Reagan-Thatcher revolution could hardly have expected that the much-vaunted globalization would fail to deliver palpable benefits to the majority of their citizens—that is, precisely to those whom they were trying to convince of the advantages of neoliberal policies compared with more protectionist welfare regimes.

But such a statement would appear even more surprising to those, including the Nobel Prize–winning economist Gunnar Myrdal, who worried in the late 1960s that the Asian masses, numbering many millions and barely able to survive on their low incomes, would remain mired in perpetual poverty. An entire literature of the 1950s and 1960s (such as Paul Ehrlich's *The Population Bomb* [1968]) had as its main theme the dangers that population growth presented for economic development in the Third World. The Asian experience of the last quarter of the twentieth century has fully contradicted such dire warnings. Instead of the "Asian Drama," which was the title of Myrdal's book, we hear today about the East Asian Miracle, the Chinese Dream, and Shining India, all coined to parallel the American Dream and the German *Wirtschaftswunder* (economic miracle).

I point to this example here, very early in the book, to highlight the difficulties that beset any long-run forecasting of economic development, particularly on a global scale. The number of variables that can and do change, the role of people in history ("free will"), and the influence of wars and natural catastrophes are so great that even forecasts of broad tendencies made by the best minds of a generation are seldom correct. We should be aware of that difficulty when in Chapter 4 we discuss the likely economic and political evolution of the world in the rest of this century and the next.

The contrast between the fortunes of the two middle classes illustrates one of the key political questions today: are the gains of the middle class in Asia related to the losses of the lower middle class of the rich world? Or, to put it differently, is the stagnation of incomes (and wages, since wages account for the lion's share of income of the lower middle and the middle class) in the West a result of the success of the Asian middle class? If this wave of globalization is holding back the income growth of the rich world's middle classes, what will be the result of the next wave, involving ever-poorer and more populous countries such as Bangladesh, Burma, and Ethiopia?

Let us now go back to Figure 1.1 and look at point C. Its interpretation is simple: we are dealing here with the people who are globally very rich (the global top 1 percent) and whose real incomes have risen substantially between 1988 and 2008. They too are the winners of globalization, almost as much as (and as we shall see in a moment, in absolute terms even more than) the Asian middle classes. People who belong to the global top 1 percent are overwhelmingly from the rich economies. The United States dominates there: half of the people in the global top 1 percent are American. (This means that approximately 12 percent of Americans are part of the global top 1 percent.)[6] The rest are almost entirely from Western Europe, Japan, and Oceania. Of the remainder, Brazil, South Africa, and Russia each contribute 1 percent of their populations. We can call those in group C the "global plutocrats."

Comparison of groups B and C allows us to address another important cleavage. We have seen that group B, with zero or negligible gains from globalization, consists mainly of the lower middle class and the poorer segments of the rich countries' populations. In contrast, group C, the winners of globalization, consists of the richer classes from these same countries. An obvious implication is that the income gaps between the top and bottom have widened in the rich world, and that globalization has favored those in the rich countries who were already better-off. This too is not entirely surprising, since it is generally acknowledged that within-nation inequalities in the rich world have increased during the past twenty-five to thirty years.[7] This is the topic we shall address in Chapter 2. But what is important, and rewarding in an epistemological sense, is to see that these effects are observable when we look at the world as a whole, too.

Figure 1.1 displays only a very rough image of the winners and losers of globalization. Many additional ways to look at these data are possible: we could look in much more minute detail at the horizontal axis (splicing the world's population into smaller "fractiles" of, say, 1 percent), or we could look at how given income groups (such as the poorest 10 percent of people in China versus the poorest 10 percent of people in Argentina) have fared over the same twenty years, or we could define income gains in standard exchange-rate dollars rather than adjusting them to take into account different price levels in different countries. But whatever adjustment we make, the essential shape of the gains and losses shown here does not change: it always appears as a reclining S curve (or what some people have called an "elephant curve," because it resembles an elephant with a raised trunk). The percentage gains are always the strongest among the middle classes in emerging economies and the global 1 percent; they are always the least among people situated around the 75–90th percentile of the global income distribution, in other words, the middle and lower middle classes in OECD countries.[8]

This shape, with a trough at the position of the relatively well-off percentiles, is very unusual in the case of individual countries. Normally, graphs such as these, which are called growth incidence curves (GIC), either rise more or less continuously, indicating that the rich have gained more than the poor, or, on the contrary, slope downward continuously, demonstrating the reverse. A reclining S curve shows that the changes in income have been such that the rich and the middle class have benefited more than those in between. Within an individual country, such changes are not likely because they would imply that either economic policies or technological change had been "calibrated" in such a way as to benefit the top 1 percent or 5 percent, to go against the interests of those placed immediately below, and then to benefit those further down. Such discontinuities are not very likely to occur in the way either new technologies or new economic policies help or hamper various income groups. For example, it is not probable that a policy that cut marginal tax rates for the top 5 percent would be accompanied by another policy that increased taxes on those just below the top 5 percent level. Here, however, we are dealing not with a single country distribution but with a global distribution that is the product of several factors: (a) the differences in countries' growth rates (or to be more specific: China's faster growth rate in comparison with that of the United States), (b) countries' original positions in the global income distribution in 1988 (when China was so much poorer than the United States), and finally (c) changes in the countries' own income distributions, which are affected not only by domestic policies but by globalization (principally by China exporting cheap goods to the United States). These factors explain how such unusually shaped curves, like the reclining S curve, are possible. What do we expect the shape of the global incidence curve to look like in the next thirty years? We shall address this issue in Chapter 4.

A very important caveat regarding the interpretation of "winners" and "losers" and of the meaning of the reclining S curve is that so far we have dealt only with relative gains across the global income distribution. The vertical axis in Figure 1.1 shows the cumulative percentage change in real income between 1988 and 2008. How would the results look if instead of *relative* change (percentage gain) we considered *absolute* change (number of dollars gained)? As we shall see, this change in perspective alters the results in a rather dramatic way.

Absolute Income Gains along the Global Income Distribution

Suppose that we take the entire increment in global income between 1988 and 2008 and call it 100. Figure 1.2 shows that 44 percent of the absolute gain has gone into the hands of the richest 5 percent of people globally, with almost one-fifth of the total increment received by the top 1 percent.[9] In contrast, people whom we have termed the main beneficiaries of the current era of globalization, the "emerging global middle class" have only received (by ventile) between 2 and 4 percent of the increase in the global pie, or in total about 12–13 percent.

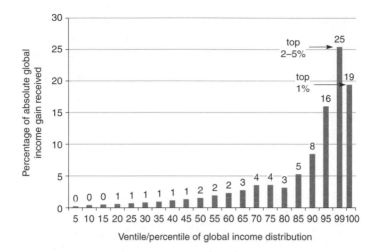

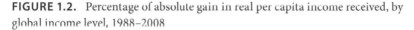

FIGURE 1.2. Percentage of absolute gain in real per capita income received, by global income level, 1988–2008

This graph shows the percentage of total absolute gain in real household per capita income (measured in 2005 international dollars) between 1988 and 2008 received by groups at different points of the global income distribution. We take the increase in total world real income as 100 and calculate how much of it was received by different ventiles (groups of 5% of the population) or percentiles of the global income distribution. The graph shows that the absolute gains in income went mostly to the richest 5% of the world population. The top 1% got 19% of the total global income increase. Data source: Lakner and Milanovic (2015).

How is this possible, and does this distribution of absolute gains invalidate our previous point regarding the winners and losers? It is possible simply because of the enormous gaps in real income that exist between the top, the median, and the bottom of the global income distribution. In 2008, the average per capita disposable (after-tax) income of the global top 1 percent was just over $71,000 per year, income at the median was around $1,400, and people who were in the poorest global decile had annual incomes under $450 (all figures are in 2005 international dollars). In looking at these numbers, we immediately see that what is but a rounding error for the incomes at the top is equivalent to the entire annual income of the poor! Now, it is clear that a very small percentage gain at the top, or around the top, will represent a huge share of the overall absolute gain. Suppose, for example that the income of the richest 1 percent increases by only 1 percent, or $710. But that amount represents one-half of the total income of the people at the global median. This is why both the large relative gains at the very top (the income of the top 1 percent grew by two-thirds between 1988 and 2008) and the almost nonexistent gains among the lower middle classes of the rich world (whose incomes increased by only 1 percent), when translated into absolute gains, look so remarkable compared with the absolute gains of the emerging global middle class. It is just a very good illustration of how hugely unequal is the distribution of incomes globally.

Does this skewed distribution in absolute gains make us revise our previous conclusion regarding the winners and losers? It does not. Rather, in some respects it emphasizes what we concluded for the richest 1 percent or 5 percent, because their considerable percentage gains appear even more stunning when we look at them in absolute amounts. (For more on absolute versus relative measures, see Excursis 1.2.) It does not make us revise our conclusion for the lower middle classes of the rich world, either, because they, like most of us, look primarily to their percentage gains (which were minimal), and when they compare their position with that of others, they are likely to contrast it with the real percentage gains realized by the top. So their income stagnation is very real. And, finally, it does not affect our conclusion about the success of the Asian middle classes either, because they too are likely to consider their relative gains first. But the introduction of the absolute measurement allows us to look at the same data from a different angle and to better perceive the immense differences in income that exist in the world today. It also highlights an important point: we should not conflate the middle classes from

EXCURSUS 1.2. Absolute versus Relative Measures of Income Inequality

In addition to highlighting the massive income gaps in the world, the comparison of relative and absolute gains in income has another value relating to the decades-old discussion of relative versus absolute measures in income distribution studies. Almost all of our inequality measures are relative, in the sense that if everybody's income increases by the same percentage, inequality is deemed unchanged. But an equal percentage increase for all corresponds to absolute gains that may be extremely unequal: a person who started the race with an income one hundred times higher will also have absolute gains that are one hundred times greater. So why are relative measures better?

First, relative income measures are conservative because they show no change in inequality in cases where absolute measures would show an increase (when all incomes go up by the same percentage) or a decrease (when they all go down by the same percentage). On inequality, which is a topic of considerable moral and political importance, and at times a very inflammatory topic indeed, we do not want to err in the direction of inflaming it further. Conservatism (in terms of measurement, not necessarily in terms of policy) is to be preferred.

Second, one of the disadvantages of absolute measures is that they are bound to increase with practically any increase in the mean: when incomes rise, the absolute distance between the rich, the middle class, and the poor becomes greater even if the relative gaps remain the same. Think of the distribution as a balloon. As the balloon expands, the absolute distance between the points on the balloon increases. Focus on absolute distances presents the disadvantage that practically every increase in the mean (blowing up the balloon) could be judged to be pro-inequality. We would lose the sharpness with which we can currently distinguish between pro-poor and pro-rich growth episodes.

With an absolute inequality criterion, it would be hard to argue that the United States entered a period of rising inequality after the 1980s (a topic which we address in Chapter 2). Since growth in the 1960s was strong, it is very likely that the absolute gaps increased then, too. So would we say that inequality in the United States started rising in 1945, or even earlier, and has not stopped since? But clearly these different periods were not the same as far as inequality is concerned.

Third, inequality and income growth are just two manifestations of the same phenomenon. Again, this point is most obvious in global inequality studies, where changes in total inequality among world citizens depend crucially on the growth rates of different countries. For the more mathematically minded, it may be easier to see this fundamental similarity between inequality and growth by thinking of the mean income as the first moment of a distribution, and of inequality as the second moment of a distribution (the variance). Growth is simply the relative increase in the first moment, and inequality is the relative increase in the second moment. The measures that we use to assess success or failure in economic development (relative change in GDP per capita) should be related to the measures we use to assess success or failure in distribution of resources (relative change in a measure of inequality). Focus on the absolutes in growth, as in inequality, would lead us to nearly always find that growth in rich countries, however small in percentage terms, would be greater than growth in poor countries, however huge. If the United States grew by 0.1 percent per capita annually, that growth would increase the absolute GDP per capita of each American by about $500, which is more than the GDP per capita of many African nations. Should we then deem Congo, in any given year, to have been as successful as the United States only if it doubles its per capita income—a feat that no human community has ever achieved in recorded history? So the logic of relativity that applies to growth should also apply to inequality.

A final argument is that relative increase in income correlates with gains in utility if we believe that personal utility functions are logarithmic in income—that for a person whose income is $10,000 to experience the same increase in welfare as a person whose income is $1,000, the absolute income gain ought to be ten times greater. In other words, one additional dollar will yield less utility, or seem less important, to a rich person than to a poor person. If we think that this is a reasonable assumption, we can then also interpret the data given in the growth incidence curve as changes in utility: an 80 percent income increase around the global median adds to the utility of people there more than a 5 to 10 percent increase in real income adds to the utility of the lower middle classes in rich countries (even if the absolute dollar gains of the latter may be larger). By this route too, we come to the conclusion that relative income changes are a more reasonable metric than absolute income changes.

the emerging market economies (people with per capita incomes of approximately between $1,000 and less than $2,000 per year) with the lower middle classes of the rich world (people with after tax incomes of approximately $5,000 to $10,000 per year; all in 2005 international dollars).

Comparison of Figure 1.1 (relative income gain) and Figure 1.2 (absolute income gain) highlights a feature that we shall often find when we analyze the changes brought about by globalization: we will very seldom be able to point to a change that has either wholly positive or wholly negative effects, or that is entirely unambiguous in its effects on all people, or in all its manifestations. In this case, we see that the much greater relative income gains for the middle classes of the emerging market economies did not always translate into greater absolute gains. By their very nature, dramatic economic movements affect various countries and groups of people differently, so that even in the case of a change that we might view as overwhelmingly positive, certain people and groups would be made worse off by it.

It is this fundamentally ambivalent nature of globalization that I hope to bring out in this book. The reader needs to be constantly aware that globalization is a force both for good and bad. Ideally, he or she, even when reading about some aspects that seem "good," should be on alert for thinking about what drawbacks or "bad" effects may lurk behind them (and conversely, when reading about "bad" effects). Our ability to comprehend and include all the "goods" and all the "bads" and to give them a subjective weighting will, in the last analysis, determine how we feel about globalization. But it is precisely this ambivalence, combined with the fact that our personal weighting schemes are by necessity different—not only because we might believe in different things, but because we ourselves or people we care about may be affected positively or negatively by globalization—that will make unanimity about the effects of globalization forever elusive.

The Effects of the Financial Crisis

We have so far discussed the changes between 1998 and 2008 because they best represent the effects of "high globalization" and because our data for that period have been well organized and made as comparable as possible. But new data and information from 2008 to 2011 are now available. In most respects, this last short period—which comes just after the financial crisis—is a continuation and even an acceleration of the globalization trends described above; but it continues the trends with a twist.

A trend that became even stronger in 2008–2011 was the growth of the global middle class, fueled during these three years, as in the previous twenty, by high growth rates in China. Between 2008 and 2011, the average urban income in China doubled, and rural incomes increased by 80 percent, driving the global growth incidence curve around the median substantially above its 1988–2008 point.

Thus the growth of the global middle class became even more visible and entrenched (see Figure 1.3).

On the other hand, the absence of growth in the rich world meant not only that the incomes of the lower middle classes in these countries continued to stagnate but also that the stagnation extended toward the top. There, too, there was no growth, and this is why point C has remained where it was in 2008 (compare Figures 1.1 and 1.3).[10]

The effect of the financial crisis on the global distribution of incomes is not surprising. What is unclear is how significant a break in global economic history this crisis, often referred to as a global financial crisis, represents. First, it should be noted that the very term

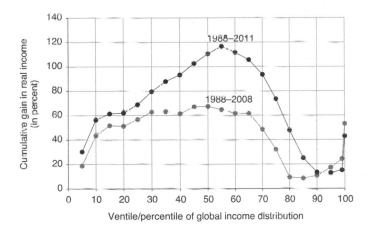

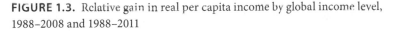

FIGURE 1.3. Relative gain in real per capita income by global income level, 1988–2008 and 1988–2011

This graph shows relative (percentage) gain in real household per capita income (measured in 2011 international dollars) at different points of the global income distribution for two different time periods: 1988–2008 (replicating the graph in Figure 1.1, except that we now use 2011 instead of 2005 international dollars) and 1988–2011. We see the continuation of very strong gains around the middle of the global income distribution but a slowdown of gains among the global top 1%. Data sources: Lakner and Milanovic (2015) and author's data.

"global" is a misnomer because the slowdown (or the recession) affected, at first, only the rich economies. It should more properly be labeled a recession among the Atlantic economies. Second, the long-term evolution of incomes at the level of nations, that is, the rebalancing of economic activity in favor of Asia and away from Europe and North America, was not interrupted but rather was reinforced by the crisis. Thus, the crisis represented not a break in this trend, but rather the reverse: reinforcement of an already existing trend. Third, the rebalancing has a counterpart in the distribution of personal incomes worldwide in the sense that it changed the shape of the global income distribution from being strongly twin-peaked (having many people at very low incomes, then practically nobody in the middle, and finally more people at very high income levels) to being fuller in the middle, such that the global income distribution is now beginning to look like the distribution of a single country. We are, of course, still far from that point, but we are certainly closer to it in 2011 (or today) than we were in 1988. This trend, too, was merely reinforced during the crisis.

Figure 1.4, which shows the distribution of world population according to income level in 1988 and 2011, illustrates very clearly the emergence of the global middle class and the diminution (flattening) of the two-humped shape of the global income distribution. What is interesting, however, is that an "emptiness in the middle" still largely characterizes the distribution of world population according to the mean income (or GDP per capita) of the country where people live, as can be seen in Figure 1.5. The contrast between the two figures illuminates the fact that while India and Indonesia, and to a somewhat lesser extent, China, remain poor countries judged by their mean incomes, income distributions in these countries are sufficiently wide and skewed to the right that a significant number of their citizens are now filling that space, the empty middle that used to exist between the two peaks.

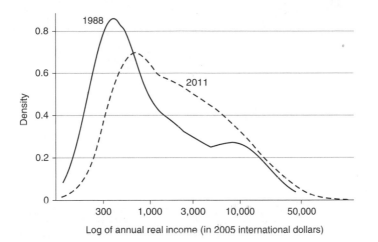

FIGURE 1.4. Distribution of world population by real per capita income, 1988 and 2011

This graph shows the distribution of world population according to real household per capita income (measured in international dollars) in 1988 and 2011, based on household surveys. The area beneath each curve is equal to total world population, respectively, in 1988 and 2011. Between 1988 and 2011, there was an expansion in the proportion of people with incomes around the middle (the "global middle class"). The graph shows that this global middle class is still relatively poor by Western standards. Data sources: Lakner and Milanovic (2015) and author's data.

The evolution of incomes in China is here again emblematic of global changes, perhaps because the increase was the fastest of any country and involved the most people. According to the household survey data for 2011, mean income in urban China has, for the first time, caught up with and even exceeded mean incomes in several European Union (EU) member countries. Urban China now has a higher mean income (in PPP terms) than Romania, Latvia, or Lithuania. In 2013, China's GDP per capita was still lower than that of the poorest EU members (Romania and Bulgaria), but the gap was less than 30 percent, and with the currently expected rates of growth, by

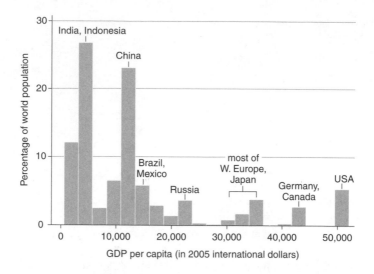

FIGURE 1.5. Distribution of world population by real GDP per capita of the country in which people live (year 2013)

This graph shows how world population would be distributed if we assigned to people their countries' mean income (GDP per capita) instead of their actual per capita income (as in Figure 1.4). Labels show selected countries. We see that there are relatively few people living in countries with "middling" levels of income. Data source: Calculated from the World Bank's World Development Indicators (WDI) database (http://data.worldbank .org/data-catalog/world-development-indicators, version September 2014).

the time the reader holds this book in his or her hands, China's GDP per capita will undoubtedly have reached the level of the poorest EU countries.[11] This is an epochal change, for although Romania, Bulgaria, and the Balkans have been the poorest part of Europe since the Middle Ages, their per capita incomes in the late nineteenth century were twice as high as China's.[12] Moreover, since we can expect that China will continue to grow faster than the core EU countries, even if its growth rate decelerates, its mean income will catch up with the EU average in another three decades.[13] This would be, in a historically very short period, a remarkable reversal of fortunes, or rather a return to a pattern of distribution characteristic of economic activity in the Eurasian space several centuries ago: per capita incomes may once again be highest in two coastal regions, one facing the Atlantic (western Europe) and the other facing the Pacific (China), while they are lowest in the hinterland of Eurasia. Peninsular Europe's exceptionalism will have come to an end.[14]

Another way to look at the change in incomes over the past several decades is to compare the mean income of people in the lower part of the US income distribution with that of people who are relatively well off in urban China (Figure 1.6). Note that since practically all of the United States is urbanized, we are de facto comparing urban

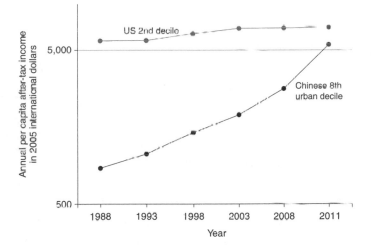

FIGURE 1.6. The convergence of Chinese and US incomes, 1988–2011

This graph shows the change in annual real household per capita after-tax income (measured in 2005 international dollars) between 1988 and 2011 for people in the US second decile and the Chinese eighth urban decile (based on household survey data). Vertical axis is in logs. Although the US second decile (while relatively poor by US standards) was still better-off than the Chinese eighth urban decile in 2011, the gap between the two has been diminishing. Data source: Author's data.

United States with urban China. The catch-up between 1988 and 2011 is quite apparent. The gap in real incomes decreased from more than 6.5 to 1 to only 1.3 to 1. (This catch-up could be illustrated by using other parts of American and Chinese distributions, but it is more striking in this example because the two income levels are becoming similar. If we used higher parts of the US distribution, the gaps would still have been very large.) There is also no doubt that this diminution of the gaps in per capita household incomes corresponds to a diminution in the real wages gap.

The Global Top 1 Percent

We have seen that although the global top 1 percent had a very good run between 1988 and 2008, their fortunes darkened between 2008 and 2011. The reason is simple: most of the people in the global top 1 percent belong to the high parts of income distributions in the rich countries (for example, 12 percent of the richest Americans are in the global top 1 percent), and their income growth slowed down or was brought to a halt by the financial crisis. This slowdown might seem surprising at first sight, given the tremendous increase in interest, awareness, and concern with top incomes in the rich world, and especially in the United States. But the contrast between the huge interest in top incomes and simultaneous slowdown in their growth is explained in part by the fact that while most incomes in rich countries declined during the crisis, top incomes remained stable or declined less. Although remaining stable might appear "good" (or perhaps even "unfair" from the point of view of other people in rich countries), it was not good enough for the global top 1 percent to maintain as high a position in comparison to the global median as before the crisis. This is because the median and the mean global income have continued to grow.

Another reason for the contrast between the recent slow growth among the global top 1 percent and popular concern with inequality is that the growth on the top was much more concentrated among the super-rich than before. In effect, if we want to focus on those who continued to gain throughout the crisis we should focus not on the global top 1 percent (which includes some 70 million people, about equal to the population of France) but on a much narrower group of super-wealthy individuals. There are, of course, many fewer of these individuals, and they are not included in household surveys.[15] We shall look at them very briefly in the next section, using an entirely different data source, *Forbes*'s list of billionaires. The list includes in 2013 and 2014 about 1,500 individuals who together with their families represent one-hundredth of one-hundredth of one percent of the world population (yes, it is 1 percent of 1 percent of 1 percent).

Let us first return to the global top 1 percent as represented in household surveys. Figure 1.7 shows the countries that have more than 1 percent of their population in the global top 1 percent. We have already seen that the United States is very well represented, with 12 percent of its population being in the global top 1 percent and accounting for about half of all the people there. Other large advanced economies, like Japan, France, and the United Kingdom, have between 3 and 7 percent of their populations in the global top 1 percent, while Germany has only 2 percent. Not shown in the graph are Brazil, Russia, and South Africa, whose top one-percenters are also in the global top 1 percent. But this is not the case for China and India, who have fewer than 1 percent of their populations in the global top 1 percent. The global top 1 percent is thus heavily dominated by the old-rich countries: China's upward march through the global income distribution has not yet spread, in sufficient numbers, to the very top.[16]

The income share of the global top 1 percent in 2008 was 15.7 percent. This number represents their share of *global* disposable income. It can be compared with *national* top 1 percent shares reported in the World Top Incomes Database (WTID), but one has to be aware that the incomes reported in WTID are before transfers and taxes and across

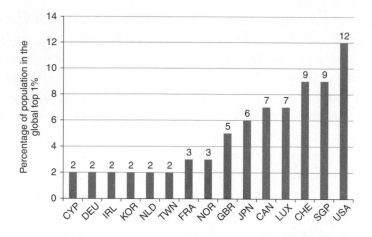

FIGURE 1.7. Percentage of national population in the global top 1% (year 2008)

This graph shows the countries that have more than 1% of their population in the global top 1%. We see that 12% of the richest Americans belong to the global top 1%. Country abbreviations: CAN Canada, CHE Switzerland, CYP Cypress, DEU Germany, FRA France, GBR United Kingdom, IRL Ireland, JPN Japan, KOR South Korea, LUX Luxembourg, NLD Netherlands, NOR Norway, SGP Singapore, TWN Taiwan, USA United States. Data source: Lakner and Milanovic (2013).

fiscal units, while incomes discussed here are after taxes and are calculated across individuals.[17] (Fiscal data cannot be used to calculate the top 1 percent share globally because fiscal data are available only for a relatively small subset of countries.) The biggest difference between the two data sources is the use of market, that is, pre-transfer and pre-tax, income by WTID rather than disposable, that is after-tax, income as used in household surveys. The share of the top 1 percent will always be greater in terms of market income than disposable income because government redistribution reduces inequality. For example, redistribution via government transfers and direct taxes in the United States in 2010 reduced the share of the top 1 percent from 9.4 percent of total market (or "pre-fisc") income to less than 7 percent of total disposable income.[18] (It should also be mentioned that the people who are in the top 1 percent according to pre-fisc income are not necessarily the same people who are in the top 1 percent according to disposable, that is post-fisc, income.) Using the United States as a comparator, we can say that the share of the global top 1 percent in world income is more than twice as high as the share of the top 1 percent in US total income (15.7 versus less than 7). This gives us a fair shorthand view of how high the concentration of income is at the global level. Yet another, more focused, view is provided by the *Forbes* annual list of billionaires.

Note, however, that when we discuss *Forbes*'s list of billionaires, we are making an important methodological move: instead of looking, as we have done so far, at incomes or consumption, which are annual flow variables, we are looking at wealth, which is a stock variable (that is, measured at one point in time) and is the result of accumulation of savings, returns on investment, and inheritance over the years. Wealth inequality is greater than inequality of income or consumption in almost every country. Not only are there tiny groups of enormously wealthy people—a phenomenon on which we shall focus in the next section—but even in the advanced countries (say, the United States or Germany), between a quarter and one-third of the population has negative or zero net wealth.[19] But very few people in these countries have zero income, and no one has zero consumption. Thus it can be seen even at an intuitive level that wealth must be much more unequally distributed than income or consumption, and that comparisons between wealth inequality and income inequality have to be made very carefully.[20] It is because the wealth data for the super-rich are of better quality (and to some extent more revealing) than the income data for the top 1 percent that we use wealth data rather than income or consumption data to shed light on the position of the super-wealthy.[21]

To see the difference between income and wealth distributions on the global level, consider Table 1.1, which shows estimates of the income and wealth shares of the global top 1 percent. For income, we have three estimates: first, the conservative one, based on household surveys alone, which (as discussed in Excursus 1.1) tend to miss the richest people and thus underestimate the share of the top 1 percent; second, an estimate which includes an adjustment that tries to correct for this problem; and third, an estimate that includes an additional correction for hidden global wealth (assets held in tax havens).[22] For the third estimate, we assume a rather strong (6 percent) return on the hidden assets, and we assume that all hidden assets belong to the global top 1 percent.[23] The income share of the richest 1 percent of people in 2010 increases from 15.7 percent under the first scenario, to 28 percent when we make an adjustment for top income underestimation in surveys, to 29 percent when we make an additional adjustment for income from hidden wealth. But all of these estimates of income share fall far short of the estimate of the global top 1 percent share in wealth made by the Credit Suisse Research Institute in 2013, which was 46 percent. From around 2000 to around 2010, the global income share of the top 1 percent either remained constant or increased slightly, while their global wealth share rose (Table 1.1).

There is thus a divergence in the evolution of income and wealth concentrations. According to the Credit Suisse Research Institute (2014), the increasing concentration in wealth is due to the strong performance of world stock markets after 2010 and to presumed higher rates of return received by the rich. The divergence between income and wealth concentrations for the top 1 percent is consistent with the picture of significant *income* gains realized by the middle of the global income distribution during the past thirty years. The growing incomes of this group have put something of a damper on the growth of the income share of the top 1 percent. But it is also very likely that the people around the global middle, who are still poor,

TABLE 1.1. Global top 1% shares in global income and global wealth

Estimate of income or wealth share	Around 2000	Around 2010
Top 1% share in global income based on household surveys alone[a]	14.5	15.7
Top 1% share in global income based on surveys and adjustment for underreporting[a]	29	28
Top 1% share in global income based on surveys, adjustment for underreporting, and adjustment for hidden wealth[b]	——	29
Top 1% share in global wealth[c]	32	46

Note: Top 1% for wealth refers to the richest 1% of adult individuals.
[a] From Lakner and Milanovic (2013); methodology of imputation explained in the paper.
[b] Additional data from Zucman (2013).
[c] For 2000 from Davies et al. (2011, 244); for 2013 from Credit Suisse Research Institute (2013, 10, table 1).

have hardly any assets at all. Consequently, their asset growth must have been very small and could not have provided any offsetting effect to the rising amounts of wealth and thus wealth share of the top 1 percent.

The Real Global Plutocrats: The Billionaires

In 2013, according to the *Forbes* list of billionaires, there were 1,426 individuals in the world whose net worth was equal to or greater than $1 billion.[24] This small and select group, together with their family members, represents one-hundredth of one-hundredth of the global 1 percent. Their total assets are estimated at $5.4 trillion. According to a 2013 Credit Suisse report (p. 5, table 1), the world's wealth is estimated

EXCURSUS 1.3. What Is a Billion?

It is very difficult to comprehend what a number such as one billion really means. A billion dollars is so far outside the usual experience of practically everybody on earth that the very quantity it implies is not easily understood—other than that it is a very large amount indeed. It might help to think of it in the following manner. Suppose that a good fairy gave you one dollar each second. How much time would elapse before you collected $1 million, and then $1 billion? For the former, you would need 11.4 days; for the latter, almost thirty-two years. Or look at it from the consumption side. Suppose now that you inherited either $1 million or $1 billion, and that you spent $1,000 every day. It would take you less than three years to run through your inheritance in the first case, and more than 2,700 years (that is, the time that separates us from Homer's *Iliad*) to blow your inheritance in the second case. Or take the problem faced by drug lords. To transport $1 million in $100 bills requires a medium-sized briefcase. To ferry $1 billion in the same banknotes would require a thousand such briefcases. Even if you used a big roller-bag, you would need about five hundred of them. And buying five hundred suitcases would attract attention that you might prefer to avoid.

at $241 trillion. This means that this super-tiny group of individuals and their families controls about 2 percent of world wealth. To put it differently, these billionaires own twice as much wealth as exists in all of Africa.

How much has the wealth of the super-rich changed during globalization? *Forbes*'s annual lists give us a good approximate means to answer that question. It is important to realize, however, that in such lists, the cut-off point is an absolute level of wealth that gradually declines in real terms if there is inflation. Thus, a registered increase in the number of such individuals is in part spurious, due simply to the lowering of the real threshold. Methodologically, this "wealth line" is identical to the poverty line: in principle, we would like to fix the poverty (or wealth) line in real terms and then check to see if the number of individuals, or their share in the total population, has gone up or down. This is indeed what we routinely do for poverty lines. Here, we have to do the same for the wealth line. In order to fix the wealth line in real terms, we use the US Consumer Price Index (CPI). Very conveniently, it turns out that the wealth line of $1 billion in 1987, when *Forbes* started publishing its global wealth lists, is equivalent in real terms to a wealth line of $2 billion in 2013 (the US price index having exactly doubled over this period). For simplicity's sake, let's call the people above that constant real level ($1 billion in 1987 prices) the hyper-wealthy or the hyper-rich.

Until 1992, *Forbes* published two separate lists: one of the four hundred richest Americans (which began in 1982), and another of global billionaires (started in 1987). In 1987, there were 49 billionaires in the United States and 96 billionaires in the rest of the world (thus in total there were 145 such individuals). *Forbes* did not calculate their combined wealth, but it may be estimated at $450 billion.[25] These two numbers (145 hyper wealthy people and $450 billion) from 1987 are what we will use to compare with the number and wealth of bi-billionaires (that is, people with net wealth in excess of $2 billion) in 2013. Conveniently, these two dates (1987 and 2013) bracket almost the same period from which we have household survey data (1988 to 2011) and thus allow us to look at what happened both on the income and the wealth sides.

In 2013, the number of bi-billionaires was 735, and their total wealth was $4.5 trillion (equivalent to $2.25 trillion in 1987 prices). Thus, both the number of hyper-wealthy people and their combined real wealth have expanded by a factor of five ($2.25 trillion versus $0.45 trillion). An obvious implication of this rough calculation is that per capita wealth of billionaires has not gone up in real terms. The average wealth of the hyper-rich was about $3 billion (in 1987 US prices) in both 1987 and 2013. There are simply many more of the hyper-rich now than there were in the late 1980s.

Meanwhile, the real world GDP has increased by 2.25 times, which is significantly less than the increase in the real wealth of the hyper-rich. As a result, the share of the hyper-wealthy individuals expressed in terms of world GDP has more than doubled, from less than 3 percent to more than 6 percent (Figure 1.8).[26]

These figures give us a reasonably firm grasp on the growth of the global plutocracy: their ranks, although tiny, have increased five-

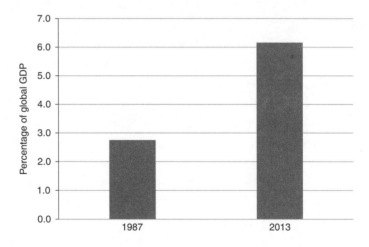

FIGURE 1.8. Wealth of hyper-wealthy individuals relative to world GDP, 1987 and 2013

This graph shows the total wealth of hyper-wealthy individuals as a share of global GDP. The hyper-wealthy are defined as people with net assets above $1 billion in 1987 US prices (equal to $2 billion in 2013 US prices). We see that their wealth increased from 1987 to 2013, relative to global GDP. Data source: Author's calculations from various *Forbes* lists.

fold, and their total wealth, measured in terms of global GDP, has more doubled. This growth, together with the expansion of the emerging global middle class, is the most significant development of the high globalization era that began in the late 1980s. What these two developments—one that may be considered hopeful, and the other perhaps ominous—might imply for the coming decades will be explored in Chapter 4. First, however, we need to address an issue that we have so far barely mentioned: income inequalities within nations and their long-term evolution. That is the subject of Chapter 2. For global inequality, inequalities within nations do play a role, but today it is a subsidiary role because their influence on global inequality is less than the influence of differential growth rates of poor, middle-income, and rich countries. However, as we shall see in Chapter 3, this rather minor role of within-nation inequality has not always been the case and in the future might change again. Moreover, so far we have intentionally focused solely on changes in global magnitudes. But national inequalities are still the most important form of inequality from the political point of view. Our world is politically organized into nation-states, and it is inequalities within nations that people most frequently debate, on which they most ardently disagree, and on whose long-term movements there exist various theories. In the next chapter I discuss within-nation inequalities and propose an alternative theory of their long-run evolution that is more complete and satisfactory, in my view, than the existing theories.

2

Inequality within Countries

Introducing Kuznets Waves to Explain Long-Term Trends in Inequality

> The long swings in income inequality must be viewed as part of a wider process of economic growth and interrelated with similar movements in other elements.
> —SIMON KUZNETS

The Origins of Dissatisfaction with the Kuznets Hypothesis

Dissatisfaction with the Kuznets hypothesis—the idea that inequality is low at very low income levels, then rises as the economy develops, and eventually falls again at high income levels—is not new, but recent developments seem to have delivered it a *coup de grâce*. While previous disenchantments had much to do with the failure to see an upswing of inequality in cross-sectional data, that is, when one moves from very poor countries to those slightly less poor, or with not finding such upswings in the historical experience of individual countries, the real blow was administered by a much graver issue on which the data are very clear: the recent increase in income inequality in the rich world. The downward-sloping portion of the Kuznets curve, which signaled declining inequality in rich countries, seemed to behave as envisaged by Kuznets until the 1980s. Since then, contrary to expectations, it has disappeared and transformed itself into an upward-sloping curve. The indubitable increase in inequality in the United States, the United Kingdom, and even in some fairly egalitarian countries like Sweden and Germany, is simply incompatible with the Kuznets hypothesis.[1]

What kept the Kuznets hypothesis alive despite this dissatisfaction was the absence of a coherent alternative explanation for the recent rise in inequality in advanced countries. One such contender was the concept of a race between education and what is known as skill-biased technological progress (that is, technological change that favors high-skilled workers), as proposed by Tinbergen (1975) and more recently reformulated by Goldin and Katz (2010). This is not a theory or a hypothesis, however, but simply an explanation of a phenomenon that we observe: the wages of more-skilled workers have increased more than the wages of the less skilled. There is no theoretical argument to tell us under what conditions to expect that the race will be won by technology (thus increasing inequality), and under what conditions by education (thus lowering inequality). In Tinbergen's original formulation, however, the race was supposed to have been won by education, with more highly skilled people becoming more numerous as countries grew richer and with skills thus swamping the effects of the technological change. This is why Tinbergen expected the skill premium to go to zero.[2] But here too, the very opposite has happened: the skill premium has shown a strong increase in most advanced countries during the past twenty years. Note also that Tinbergen's theory, like Kuznets's, holds that inequality should be expected to decrease with development—a conclusion that is unambiguously contradicted by the facts.

It was Thomas Piketty's *Capital in the Twenty-First Century,* a book of extraordinary breadth and influence, that presented a theory to effectively displace Kuznets's. The problem was how to explain both the decrease in inequality in rich countries in the period 1918–1980 and its subsequent increase. Piketty argued that the decrease was a special and unusual event driven by the political forces of wars, taxation to finance the wars, socialist ideology and movements, and economic convergence (which kept the growth rate of wages above the growth rate of income from property). The "normal" capitalist constellation, under which we live today, yields, in Piketty's view, rising inequality, as it did in the pre–World War I period. This theory thus explains both portions of the Kuznets curve—which, in Piketty's view, is U-shaped rather than inverted-U-shaped as Kuznets thought.

But can Piketty's approach explain changes in inequality in the preindustrial period? Consider Figure 2.1, which plots inequality levels (measured by Gini coefficients)[3] for the past two to three centuries for the United States and the United Kingdom, the two countries that are exemplars of capitalist development and where the data are most plentiful. If one looks at the period 1850–1980, the results are almost fully consistent with the inverted-U-shaped curve that Kuznets's theory predicts (as well as any empirical data can come close to theory). The problem with Kuznets's approach is that it cannot explain the rising inequality that occurred after 1980. In contrast, Piketty's ideas explain the trajectory of inequality in the United States and the United Kingdom over the period of almost one hundred years from the early twentieth to the early twenty-first century, but if we extend our gaze further back, into the eighteenth and nineteenth centuries, we see an increase in inequality that Piketty's theory does not explain. It could perhaps be said that inequality during that period followed the usual pattern of increase with capitalist development (similar to what is happening today), but that explanation implies that inequality in a capitalist system inexorably rises unless it is checked by wars, other calamities, or political

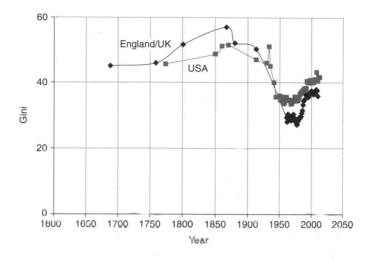

FIGURE 2.1. Inequality in England/UK and the United States from the 17th century to the 21st century

This graph shows the long-term evolution of the Gini, a measure of income inequality ranging from 0 = full equality to 100 = full inequality, in England (United Kingdom in the twentieth century) and the United States. Data sources: See sources listed for Figures 2.10 and 2.11.

action, a statement which is manifestly at odds with reality: periods of decreasing inequality driven by economic forces have occurred under capitalism. Even technically, inequality (whether estimated by top income shares or by Gini coefficients), is, unlike GDP per capita, bounded from above and cannot keep on rising forever. More realistically (not simply because the Gini coefficient ranges in value from 0 to 1), it is bounded from above by such factors as the complexity of modern societies, social norms, large social transfer systems funded by taxation, and the threat of rebellion. Thus, to say that inequality must always increase under capitalism, as some of Piketty's commentators have averred either as a compliment or a criticism (Varoufakis 2014; Mankiw 2015), does not make much sense and is factually incorrect.[4] But Piketty leaves unexplained what forces will check the rise of inequality under capitalism other than wars or political agitation.

In conclusion, the three most influential theories of income inequality all have a *prima facie* problem explaining the modern facts. Kuznets's and Tinbergen's problem is with the most recent period, and Piketty's with the period before the twentieth century.

Kuznets Waves: A Definition

The objective of this chapter is to propose an extension of the Kuznets hypothesis which I label the Kuznets wave or cycle (the terms will be used interchangeably), and which I believe is able to explain, in general terms, changes in inequality in the period prior to the Industrial Revolution, the subsequent period up to the Reagan-Thatcher revolution, and the most recent period. I shall argue that the modern historical era, the past five hundred years, is characterized by Kuznets waves of alternating increases and decreases in inequality.

Before the Industrial Revolution, when mean income was stagnant, there was no relationship between mean income level and the level of inequality. Wages and inequality were driven up or down by idiosyncratic events such as epidemics, new discoveries (of the Americas or of new trade routes between Europe and Asia), invasions, and wars. If inequality decreased as mean income and wages went up and the poor became slightly better off, Malthusian checks would be triggered: the population would increase to unsustainable levels and would ultimately be driven down (as the average per capita income declined) by higher mortality rates among the poor. This would push the poor back to subsistence level and raise inequality to its previous (higher) level. In the case of wars, when the mean income of a society is very low, there are only two possibilities: either most of the costs are borne by the rich and inequality decreases, or the income of the poor falls below the subsistence level, in which case population drops. It is not unreasonable to assume that, no matter how exploitative rulers were, and how indifferent to the fate of the poor, very few societies could afford the second solution. It is also a self-defeating policy, since a population decline means a reduction in the number of able-bodied males who could be pressed into the military. This is why the first solution would be preferable, and why we expect wars in preindustrial societies to have often led to a reduction in inequality.[5]

In a nutshell, for the period before the Industrial Revolution, I argue that inequality moved in Kuznets waves undulating around a basically fixed average income level. Kuznets waves are related to but not the same as Malthusian waves. In a Malthusian cycle, higher mean income and lower inequality (with real wages going up) triggers a population increase among the poor that, in turn, reduces their wages, pushes inequality up, and checks further population growth. Unlike Malthusian cycles, however, Kuznets cycles can be driven by nondemographic factors, such as modest growth or an influx of gold, which at first increase the gap between landlords and traders on the one hand, and workers on the other, but then push inequality down as labor gets scarcer. Kuznets cycles may be thought of as a broad concept that subsumes Malthusian cycles in special cases where the "action" that drives inequality up or down takes place almost entirely through the change in the denominator (population).

With the Industrial Revolution and the sustained increase in the mean income, the situation changes and wages generally increase *pari passu* with income (or, during the Golden Age of Capitalism, even faster). There are two important implications of the Industrial Revolution for the behavior of income inequality.

First, inequality now can increase more than before because a higher total income allows a part of the population to enjoy much higher incomes without driving everybody else below the starvation point. Higher total income simply gives more "space" for inequality to increase, assuming that everybody must have at least a subsistence income. This idea underlies the "inequality possibility frontier" as defined by Milanovic, Lindert, and Williamson (2011): when the mean income is just slightly above subsistence and we "require" that population not decline, then the surplus above subsistence must be small, and even if entirely taken by the elite, it cannot result in huge inequality (measured across the entire population). This is because all but a tiny elite will have the same income. But as the mean income rises, the surplus above the subsistence level increases as well, and the possible, or feasible, inequality becomes greater. The inequality possibility frontier is a locus of *maximum feasible* inequality levels (measured by the Gini coefficient) that obtain for different values of mean income. The frontier is concave: maximum feasible inequality increases with mean income but at a decreasing rate. Figure 2.2 shows the relationship: for a mean income level equal to subsistence, the

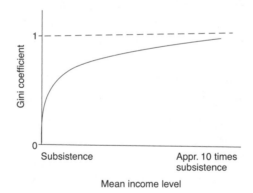

FIGURE 2.2. Inequality possibility frontier: the locus of maximum feasible Gini coefficients as a function of mean income level

This graph shows the maximum feasible inequality (measured by the Gini coefficient) for various levels of average per capita income. Maximum feasible inequality is defined as maximum inequality under the condition that no person has an income lower than subsistence.

maximum Gini coefficient is 0. It then gradually increases as mean income exceeds subsistence, and when it exceeds it by 15–20 times, the maximum Gini coefficient is close to 1 (or to 100 if expressed in percent).[6]

Second, after the Industrial Revolution, inequality and mean income entered into a relationship that was absent before, when the mean income was fixed. I argue that a structural change (movement into a much more diversified manufacturing sector) and urbanization, along the lines proposed by Kuznets, drove inequality up starting from the time of the Industrial Revolution to a peak in the rich countries which occurred at the end of the nineteenth century or the beginning of the twentieth.

After that point, again as proposed by Kuznets, inequality decreased as the supply of more-educated labor and the demand for redistribution increased, and return on capital (which was always closely associated with higher inequality) went down.[7] This was a "benign" mechanism (resulting from economic and demographic forces) that reduced inequality. But there was also a "malign" mechanism (consisting of wars and revolutions) that pushed inequality down in the rich countries after World War I. I argue that it is the interplay of these two mechanisms (malign and benign) that explains the downward portion of the first Kuznets wave—the decline in inequality that occurred throughout the rich world during most of the twentieth century and is often referred to as the Great Leveling. The downward movement was precipitated by a malign mechanism (the First World War), which itself, as we shall see later in this chapter, was the product of large domestic inequalities. The downward slide then continued thanks to the economic and social forces set into motion by the war. The combination of malign and benign forces, or war and welfare—the two ways by which inequality can be reduced in modern societies—will play an important role in our explanation of past, but also future, changes in inequality.[8]

The forces that drove inequality down after World War I had come to an end by the 1980s, the period around which we date the beginning of the second Kuznets curve for the rich countries (i.e., for postindustrial societies). The 1980s ushered in a new (second) technological revolution, characterized by remarkable changes in information technology, globalization, and the rising importance of heterogeneous jobs in the service sector. This revolution, like the Industrial Revolution of the early nineteenth century, widened income disparities. The increase in inequality happened in part because the new technologies strongly rewarded more highly skilled labor; drove up the share of, and the return to, capital; and increasingly opened the economies of rich countries to competition from China and India (the effects of which we saw in Chapter 1). The structure of demand, and thus of jobs, moved toward services, which in turn were staffed by less qualified and worse-paid labor. On the other hand, some service sector jobs, as in finance, were extremely highly paid. This widened wage, and ultimately income, distribution.[9]

In addition, pro-rich policies reinforced these trends. One could regard such policies as exogenous to the technological revolution and globalization, but that would be wrong. The new policies that started in the early 1980s were not driven so much by dissatisfaction with the performance of the welfare state (which was their original and ostensible rationale) as by the process of globalization, inherent in the information revolution. If dislike of a bloated welfare state had been the reason for reducing tax rates on high incomes and for taxing capital income at a lower rate than labor income (in a throwback to the period before the French Revolution), then the size of the state would have been diminished and the process would eventually have come to a halt once the "government" was sufficiently reduced in size. But neither happened. The size of the welfare state, despite attracting much criticism during the Reagan-Thatcher era, and even later during the "New Labour" or the "new Democrat" eras of Tony

Blair and Bill Clinton, did not change much.[10] The tax policies, however, remained in place. The reason why they did so was economic necessity. In the era of information technology and globalization, it is simply more difficult to tax mobile capital that, with freely accessible information and the global reach of banks and stock markets, can easily move from one jurisdiction to another.[11] In a reversal of the well-known adage of Karl Marx that "proletarians have no homeland," it could be said that in the present era, capital and capitalists have no homeland. Capital has thus become much more difficult to control and tax. This has exacerbated the increase in inequality.

A summary of the malign and benign forces that lower inequality in preindustrial, industrial, and postindustrial societies is shown in Table 2.1. The main difference between the two types of forces is that benign forces are lacking in societies with a stagnant mean income. It is only in growing economies that forces of rising education, greater political participation, and an aging population demanding social protection impart downward pressure on income inequality. In other words, it is not accidental that societies with higher (and growing) income are also societies that have a higher level of education and greater political rights and have gone through the demographic transition. Among the benign forces, I also list low-skill-biased technological change. I will have more to say about it at the end of this chapter, but this force is one, I believe, that has not been sufficiently explored and might hold some promise for the future. For historical reasons, we are used to thinking of technological progress as capital-driven, embodied in machines, and either complementing high-skilled labor (and thus raising the wage premium) and/or replacing low-skilled labor and thus producing the same effect of increasing the wage gap. We cannot exclude the possibility that some types of technological progress may enhance the productivity of low-skilled labor and thus be pro-poor. But it has been hard to identify what these might be.

TABLE 2.1. Malign and benign forces that reduce inequality

Type of society	Malign forces	Benign forces
Societies with stagnant mean income	*Idiosyncratic events* Wars (through destruction) Civil conflict (state breakdown) Epidemics	
Societies with a rising mean income	Wars (through destruction and higher taxation) Civil conflict (state breakdown)	Social pressure through politics (socialism, trade unions) Widespread education Aging population (demand for social protection) Technological change that favors low-skilled workers

When it comes to malign forces, however, there is more similarity between preindustrial and modern societies because war and civil conflict play a role in both stagnant and expanding economies. The effect of wars on inequality in preindustrial societies probably varied depending on whether they were wars of conquest, like the ones prosecuted by the Roman Empire at its peak, which led to increased inequality through the creation of servile labor, or wars that resulted in state collapse and thus reduced inequality. In other words, in preindustrial economies wars could be either pro- or anti-inequality. In modern times, because of mass mobilization, destruction of property, and progressive taxation, wars are (or have been so far) inequality-reducing. However, as the nature of war changes and as wars begin to affect fewer people because of the formation of professional armies, the future effects of wars on inequality might change too.

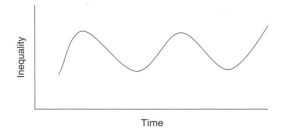

FIGURE 2.3. Expected pattern of changes in inequality over time, from the preindustrial through the postindustrial period

This graph shows regular cycles of inequality unfolding over time.

Another malign force, disease, has been more important in stagnant than in expanding economies. The massive epidemics that have destroyed so many lives in preindustrial societies and thus have often led to increases in real wages and declines in inequality have, luckily, been absent in more developed societies. Outbreaks of diseases like HIV/AIDS and Ebola have not had a demonstrable effect on reducing inequality in rich countries.

In a highly stylized way, what we expect to find when we consider inequality over time is a cyclical pattern, as shown in Figure 2.3.

But when we look at changes in inequality versus income per capita (where income is really a proxy for structural changes such as industrialization or the movement of people from rural to urban areas), we expect to find a pattern such as that shown in Figure 2.4.[12]

At low income levels (say, below $1,000 or $2,000 per year in 1990 international dollars), there would be both increases and decreases of inequality while the mean income is stagnant, resulting in a scrambled picture resembling a noise signal.[13] But with the first and second technological revolutions, we would expect to find a much clearer picture of rises and then declines in inequality with increasing income.

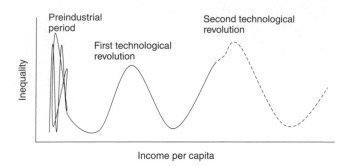

FIGURE 2.4. Expected pattern of changes in inequality versus income per capita from the preindustrial through the postindustrial period and into the future (dotted line)

This graph shows that the pattern of regular cycles of inequality unfolding over time (as shown in Figure 2.3) changes when inequality is plotted against mean income instead of time. Changes in inequality versus mean income are irregular in preindustrial societies but shift into regular cycles in industrial and postindustrial societies.

An interesting question to ask is what might happen if the growth rate decelerated and fell to zero, and the economy became stagnant, but at a much higher level of income than in stagnant preindustrial economies. It is not inconceivable that Kuznets cycles would continue to take place against the background of an unchanging mean income, producing a picture similar to the one we have for preindustrial economies.

In the next section, I discuss the movement of Kuznets waves before the Industrial Revolution. I shall, rather conventionally, set the middle of the nineteenth century as the borderline between preindustrial and modern times (for societies that underwent the Industrial Revolution at that time).[14] As in many similar works on inequality which operate at a high level of abstraction, I have to rely on relatively few pieces of evidence. Even so, the evidence is incomparably more abundant than when Kuznets was writing in 1955. We can chart probable movements of inequality over several centuries for a dozen countries. To this empirical substantiation of my claim I now turn.

Inequality in Societies with a Stagnant Mean Income

Figure 2.5 shows inequality of income (approximated by the ratio of land rent to wages) in Spain over a period of more than five centuries, as calculated in seminal works by two Spanish economists, Carlos Álvarez-Nogal and Leandro Prados de la Escosura (2007, 2009, and 2013). The graph, which plots inequality on the vertical axis against time on the horizontal axis, shows the usual features of a Kuznets curve: alternating upswings and downswings in inequality. Kuznets graphs are often presented in this way, as inequality against time (e.g., in Figure 2.1), but they can be interpreted within the context of the Kuznets hypothesis only so long as the passage of time is accompanied by a steady increase in per capita income or another relevant structural change. Increasing income with time is what we usually expect in the modern era, where the long-term growth rate in advanced economies over the period 1820–2010 was around 1–1.5 percent per capita annually. In this case, there is not much difference between looking at the evolution of inequality over time versus looking at it over GDP per capita since, over the long term, time and income progress together. (It is still preferable to use income rather than time, however, because it is a much better proxy of the structural transformation that underlies the Kuznets hypothesis.)

So when we use the results produced by Álvarez-Nogal and Prados de la Escosura to investigate the Kuznets hypothesis in its standard formulation, we have to plot inequality against an estimate of real income. This is done in Figure 2.6. The striking feature of this graph is the absence of any regularity: our measure of inequality goes up and down, that is, it oscillates around an average number without any relationship to the mean income (GDP per capita). This lack of a

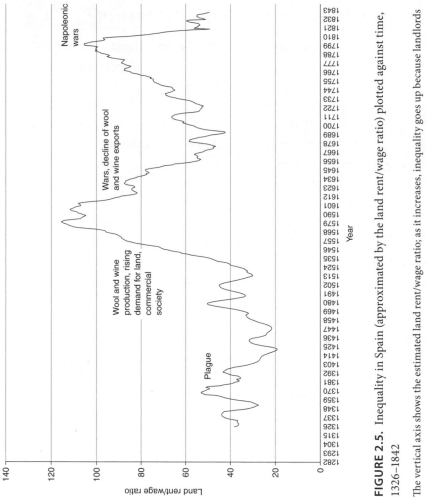

FIGURE 2.5. Inequality in Spain (approximated by the land rent/wage ratio) plotted against time, 1326–1842

The vertical axis shows the estimated land rent/wage ratio; as it increases, inequality goes up because landlords gain relative to workers. Data source: Álvarez-Nogal and Prados de la Escosura (2007, 2013).

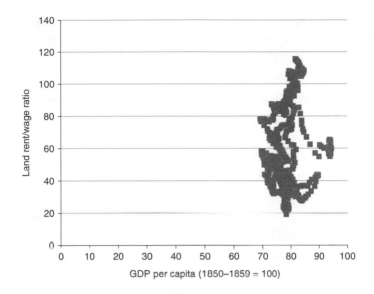

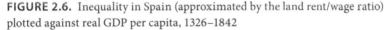

FIGURE 2.6. Inequality in Spain (approximated by the land rent/wage ratio) plotted against real GDP per capita, 1326–1842

The vertical axis shows the estimated land rent/wage ratio (from Figure 2.5); as it increases, inequality goes up because landlords gain relative to workers. The horizontal axis shows the estimated GDP per capita with level = 100 fixed for the years 1850–1859. Data source: Álvarez-Nogal and Prados de la Escosura (2007, 2013).

relationship results from the fact that income was essentially stagnant in Spain during the five centuries covered by the Álvarez-Nogal and Prados de la Escosura study.[15] Thus, not surprisingly, there is no relationship between income inequality and mean income, or for that matter any other structural parameter that could be regarded as associated with income. Upward and downward swings in inequality appear just as many blurred dots against the background of a more or less constant number on the horizontal axis.

This point corroborates our hypothesis that while ups and downs in inequality did occur during the period before the Industrial

Revolution, they cannot be interpreted as having been driven by rising or declining income, or, to stay closer to Kuznets's original formulation, by the "structural" laws of motion. In other words, the hypothesis of Kuznets cycles, as reformulated for the period before the Industrial Revolution (or for any period of stagnant incomes) is very different from the Kuznets hypothesis as formulated for the modern period of sustained growth in average incomes.

What pushes inequality down in preindustrial societies?   If it is not income change or structural transformation that pushes inequality up or down in preindustrial societies, then what is it? A look at the data from Spain in Figure 2.5 can give us a clue about what forces reduce inequality. The decrease in inequality after 1350 was due to the plague. The second and very long downward inequality movement that started around 1570 was caused, as Álvarez-Nogal and Prados de la Escosura (2007) argue, by wars conducted by Spain (against the Low Countries, the Ottoman Empire, and England) and by the destruction of wool and wine export networks caused by these wars. Finally, the third period of inequality decline, after 1800, is directly related to the Napoleonic wars (Leandro Prados de la Escosura, pers. comm.). We shall find the same effects in other historical cases: inequality generally declines, in preindustrial societies, in the face of cataclysmic events like plagues, wars, and revolutions.

In a recent work, Guido Alfani (2014), who studied northern Italian towns from the fourteenth to the eighteenth century, finds decreases in wealth inequality around the 1350s during the Black Death, and then three centuries later, around 1630, during the last big plague that affected this part of Europe. Alfani and Ammannati have presented very similar evidence for the effects of the plague in the Florentine state: "the terrible pandemic [of 1348] seems to be at the root of a fairly long phase of inequality decline, which in the [Tuscan] cities lasted until about 1450" (2014, 22). Particularly instructive for our purposes is Alfani's figure, reproduced here as Figure 2.7, which shows

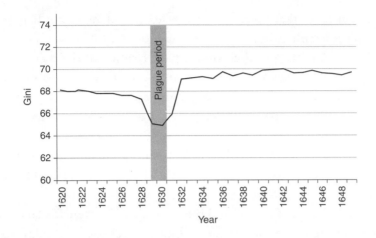

FIGURE 2.7. Wealth inequality in the city of Ivrea, northern Italy, 1620–1650

This graph shows inequality in wealth (measured by Gini values) in a northern Italian city affected by the plague in the Middle Ages. Inequality decreased during the plague. Data source: Adapted with permission from Alfani 2014.

that the decline in inequality occurred at the same time as the plague of 1628–1631.[16] Alfani's work on the impact of the plague is important because he was able to follow the yearly evolution of family fortunes before, during, and after the crisis over a period of thirty years.

What makes inequality go down in the face of catastrophic events such as plague? The most common explanation, as proposed by Pamuk (2007) and Álvarez-Nogal and Prados de la Escosura (2007), is that real wages increase as labor becomes more scarce. This increase leads to a decline in the land rent/wage ratio, as we saw in the case of Spain (Figure 2.5). On the side of wealth, high mortality results in the fragmentation of property, including among large landholders whose land becomes split among family members (Alfani 2010). Hülya Canbakal (2012) links the decline in wealth inequality in the large Ottoman city of Bursa (estimated from probate records over several centuries) to the period of "state breakdown" between 1580 and 1640, characterized by hyperinflation and political instability.

She concludes that there is a "positive, if moderate, link between [average] wealth, inequality and population" (p. 15).[17]

To be sure, the reaction to the Black Death and the increase in wages was not the same everywhere, and that's where institutions matter. As Mattia Fochesato (2014) argues, landowners in different parts of Europe responded differently to a more or less identical wage shock caused by the plague. In southern Europe, where feudal institutions were stronger, landowners renegotiated sharecropping contracts, restrained the movement of labor, and did everything they could to reduce wages through extra-market mechanisms. In northern Europe (England and the Netherlands), where feudal institutions were weaker, it was more difficult to check wage increases. Inequality as measured by the land rent/wage ratio probably went down in both cases, but not equally.[18]

Another type of catastrophic event that reduces inequality is war. For modern societies, the argument that war can be a force for equality, if an unwelcome one, recently received much attention in Piketty's *Capital in the Twenty-First Century*. It was already present in Piketty's earlier work on French inequality (2001a), which showed how inequality was affected by World War I and its aftermath. War reduces inequality through physical destruction of capital and inflation (creating real losses for creditors), resulting in a general decrease of income received from property. David Ricardo, in the famous chapter 31 of his *Principles of Political Economy and Taxation* (1817), proposed another channel, which has not been much explored, through which war reduces inequality. Government war spending, financed out of additional taxes paid by the rich, creates a greater demand for labor than does the normal consumption pattern of the rich. Thus, a given amount of money, now in the hands of the government rather than capitalists, is used to hire more people, many of them as soldiers, increasing the overall demand for labor, raising wages, and reducing inequality.

In summary, in the premodern era, income inequality goes down when there are catastrophic events. They can be associated with transitory increases in mean income (as in the case of epidemics) or with state breakdown when mean income goes down (see Excursus 2.1 on the Roman Empire). It could be argued that the new feature introduced in the modern era is, as we shall see later in this chapter, a decline of inequality when mean income is steadily rising.

What pushes inequality up in preindustrial societies? Wouter Ryckbosch (2014) provides inequality estimates for cities in the Low Countries between 1400 and 1900. His results are illustrated in Figure 2.8a. The inequality data, based on capitalized housing rents (indicating inequality in housing wealth), show a general, if weak, tendency toward increase until the onset of the Industrial Revolution. But after approximately 1800, inequality seems to be on the increase overall. This is, as mentioned before, one of our (and of course, Kuznets's) key arguments: that the Industrial Revolution gave a significant upward push to inequality. In the expanding economies of western Europe and its offshoots (to use Angus Maddison's terminology for western Europe and its former colonies of settlement), the upward push continued until inequality reached its peak between the end of the nineteenth century and the onset of World War I. In countries that were latecomers to industrialization, like Brazil and China, the peak might not have been reached until a century later or even the present day.

But let us return to the preindustrial societies. What makes inequality go up when mean income stays more or less constant? If average income is close to subsistence, there is clearly very little "space" for inequality to increase without leading to the loss of population (as we have seen in the discussion of the inequality possibility frontier). But inequality can increase if there are temporary increases (even if small by today's standard) in the mean income, as exemplified by the case of Spain, when wool production increased in the sixteenth century (Figure 2.5), or by the case of cities in northern Italy after 1500, during the period of the Commercial Revolution (Figure 2.8b).

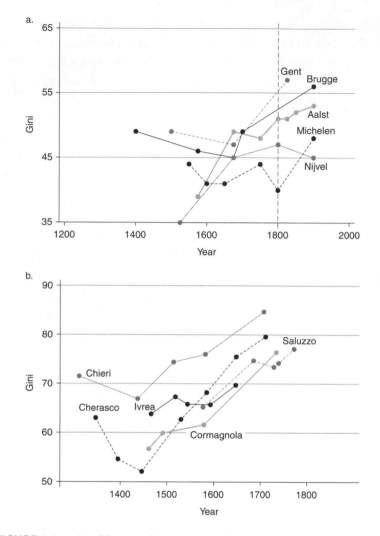

FIGURE 2.8. a. Wealth inequality in cities in the Low Countries, 1400–1850. b. Wealth inequality in northern Italian cities, 1311–1772

These graphs show inequality in wealth (measured by Gini values) during the Middle Ages in cities in today's Low Countries and northern Italy. The year 1800 marks the beginning of the Industrial Revolution. Data sources: a: Ryckbosch (2014); b: Alfani (2014).

The weakening and dissolution of the Western Roman Empire provides an instructive case of decline in real per capita income occurring simultaneously with a decline in income inequality. The material standard of living was on the decline by the end of Marcus Aurelius's reign (180), and that decline accelerated and became generalized everywhere in the West as Rome itself was sacked in 410 and ultimately fell to the Goths in 476. In most regions of western Europe, mean incomes went down and regional income gaps declined (Ward-Perkins 2005; Goldsworthy 2009; Jongman 2014). It is estimated that at the time of Octavian's death in the year 14, Italy had an average income of 2.2 times the subsistence level, almost twice as high as Britain's; by the year 700, average income in Italy was only 20 percent above subsistence, while in Britain it was merely 7 percent above.[19]

The decrease in regional mean incomes (and consequently in the mean income of the entire territory controlled by the Roman Empire in the first and second centuries) meant that interpersonal inequality also decreased. Inequality in the Roman Empire at Octavian's death is estimated to have been around 40 Gini points (Milanovic, Lindert, and Williamson 2007, appendix 2). Scheidel and Friesen (2009), using more detailed social tables, estimated a Gini of 41 at around the mid-second century.[20] But by the time of the fall of Rome, inequality had declined to about half that amount, and around the year 700, it might have been as low as 15–16 Gini points. Figure 2.9 shows the decline in inequality over the territory of the former Roman Empire during the first seven centuries of the Common Era. When incomes were so low, there was simply, as suggested by the inequality possibility frontier, very little "space" for inequality to exist; that is, there were fewer people who could command higher incomes without driving others to starvation. When the mean income is equal to subsistence, the only Gini coefficient that is compatible with the survival of all is zero.

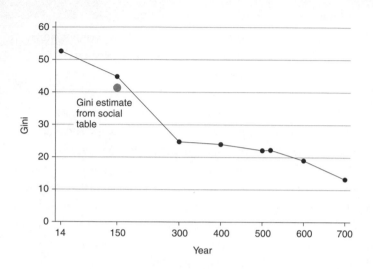

FIGURE 2.9. Estimate of interpersonal income inequality in the territory of the Roman Empire, 14–700 CE

This graph shows the upper-bound estimate of income inequality (measured by Gini values) in ancient Rome and its successor states. The point denoted "Gini estimate from social table" shows the actual estimate of inequality based on a detailed social table from the mid-second century. Data sources: Graph from Milanovic (2010b); social table Gini from Scheidel and Friesen (2009).

The Roman story provides a very powerful example of simultaneous immiseration and inequality reduction. The highest inequality probably occurred at the time when income levels were the highest. The subsequent sustained reduction of income eventually led to the leveling of almost everyone into a common state of poverty.[21]

The historical upward movement in inequality described by Ryckbosch (2014) for the Low Countries proceeded precisely as explained here using the idea of the inequality possibility frontier. The growth of the economy, or more exactly of cities, from the late Middle Ages onward was associated with the creation of a surplus over subsistence. (It is tricky to determine causation here: a more likely scenario is that the existence of the surplus enabled the creation of cities, which then enabled further increase of the surplus.) This situation produced an increase in the r/w ratio (rate of return to capital-over-wage), with the surplus ending up in the hands of the capitalists, and an overall increase in inequality. Ryckbosch thus relates personal income distribution directly to movements in the profit-wage ratio. Because mean income is increasing, this movement corresponds to a movement to the right along a given inequality possibility frontier (see Figure 2.2), allowing for an increase in inequality.

In summary, inequality expands and contracts in preindustrial economies against a broadly unchanging mean income, driven by accidental or exogenous events such as epidemics, discoveries, or wars. Absent are the endogenous forces of economic development that we in the modern era assume to be the forces that affect inequality.

In an influential paper, van Zanden (1995) used the term "super Kuznets curve" to describe the rise in income inequality that occurred during the Commercial Revolution, starting around 1500, suggesting that it was a Kuznets curve *avant la lettre*. I present here a similar argument but consider the preindustrial and the modern epochs together as a continuum, arguing that Kuznets waves occur during the entire period, though driven by very different forces at different times. In preindustrial times, there were no systematic forces: change was driven by the vagaries of accidents, from catastrophic events to those that partially relieved the constraints of subsistence, leading to alternating decreases and increases in income and wealth inequality. Only in societies with a sustained increase in the average income did economic forces, in the form of rapid technological change and its "inequality offsets" (widespread education, reduced rate of return to capital, social insurance), begin to exert systematic effects on inequality. In the next section we shall review some of the long-term data that demonstrate Kuznets waves in modern societies, which we divide into industrial and postindustrial, corresponding respectively to the first and the second technological revolutions.

Inequality in Societies with a Steadily Rising Mean Income

Societies with a steadily rising mean income are fundamentally different from stagnant societies. A rise in the average income opens the "space" for a rise in inequality, as suggested by the inequality possibility frontier. That does not mean, of course, that higher inequality is inevitable, but it does make it possible (unlike in stagnant societies, where a significant increase in inequality is possible only if a part of the population does not survive).

But did inequality go up? The Kuznets hypothesis is our key workhorse for answering this question. As Kuznets argued, it is the structural movement, the transfer of labor from the low-income, low-inequality agricultural sector to the higher-income, higher-inequality industrial sector (and concomitantly, from rural to urban areas) that increases income inequality. Figure 2.1, which shows estimates of inequality for the United States and the United Kingdom/England over a period of several centuries, does indicate that the curve continued to rise upward until the late nineteenth century or early twentieth century. Similar long-term series are now available for other countries as well, and they are in broad agreement with the Kuznets hypothesis—all the way up to the late 1970s.

In the next five subsections I review evidence on long-term changes in inequality for ten countries from around the world, presenting the data in graphs that show estimates of income inequality plotted against mean income, precisely the variables for which we could detect no relationship in the preindustrial era. We consider first the relationships for the United States and the United Kingdom, where we look at inequality of disposable per capita income (that is, income after social transfers and direct taxes) versus GDP per capita.

Kuznets waves: United States and United Kingdom. Inequality in the United States increased between Independence (the social tables data are for 1774) and the Civil War (the data are for 1860) and then continued to rise until the early twentieth century, when it is generally considered to have reached its peak. The exact year is hard to pinpoint. According to an estimate by Smolensky and Plotnick (1992), based on various macrodata, US inequality peaked in 1933, driven by the highest-ever rate of unemployment and thus low incomes for many families (see Figure 2.10).[22] Peter Lindert and Jeffrey Williamson, however, contend that US inequality remained at a high plateau of around 50 Gini points, with slight oscillations, from the late nineteenth century to the Great Depression (Williamson and Lindert 1980; Lindert and Williamson 2016). They do not report any changes in inequality between 1929 and 1933. What seems clear is that inequality peaked at slightly over 50 Gini points, at an income level of $5,000 per capita (in 1990 international dollars). After the Great Depression, US inequality decreased steadily until the end of World War II. Notice also the leftward movement of the curve during the Great Depression, just after the end of World War II, and again during the Great Recession: these movements reflect declines in real GDP per capita.

Inequality remained at a historically low level of about 35 Gini points until the trough in 1979. After that it rose steadily, reaching over 40 Gini points by the second decade of the twenty-first century. During the downward portion of the Kuznets curve, from the Great Depression to 1979, real GDP per capita almost quadrupled. Kuznets's

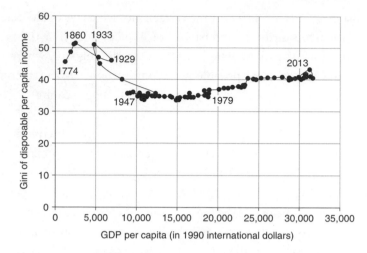

FIGURE 2.10. The relationship between income inequality and mean income (the Kuznets relationship) for the United States, 1774–2013

Data sources: Ginis: 1774, 1850, 1860, and 1870 from social tables created by Lindert and Williamson (2012); 1929 from Radner and Hinrichs (1974); 1931 and 1933 from Smolensky and Plotnick (1992); 1935 to 1950 from Goldsmith et al. (1954); after 1950, from US Census Bureau, *Income, poverty and health insurance coverage in the United States* (various issues); gross income data adjusted to reflect disposable income. GDP per capita from Maddison Project (2013).

original hypothesis is consistent with the data through 1979 but does not explain the rise in both inequality and income that has occurred over the past forty years. The concept of Kuznets waves, with recent changes being driven by the second technological revolution, makes sense of this upsurge of inequality since 1980.

The political and economic elements that underlie the changes of the past hundred years—from the New Deal, the power of organized labor, and high tax rates (driven by the need to pay for the two world wars) to the recent forces of globalization, reduced taxation, and the weakened bargaining power of labor—are too well known to be re-told one more time. However, it is this interplay between, on the one

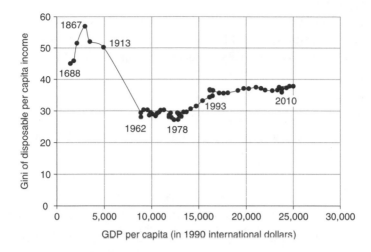

FIGURE 2.11. The relationship between income inequality and mean income (the Kuznets relationship) for the United Kingdom/England, 1688–2010

Data sources: Ginis: for 1688, 1759, 1801, and 1867 from social tables for England/UK reported in Milanovic, Lindert, and Williamson (2011); 1880 and 1913 from Lindert and Williamson (1983, table 2); 1961 to 2010, official UK data (disposable per capita income) kindly calculated and provided by Jonathan Cribb, Institute for Fiscal Studies. GDP per capita from Maddison Project (2013).

hand, these apparently determinative economic forces, and, on the other hand, political and social forces, that shapes the movement of Kuznets waves. The increase in the mean income that we observe is only a proxy for the economic forces at play; the change in inequality that we observe is the product of both these economic forces and political decisions.[23] Naïve "economicism" that looks only at the forces of supply and demand is insufficient to explain movements in income distribution. It is also wrong to focus only on institutions. Institutions and policies work within what economics allows: they are, if one wishes to use this term, "endogenous," that is, largely dependent on income level, and they can only vary within what income permits. They break out of that framework only in exceptional cases of "political voluntarism," which holds that it can dispense with economic limitations. But this seldom happens in capitalist societies and even less often (or never) in capitalist *and* democratic societies.[24]

Let us now move to the British data (Figure 2.11). The shape of the graph is remarkably similar to that for the United States. The peak of inequality came in 1867, at a Gini value of almost 60 (that is, 10 points higher than at the same time in the United States), according to the social tables from which we calculate income distribution.[25] Note that inequality in the United Kingdom has declined from being drastically higher than in the United States (and higher than in today's Brazil) to being lower than in the United States. As argued many years ago by Lindert and Williamson (1985), by Polak and Williamson (1993), and more recently by Williamson in his book *Trade and Poverty* (2011), US inequality continued to increase after British inequality peaked because the arrival of new immigrants in the 1910s kept wages for low-skill jobs relatively low and caused overall US wage distribution to widen, or stretch out. This is the wage-stretching explanation for increased inequality, as contrasted with what van Zanden (1995) called the classical explanation, which sees an increasing share of capital in functional income distribution gradually leading to greater interpersonal inequality. We shall also find the echoes of these two different explanations in the recent increase in inequality in the United States: most of the increase until about the year 2000 was due to wage-stretching, but since 2000, it may have been driven in addition by a rise in the share of income coming from capital.

Immigration and wage-stretching explain why the peak of inequality in the United States came some time between 1910 and 1933, while British inequality is generally thought to have reached its zenith earlier, in the last quarter of the nineteenth century. The forces that pushed US inequality up in the roaring twenties were, in many ways, similar to the forces that pushed it up in the 1990s: downward pressure on wages (from immigration and/or increased trade), capital-biased technological change (Taylorism and the Internet), monopolization of the economy (Standard Oil and large banks), suppression or decreasing attractiveness of trade unions, and a shift toward plutocracy in government.

For about half a century before World War I, a gradual and modest decrease in British income inequality occurred. It is estimated that by 1913, the Gini value was at around 50, some 10 points below its 1867 peak. These estimates are corroborated by what we know about the upward movement of British real wages and the emergence of the so-called labor aristocracy in the last decades of the nineteenth century (on which more in Chapter 3).[26] The next data point that we have for British inequality is unfortunately almost half a century later (1962). The level of inequality by then had halved, to less than 30 Gini points. The effects of the two world wars, much higher taxation, and reduced income from capital, combined with the rising strength of unions and the expansion of the welfare state, were behind this remarkable reduction in inequality. After the Second World War, in an evolution that almost blow-by-blow replicates the American experience, British inequality went down until 1978 and then increased, even faster than in the United States, to end up at a Gini value slightly below 40 in 2010.

The similarity between the United States and the United Kingdom extends beyond the timing and shape of changes in inequality. The peak inequality was reached at income levels between $3,000 and $5,000 (in 1990 international dollars), although, as we have just seen, the peaks were some fifty to sixty years apart. At GDP per capita between $10,000 and $15,000 (or $20,000 in the case of the United States), inequality was remarkably stable and low. One should not, however, read in these numbers some general rule about turning points in the Kuznets curve, which previous generations of economists tried in vain to discover. The United States and the United Kingdom followed very similar inequality trajectories because they were at about the same income level, were similarly organized politically, and were exposed to the same forces of international competition and wars. But it is reassuring that we find the same evolution of inequality in countries with similar economic and political structures. The three forces that we view as broadly shaping the evolution of inequality, namely, technology, openness (or globalization), and policy (or politics), which we shall bundle together under the acronym TOP, were similar—indicating in turn that policy may to a large extent be regarded as endogenous, that is, responsive to the forces of economic change. Similar evolution of economic and political forces produced similar evolution of income inequality.

Kuznets waves: Spain and Italy.   But we cannot base our general conclusions on only two examples, however important. Luckily, in the recent period there has been an expansion in the long-term data on inequality. From Leandro Prados de la Escosura's (2008) work, we have estimates of Spanish inequality for the period 1850–1985; after that date we use Spanish household surveys. From 1850 all the way to the 1950s—a period that although "modern" resembles in many aspects the Spanish preindustrial era, with violent swings in inequality and very little growth in real income—we indeed find a pattern similar to what we saw for the United States and the United Kingdom (Figure 2.12). Inequality reached a peak in 1953, at a very high value exceeding 50 Gini points.[27] The subsequent downward slide extended to the mid-1980s, when the Gini was reduced by more than 20 points. Within the span of about three decades, during which

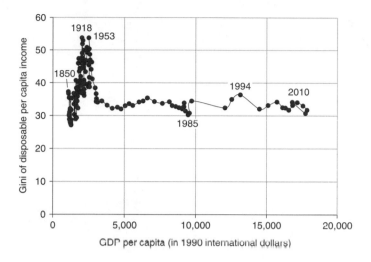

FIGURE 2.12. The relationship between income inequality and mean income (the Kuznets relationship) for Spain, 1850–2010

Data sources: Ginis: 1850 to 1985 from Prados de la Escosura (2008); 1985 to 2010 from Luxembourg Income Study (http://www.lisdatacenter.org/) and All the Ginis database (http://www.gc.cuny.edu/branko-milanovic). GDP per capita from Maddison Project (2013).

Spain was on a downward inequality trajectory, real GDP per capita quadrupled. Inequality stabilized (or increased slightly) in the last decade of the twentieth and the first decade of the twenty-first century. We can easily see the first inverted-U Kuznets curve for the period from 1850 to 1980, but after that, the upward portion of a second Kuznets curve is not as apparent as in the United States and the United Kingdom.

The relationship between inequality and income for Italy, with data that start at unification in 1860–61, shows essentially a continuous downward trend until the 1980s (Figure 2.13).[28] Like other advanced economies, Italy experienced the Great Leveling for most of

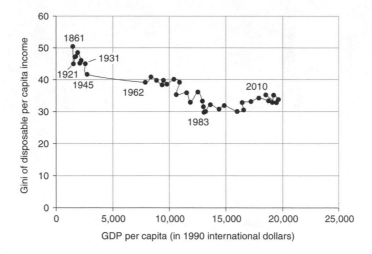

FIGURE 2.13. The relationship between income inequality and mean income (the Kuznets relationship) for Italy, 1861–2010

Data sources: Ginis: 1861 to 2008 from Brandolini and Vecchi (2011) and personal communication from both authors; 2010 from Luxembourg Income Study (http://www .lisdatacenter.org/). GDP per capita from Maddison Project (2013).

the twentieth century. As elsewhere, the lowest point of inequality occurred in the early 1980s, followed by a strong increase since. In the case of Italy, we can ask if it is possible to detect any influence of fascism. Although Gini values are available only for 1921 (on the eve of Mussolini's takeover), 1931 (the point of high fascism), and 1945 (the end of the war), we see that there was no change in the Gini value between 1921 and 1931. A strong decrease between 1931 and 1945 is most likely explained, as in the other countries, by the effect of war and not by fascism per se.

Kuznets waves: Germany and the Netherlands. The data for Germany are fragmentary and less consistent over time than those we have for other countries (Figure 2.14). There is also a long hiatus

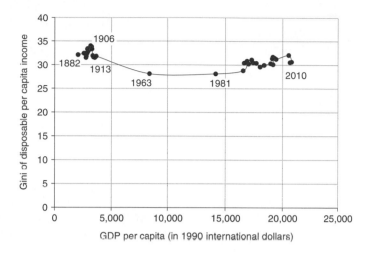

FIGURE 2.14. The relationship between income inequality and mean income (the Kuznets relationship) for Germany, 1882–2010

Data sources. Ginis: 1882 to 1913 from Grant (2002); 1981 to 2010 from All the Ginis database (http://www.gc.cuny.edu/branko-milanovic). GDP per capita from Maddison Project (2013).

between 1931 and 1963, when the data on inequality become available again (for West Germany). The borders of the country also changed several times in the period covered here. The graph shows a rise in inequality in the early twentieth century, but the level was substantially lower than in the United Kingdom and the United States. We can also infer a long-term process of income equalization, in line with Kuznets's hypothesis, by comparing the 1906 and 1981 values (a drop of 6 Gini points). As elsewhere in the rich world, there has been an upward movement of Gini values in the past twenty years; this movement has not been as strong, however, as in the Anglo-Saxon countries.

The data for the Netherlands/Holland go back to the sixteenth century (Figure 2.15). The three early data points (1561, 1732, and

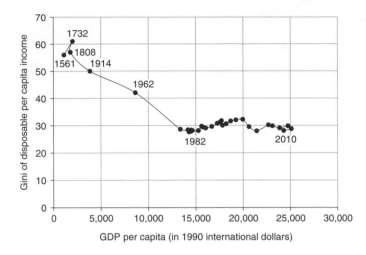

FIGURE 2.15. The relationship between income inequality and mean income (the Kuznets relationship) for the Netherlands/Holland, 1561–2010

Data sources: Ginis: 1561 to 1914 from Soltow and van Zanden (1998); 1962 to 2010 from All the Ginis database (http://www.gc.cuny.edu/branko-milanovic). GDP per capita from Maddison Project (2013).

1808) are obtained from distributions of housing rents, which are assumed to be correlated with income. (This same approach was used for the data from medieval northern Italy and the Low Countries discussed above.) Such distributions come from data on taxes that were imposed on houses. The data show both inequality and income rising during the Dutch Golden Age, driven by the factors outlined by van Zanden's (1995) classical explanation—that is, a shift in the functional distribution of income toward property owners and away from labor. Both income and inequality declined during the Napoleonic wars (as can be seen in a comparison of the data points for 1732 and 1808), as we would expect from our discussion of the malign forces that drive inequality down. The twentieth-century data (from household surveys) illustrate the well-known equalization of incomes in the Netherlands, again, as elsewhere in the West, a process explained by socialist agitation, full voting rights, the introduction of the eight-hour workday, and rising real wages. This was accompanied by a remarkable increase in mean income (three-fold between 1914 and 1980). As in the other countries we have considered, the decline in inequality ends in the early 1980s. The Gini had by then reached its minimum value of 28 points. After that there was a very mild increase, with the Gini reaching a value of 30 points before the Great Recession. As in Germany, the upward portion of the second Kuznets wave is indeed very modest.

Kuznets waves: Brazil and Chile. We move next to South America, where we have long-term data for Brazil and Chile (Figures 2.16 and 2.17). Two data sets are available for Brazil, one from Prados de la Escosura (2007; based on the use of the Williamson ratio to estimate Gini coefficients)[29] and another from Bértola et al. (2009) (based on social tables). Although the two data sets do not show exactly the same pattern of increasing inequality in the mid-nineteenth and early twentieth centuries, they both show that there was a period of increasing inequality until around 1950, followed by stabilization at a very high level. In the 1970s to 1980s, Brazil was probably one of the two most unequal countries in the world, the other being South Africa. There has been a steady decline in inequality since the late 1990s. The governments of Fernando Henrique Cardoso and Luiz Inácio Lula da Silva are credited for this unusual trend, bucking the trends in practically every other country of the world (excluding a few other Latin American countries, such as Argentina and Mexico). The decrease has by now lasted sufficiently long, more than a decade, that we can see it as a real and important development. This does not mean that this development cannot be overturned. But the overall shape of changes in inequality in Brazil over the past 150 years, including the most recent period, is fully compatible with the first

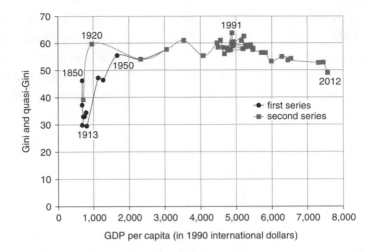

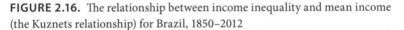

FIGURE 2.16. The relationship between income inequality and mean income (the Kuznets relationship) for Brazil, 1850–2012

This graph shows the Kuznets relationship for Brazil from two different data sets. The first series estimates Ginis from the Williamson ratio (mean income divided by the average unskilled wage); such estimates are called quasi-Ginis. Data sources: Ginis: 1850 to 1950 (first series) from Prados de la Escosura (2007); 1870 to 1920 (second series) from Bértola et al. (2009, table 4); 1960 to 2012, from All the Ginis database (http://www.gc .cuny.edu/branko-milanovic). GDP per capita from Maddison Project (2013).

Kuznets wave. Moreover, the economic forces that Kuznets had in mind—broader education, higher minimum wages, increased social transfers—are precisely the forces credited with having brought inequality down in Brazil (see Gasparini, Cruces, and Tornarolli 2011; Ferreira, Leite, and Litchfield 2008).

The data for Chile are most interesting. They have been developed by Javier Rodríguez Weber (2014) by an ingenious application of social tables. Using a method he calls dynamic social tables, Rodríguez Weber created very detailed social tables with estimated populations and incomes for several hundred social groups or occupations for certain economically or politically salient years—those for which

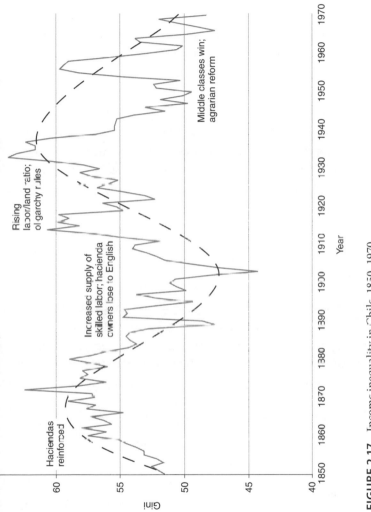

FIGURE 2.17. Income inequality in Chile, 1850–1970

This figure shows the evolution of Gini value over time in Chile. The Gini values are calculated from dynamic social tables, which list annual mean incomes and populations by social class or occupation. The distinctive features of each period are indicated in the graph. The dashed line shows a stylized (average) evolution of inequality over the period. Data source: Rodríguez Weber (2014).

data are more plentiful and that stand at the turning points of different political and economic phases. Rodríguez Weber starts with very complete income and wage data (including wages for both men and women) and then lets income sources of these social groups increase at the rates obtained from the general wage or income macrodata. For example, if the income of a group is composed mostly of unskilled workers' wages, then Rodríguez Weber shows the evolution of the group's income following the average construction worker wage. The social composition is thus kept fixed over a period of time, but incomes of various social groups are allowed to vary at different rates, generating changes in inequality over time. We thus get a much more exciting ("dynamic"; annual) picture than we would get from individual "static" (one year only) social tables. Chile has thus probably one of the most complete data sets detailing the evolution of inequality over the long run.

Rodríguez Weber's results for the period 1850–1970 are shown in Figure 2.17. Over time, there is a clear succession of Kuznets waves. However, these changes are explained by a combination of economic and political forces (and this is one of the great virtues of Rodríguez Weber's work). The first Kuznets wave, from 1850 to 1903, is explained, in its upward portion, by the political stranglehold of hacienda owners, who were able to keep peons at the subsistence level. The downward portion of the curve, from 1873 to 1903, was caused by declines in incomes of the hacienda owners as a result of lower copper prices, the purchase of mines by British capitalists, and, finally, an increased land-to-labor ratio (which drove wages up) when Chile expanded its territory by two-thirds after winning the war against Peru and Bolivia.[30] The second Kuznets wave, from 1903 to 1970, displays a similar interaction of economic and political factors, with the downswing portion reflecting the usual political and social factors: expansion of education, strong trade unions, and increased minimum wages—all the same elements common to episodes of the Great Leveling in the advanced capitalist economies over exactly the same period. (In Chile, the "bookends" to this episode were the victory of the left-wing Frente Nacional in 1938 and the coming to power of Salvador Allende in 1970.)[31]

Kuznets waves: Japan.   In Asia, we have long-term data only for Japan and only from the end of the nineteenth century (Figure 2.18). The data show a strong upswing in inequality lasting for about forty years, with the peak occurring just before World War II. The war dramatically reduced inequality and after 1945, Japan, like all developed countries, entered a long period of relatively low inequality, so that by 1962 (when more regular data are available), its Gini value was at about 35 points (the approximate level at which it has

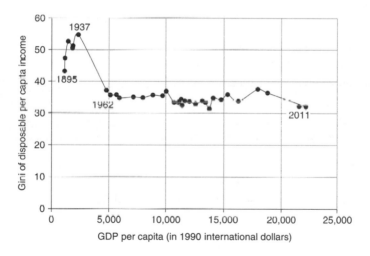

FIGURE 2.18. The relationship between income inequality and mean income (the Kuznets relationship) for Japan, 1895–2011

Data sources: Ginis: 1895–1937 from Minami (1998, 2008); 1962–2011 from All the Ginis database (http://www.gc.cuny.edu/branko-milanovic). GDP per capita from Maddison Project (2013).

stayed ever since).[32] This is some 20 Gini points below the pre–World War II peak. Japan's maximum inequality during the first Kuznets wave occurs at an income level of $2,300 (in 1990 international dollars), a value not dissimilar to that in the United Kingdom and Spain.

The logic of Kuznets waves.   It is the interplay between economic and political factors that drives Kuznets waves, or cycles. A narrow focus on "benign" economic forces alone is insufficient and naïve. Income inequality is, almost by definition, an outcome of social and political struggles, sometimes violent ones. These struggles are not limited to today's or yesterday's "Third World": one need only remember the extremely bloody Paris Commune, the 1886 Haymarket demonstrations in Chicago, which gave rise to International Labor Day, or the harsh British responses to several miners' strikes. Although labor lost in all these cases, and many more that could be adduced from various countries, the pressure it exerted ultimately proved too strong and resulted in a sustained decrease in inequality during what is often called the short twentieth century (from World War I to the collapse of the Soviet Union).

Most political battles are fought over the distribution of income. But we should remember that political battles take place in a much broader economic environment, within parameters set by such factors as the existence or nonexistence of globalization, the supply of skilled labor, the abundance or not of capital, and the presence or absence of easily exploitable resources. These parameters cannot be changed overnight; and they set the context for political and social struggle. Political forces that push for greater inequality will, of course, be emboldened and stronger when the economic trends work in their favor—if labor becomes more plentiful, if technological change is capital- or high-skill-biased. But such a situation does not guarantee their victory.

As is nicely illustrated in Europe and the United States for the period after the Great Depression and World War II, the strength of trade unions, the political power of socialist and communist parties, and the example and military threat of the Soviet Union all curbed pro-rich policies by constraining the power of capital.[33] But once these political limitations weakened or disappeared and economic factors became more favorable to capital, including skill-biased technological change and the large expansion of global labor that came with the opening of China and the fall of communism, the situation reversed, and the advanced economies entered a period of rising inequality, the second Kuznets wave, which is still in force.

Table 2.2 summarizes the key features of the downswing of the first Kuznets wave and the upswing of the second in advanced economics. Unlike in the earlier literature on the Kuznets curve, we are not looking here to discover the common date or income level at which the cycle peaked. Because of the complex interplay of political and economic forces, the dates and income levels differ. However, the shape of the changes, or cycles, is similar. In all countries (except the Netherlands), inequality peaked at around 50–55 Gini points; only in the Netherlands, the earliest industrializer, did peak inequality reach 60 Gini points, the level of contemporary inequality in Latin America. Nor were any of the peaks ever very low, at, say, 40 Gini points, which is approximately the present US level.

The downward portion, measured from the peak to the approximate trough, lasted the longest (again with the exception of the Netherlands) in Italy and the United Kingdom, where the broad downward trend took place over more than a century: in Italy, from the unification of the country until the early 1980s; in the United Kingdom, from 1867 until the advent of Margaret Thatcher. The United States had a relatively short downswing of some fifty years (1933 to 1979). The shortest downswing was in Spain (about thirty years), because Spain had atypically high inequality in 1953. That

TABLE 2.2. The first and the second Kuznets waves in advanced economies

Country	Peak of Kuznets wave 1			Trough of Kuznets wave 1			Growth-inequality trade-off during the downswing			Kuznets wave 2 (upward portion; Gini point increase so far)
	Year of maximum inequality	Level of maximum inequality (Gini points)	GDP per capita in year of maximum inequality ($PPP)	Year of minimum inequality	Level of minimum inequality (Gini points)	GDP per capita in year of minimum inequality ($PPP)	Approximate # of years of downswing of Kuznets wave 1	Gini decrease (in points)	GDP increase (# of times)	
United States	1933	51	4,800	1979	35	19,000	50	16	4	strong (+8)
United Kingdom	1867	57	3,000	1978	27	13,000	110	30	>4	strong (+11)
Spain	1953	55	2,500	1985	31	10,000	30	24	4	modest (+3)
Italy	1861	51	1,500	1983	30	13,000	120	21	<9	strong (+5)
Japan	1937	55	2,300	1981	31	14,000	45	24	6	modest (+1)
Netherlands	1732	61	2,000	1982	28	14,000	250	33	7	modest (+2)

Note: GDP per capita in 1990 international dollars, from Maddison Project (2013).

Sources: See sources listed for Figures 2.10–2.13, 2.15, and 2.18.

level, however, was about the same as in 1918, and with a different and equally plausible reckoning (placing the peak of the first wave around 1918), we could argue that the Spanish downswing lasted more than sixty years. But Spain is also a very interesting case because of the absence of the typical effects of wars (decreased inequality), since the country did not participate in either of the two world wars (although it did experience a civil war, from 1936 to 1939). Moreover, its high inequality in the 1950s is atypical because it was ruled by a quasi-fascist regime that kept inequality, and to some extent the social structure, in the same form as it had been elsewhere in the rich world in the early twentieth century. Spain's apparent atypicality actually helps to highlight the key factors that were crucial for the reduction of inequality in other developed countries: wars, left-wing political pressure, and social policy.

The inequality downswing coincided with a major increase in real per capita income in all countries. The increase was the largest in Italy (almost nine times) because of the long duration of the downswing and Italy's fast post–World War II growth. The Netherlands's mean income expanded by six times, but (it should be recalled) its inequality peak occurred almost a century before that of other countries. The American, British, and Spanish economies each expanded by four times (as measured by per capita income), while their income inequalities declined by between 15 Gini points (in the United States) and 30 Gini points (in the United Kingdom). In all countries, there were indeed massive declines in inequality, cutting its level, measured by the Gini coefficient, almost in half and in the Netherlands and the United Kingdom by more than half. The fact that the downswing in inequality coincided with enormous increases in per capita incomes, despite wars in which all countries considered here were involved, shows that over the long term, growth does not require rising inequality. Historical data certainly do not support the hypothesis of a trade-off between the two.

Figure 2.19 illustrates these relationships. Both growth and inequality are "normalized"; growth is indicated on the horizontal axis by the average per capita growth rate per decade, and inequality is indicated on the vertical axis by the average reduction in Gini points per decade.[34] It is remarkable that the countries are aligned almost on a straight line, with those that had faster growth having also had greater reductions in inequality. One cannot make too much of this relationship, since the duration of the downswing portion of the first Kuznets wave was very different between the countries: surely it would be unrealistic, for example, to expect the Netherlands to have had a very high growth rate during more than two centuries. The graph also shows the fairly strong position of the United States,

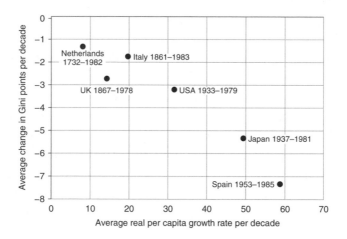

FIGURE 2.19. Relationship between change in inequality and growth during the downward portion of the first Kuznets wave

This graph shows average per capita GDP growth rate per decade during the period of the Great Leveling on the horizontal axis, and on the vertical axis, the average decline in Gini points per decade during the same period. Countries that had higher growth rates generally also had larger declines in inequality. Data sources: See sources for Figures 2.10–2.13, 2.15, and 2.18.

which, rather against the grain of what is assumed nowadays, experienced very high growth (more than 30 percent per decade) and a very strong reduction in inequality (more than 3 Gini points per decade)—simultaneously.

Most interesting, and revealing, is the date of the trough of the first Kuznets wave, and thus the date when the second wave began. In all countries, the trough occurred in the late 1970s or early 1980s. The timing differs by at most a couple of years, and since, by the early 1980s, all the countries considered here had similar income levels (except the United States, which was richer), the turning point, both in terms of time and level of income, occurred at the same point for all. The upswing was not, however, equally strong everywhere. The United States, the United Kingdom, and Italy show the strongest evidence of the second Kuznets wave, with the US and Italian Ginis having risen by at least 5 points and the British Gini by more than 10 points. The inequality upswing is more modest in Spain, Germany, Japan, and the Netherlands, where we can speak of a rise of at most a couple of Gini points. Yet all countries' Ginis are clearly following an upward trajectory—so the second Kuznets wave is on.

This pattern is displayed in Figure 2.20, a counterpart to the Figure 2.19, with growth and inequality now positively correlated but in a very particular way which illustrates the differences in country experiences. The countries that lie above an imaginary line drawn through the figure (the United Kingdom, the United States, and Italy) all "required" a greater increase in inequality for a given rate of growth than the countries that lie below this line (Japan, the Netherlands, and Spain).

What Drove the Downswing of the First Kuznets Wave?

The first Kuznets wave in technologically advanced societies (that is, countries with rising mean incomes) lasted from the beginning of the

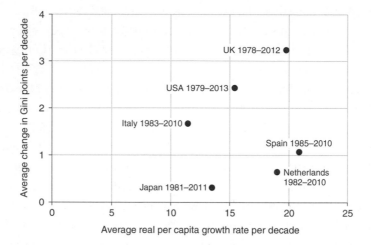

FIGURE 2.20. Relationship between change in inequality and growth during the upward portion of the second Kuznets wave

This graph shows the average per capita GDP growth rate per decade during the period of the recent upswing in inequality (starting around 1980) on the horizontal axis, and on the vertical axis, the average increase in Gini points per decade during the same period. All countries experienced increases in inequality, and those with the greatest amount of increase (the UK, USA, and Italy) registered greater increases in Gini points per unit of growth. Data sources: See sources for Figures 2.10–2.13, 2.15, and 2.18.

Industrial Revolution to approximately the 1980s. This long period of some 150 years involved, as we have seen, an increase in inequality, peaking variously between the late nineteenth century and the early twentieth, and then decreasing more or less continuously during the next seventy or eighty years. Thus the upward and the downward portion seemed to have lasted approximately the same amount of time.

It is the subsequent upward swing in inequality in rich countries, which started around 1980, that is difficult to reconcile with Kuznets's original hypothesis that inequality would decline and stay at that lower level after income became sufficiently high. It is for this reason that I think that it is more appropriate to speak of Kuznets cycles, or waves, and to view the current upward swing in advanced countries as the beginning of the second Kuznets wave. Like the first wave, it is the product of technological innovation and change, of the substitution of labor by capital (the "second machine age"), and the transfer of labor from one sector to another. In the first Kuznets wave, the transfer was from agriculture (and thus rural areas) to manufacturing (and thus urban areas); in the second, it is from manufacturing to services. As discussed before, this second wave is also driven by pro-rich changes in economic policies.

But while the factors that are currently pushing inequality up in the advanced world may be generally well understood (even if there is no consensus on their relative importance), it is much less clear what might lead inequality to go down, as in a Kuznets wave we would expect to happen. What forces may be set in motion by the system itself that would limit the increase in income inequality and ultimately overturn it? We shall look at some of these forces at the end of this chapter; and indeed when it comes to the United States (Chapter 4), I am somewhat skeptical that they can be easily identified. But before we look at the future, it is instructive to look at the past and to identify the reasons why the first upswing in inequality came to an end. For this exercise might contain implications for the second wave.

Domestic inequalities and World War I. There are two distinct views of why inequality decreased in the twentieth century. The traditional one, espoused largely by Kuznets himself, is that it was a product of various economic forces: a gradual end to the structural transformation whereby most of the population moved into urban areas and into manufacturing (thus eliminating the rural/urban gap that is one of the important contributors to inequality); increased schooling, which reduced the education premium (an explanation especially favored by Tinbergen [1975] and Goldin and Katz [2010]); the aging of the population, and thus greater demand for social services (social security, nationalized health), which in turn required greater taxation of the rich; and, possibly in the background, the need for greater social cohesion in the context of wars, including the Cold War, which meant that financing of wars should fall mostly on the rich.[35]

The second explanation, favored by Piketty, not only in his most recent book, *Capital in the Twenty-First Century,* but also in his earlier book *Les Hauts revenus en France,* published in 2001, is, unlike Kuznets's theory, primarily a political theory. According to Piketty, the two world wars not only led to higher taxes but also destroyed property and reduced large fortunes. This was particularly true in France, which provided a template for his later work.[36] In his book on France, Piketty shows that the concentration of capital declined after the wars and the largest French fortunes never recovered: around the year 2000, the highest-valued estates were still worth less than before World War I.[37] The lower concentration of wealth combined with a lower capital-output ratio (because of the destruction of capital) resulted in a reduction of revenues from capital and a reduction of inequality. In Piketty's story, the shocks of war, as well as the ensuing "shock" of socialist and communist parties that, thanks to their new-found political influence, introduced much pro-labor legislation, are presented as exogenous events, that is as political elements outside economics proper.

It is on this question, the reason why the crest of the inequality wave broke, that the interpretation proposed here differs from Piketty's. I argue that the outbreak of World War I and thus the reduction of inequality subsequent to that war are to be "endogenized" in the economic conditions predating the war, by which I mean that domestic inequalities played an important role in the run-up to the war. In making this argument I go back to an older, and in my opinion, most persuasive, interpretation of the outbreak of World War I. According to this interpretation the war was caused by imperialist competition, embedded in the domestic economic conditions of the time: very high income and wealth inequality, high savings of the upper classes, insufficient domestic aggregate demand, and the need of capitalists to find profitable uses for surplus savings outside their own country.

In the early twentieth century, finding an external investment outlet for the surplus savings meant being in physical control of a place, and making such investment profitable required that other possible competitors be excluded even at the cost of a war. Let me quote Keynes (|1936| 1964, 381–382), an author who does not exactly spring to mind when we think of critics of imperialism: "but, over and above this [dictators as causes of wars] . . . are the economic causes of war, namely the pressure of population and the competitive struggle for markets. It is the second factor, which probably played a predominant part in the nineteenth century, and might again."

This "competitive struggle for markets" led to the exploitation of the colonies.[38] Economic success required creating colonies, protectorates, or dependencies, and introducing what Paul Bairoch has called the colonial contract. The colonial contract was defined by the following elements: colonies could trade only with the metropolis, with goods transported on the metropolis's ships, and colonies could not produce manufactured goods (Bairoch 1997, 2:665–669; see also Milanovic 2002b). The scramble for colonies in Africa was fueled by the interests of European capitalists (see Wesseling 1996). A similar, almost equally brutal, scramble for new territories took place in Siberia, where Russia expanded eastward, and in the Americas, where the United States expanded westward to annex Mexican territories and southward to reinforce political control. Ghana, Sudan, Vietnam, Algeria, the Philippines, California, and Siberia are all part of the same process. In the apt terminology introduced by McGuire and Olson (1996), colonies were ruled by "roving" rather than "stationary" bandits.

The broad outline of the argument I present here is not new. Placing it within the framework of Kuznets waves is what is new. At the turn of the twentieth century, the argument linking colonialism to domestic maldistribution of income was made by John Hobson in his book *Imperialism: A Study* ([1902] 1965). It was followed by works by Rosa Luxemburg in 1913 *(The Accumulation of Capital)* and Vladimir I. Lenin in 1916 *(Imperialism, the Highest Stage of Capitalism)*. As Hobson put it, "it is not industrial progress that demands the opening up of new markets and areas of investment, but *maldistribution of consuming power* [my emphasis] which prevents the absorption of commodities and capital within the country" (p. 85). There is an entire tradition of linking domestic maldistribution of income to foreign expansion going back to Marx, even if Marx did not develop it as thoroughly as did Hobson, Luxemburg, and Lenin.[39] The objective of this book is not to discuss this view and compare it with others, but to point out that, in this reading of the causes that led to World War I, domestic issues and especially high inequality are of key importance.[40] The Great War did not come out of nowhere, nor did it result from individuals making this or that misreading of the events; it was caused by much deeper structural factors, among which domestic "mal-distribution of consuming power" is perhaps the most important.[41] To be quite clear, because it is an important point: the malign forces that broke the first Kuznets cycle and set the rich world's inequality on its downward path for the next seventy years were contained in the unsustainably high domestic inequality that existed before.

As indirect support for the hypothesis that domestic factors were crucial for the outbreak of the war, I would like to mention Niall Ferguson's *Pity of War* (1999), which deals with the war on the western front (the eastern front is mentioned only in passing) and starts from an entirely different hypothesis: the war was the result of an accident, a malentendu, and the fact that it arrayed one set of powers against another set of powers was not preordained.[42] In other words, both the war and the combination of belligerents on each side were a product of chance. But, and this is crucial for us, at the end of his book Ferguson falls back, reluctantly and probably without fully realizing it himself, to the Marxist explanation that sees both the causes and the outcome of the war as internally driven.[43] In Ferguson's view, the domestic origin of the war lay in longer-term financial weakness in Germany, which constrained its military capacity and demanded an early "defensive preemptive war"; the domestic explanation for the outcome of the war lay in the political strength of the German upper class, which did not want to pay as much for the war as was needed to win it and was sufficiently influential to prevent the government from imposing higher taxes. Since funding the war by borrowing was not possible either domestically, because of the shallowness of the German market, or internationally, after the United States entered the war and Germany was cut off from the New York financial market, Germany basically ran out of money to pay for the war. But note that in both explanations, it is German *domestic* economic and political "correlations of forces" that explain military actions. I focus on Ferguson because his book is one of the best of the recent books on World War I, and it serves to illustrate how even those who seem to explicitly reject domestic factors in the explanation of the war eventually come to acknowledge the importance of those factors.

Malign and benign forces in the era of the Great Leveling. If the First World War is endogenized in the economic conditions of early-twentieth-century Europe (and the world), then our reading of the downward-sloping Kuznets curve is very different from both Kuznets's and Piketty's readings. The internal contradictions between different social classes found an outlet in the war, and once the war unleashed other forces (including the growth of the socialist movement, the Russian revolution, and of course the destruction of physical and financial capital), the downward-sloping part of the first Kuznets wave occurred—not, as is implicit in Piketty's interpretation, as an event exogenous to economics, but as part-and-parcel of economics, and especially part-and-parcel of the high social and economic inequality that preceded the war. This interpretation is also different from that of Kuznets, who essentially ignores the role of wars.

Other real economic gains that came after the war and that reduced income inequality, from social democracy in Sweden, to the New Deal in the United States, to high taxation and trade union density in most of Western Europe, were indeed economic forces or, as we termed them, benign forces, that were rightly emphasized by Kuznets—but they happened because they were precipitated by the war, and the war itself happened because income inequality led to it.

This reading of history at the end of the previous era of globalization is crucial, not only because it addresses the forces that brought globalization to an end and set the Kuznets curve on its downward path, but because it helps to illuminate today's situation. Rising inequality indeed sets in motion forces, often of a destructive nature, that ultimately lead to its decrease but in the process destroy much else, including millions of human lives and huge amounts of wealth. A very high inequality eventually becomes unsustainable, but it does not go down by itself; rather, it generates processes, like wars, social strife, and revolutions, that lower it.

This perspective enables us to notice the similarity between the declines in inequality in the preindustrial era, which were most often caused by cataclysmic events such as wars, epidemics, or natural catastrophes, and the decline of inequality during the first Kuznets wave. Between 1914 and 1980, the decrease in inequality was brought about through a wrenching process, a combination of malign forces like wars and benign economic policies that were characterized by the confluence of interests between left-wing political parties (which emphasized free education, health care, and so on) and property-owning classes that, out of fear of new socialist movements and possible expropriation of capital, accepted measures that created a broad-based middle class. I do not have in mind here only the rich world, but everybody else as well. In developmental states like Turkey, Brazil, and South Korea, the same process occurred even during right-wing dictatorships. This process was also promoted by US international development policies throughout the 1950s, 1960s, and 1970s, when the United States supported right-wing oligarchic regimes, but, in a quid pro quo for that support, urged, and in some cases pressed, these regimes to open themselves up to the middle classes. The United States backed, and even implemented, agrarian reforms in Japan, Taiwan, and South Korea, and it also supported land redistribution schemes in Latin America after John F. Kennedy created the Alliance for Progress in 1961 (not coincidentally, shortly after the Cuban revolution). The same process existed in communist countries, where left-wing dictatorships came to power by nationalizing capital and promising equality and then could not renege on these essential features; thus they continued policies that kept inequality in check, including massive expansion of education and transfer of labor from agriculture to industry—the quintessential Kuznetsian processes. It is therefore wrong to see the downward slide of the first Kuznets wave as pertaining only to rich economies. The era of broadly declining inequality—be it through nationalization, expansion of education, agrarian reform, or the welfare state—was a feature of the third quarter of the twentieth century almost worldwide.

I do not want to downplay the purely economic (or benign) elements that Kuznets emphasized, but it is important to recognize that they occurred within a specific social framework. For example, the

A great leveling that was more radical than the one that occurred in
the West took place in countries that, following Russia in 1917–22,
became socialist after World War II. The socialist great leveling may
have influenced the Western Great Leveling through the impact of
socialist and communist parties in the West, but whatever the exact
relationship, the two leveling processes, together with similar processes
produced by decolonization or in developmental states such as Turkey
and Brazil, should all be viewed as part of the same trend, characteristic
of the short twentieth century.

The socialist great leveling was produced in a simple manner.
First, most enterprises were nationalized, which, as in state-owned
enterprises in the West, resulted in a more compressed wage distribution. (Data on wage distributions in socialist economies are plentiful,
and a number of studies have documented the wage compression.)[44]
The education premium was also reduced. Since most of the
countries that became socialist were less developed than Western
Europe and the United States, one might expect the skill premium to
have been high (say, similar to what it was in Latin America). But
nationalization of enterprises changed that: wages of low-skilled
workers were relatively high and wages of high-skilled workers
relatively low. Massive increase in schooling on the supply side,
however, would have produced some reduction in the high-skill wage
premium even if these were market economies.

Nationalization of the means of production had two other effects on
income distribution. It abolished income from property, income that is
always heavily skewed toward the rich, and it almost eliminated the
entrepreneurial return, since private entrepreneurship was banned or
pushed to the margins. Entrepreneurial income remained in existence

only in small-scale service sectors (hotels, repair shops, etc.), and, in Yugoslavia and Poland, in agriculture, where land stayed largely in private hands but was divided into small parcels. In countries such as Russia and Hungary where large land holdings had dominated in the past, nationalization of land eliminated the high incomes of the landed aristocracy.

Finally, guaranteed jobs and thus the absence of unemployment (with a few exceptions), widespread pensions (often with the exception of agriculture), and subsidization of staple goods (thus ensuring that subsidies were progressive) completed this picture. It is not surprising that, according to Czech sociologist Jiři Večernik (1994), it was possible to estimate total household income by taking into account only the demographic characteristics of a household: how many members it had and how old they were. In other words, education and property ownership, the two most powerful determinants of income in market economies, were made irrelevant.

Was this radical leveling a success? In terms of inequality reduction, undoubtedly yes. But in terms of growth and innovation, no. For a long time, socialist policy-makers held that too much wage equalization eliminated incentives for acquiring new skills and working hard. In the "heroic" phase of socialism, this could be compensated for through "socialist emulation"—psychic income and social esteem acquired by those who, like the miner Aleksei Stakhanov, eponymous hero of the Stakhanovite movement, worked hard for no pecuniary return. But, in the long run, this system was unsustainable. A slew of socialist reforms in the 1960s were supposed to address defects in the system; allowing enterprises to keep more money and distribute it to the best workers was supposed to increase productivity. But the reforms failed on the bedrock of a system that, ideologically, could not afford large differences in income between people and whose political elite did not want to relinquish control of enterprises.

The socialist leveling, or *uravnilovka* in Russian, as it was known in the Eastern bloc, was also inimical to technological progress. As the years went by and the nature of technological progress itself changed, from being embodied in large network industries such as electricity and railroads to much more decentralized ones, the socialist economies fell farther behind their capitalist counterparts. They faced the so-called *zastoi,* or stagnation, of the Brezhnev era, which ultimately brought the system to its collapse.

The example of socialist economies holds several lessons. First, there are limits to voluntaristic policies whereby inequality is reduced out of step with economic conditions. In some deeper sense, such policies were anti-Marxist because they violated the interdependency between the development of the forces of production and the relations of production. Perhaps the "original sin" was that the first Marxist revolution took place in a less-developed country like Russia. Second, equality can be pushed too far: it discourages hard work, education, and innovation. Third, ideology matters, and, contrary to the claims of modern institutionalists like Acemoglu and Robinson (2012), concentrated political power does not necessarily entail concentrated economic power.

ideology of mass education in developing countries, which might have been predicated on the need to create a strong middle class as a bulwark against communism, led, in a purely economic reaction, to a decrease in the education premium and thus lowered inequality. But perhaps none of these developments would have occurred had high inequality not led to a paroxysm that propelled the world into war.

Recognizing the role of ideology and of the economic elements that contributed to the decrease in inequality from 1950 to 1980 gives us hope that humanity, facing a very similar situation today as one hundred years ago, will not allow the cataclysm of a world war to be the remedy for the ills of inequality. Awareness of the destructive nature of increasing inequality and knowledge of the "benign" means to reduce it, combined with the ongoing process of income convergence between populous and relatively poor countries like China and India and the rich world—these factors make one optimistic that a peaceful process of decreasing global inequality could be managed in this century. We shall return to this theme in Chapter 4.

What Is Driving the Second Kuznets Wave Up, and What Might Drive It Down?

How to explain the upward portion? The second Kuznets wave has many similarities with the first. Its rise was driven by a second technological revolution (resulting primarily from progress in information technology) and by globalization (which, as we have seen, also accompanied the first technological revolution).[45] Both technological revolutions created rents; in the case of the second, these rents have been generated in telecommunications, pharmaceuticals, and the financial sector, both for technological leaders and for those who used political power to acquire monopoly power and protection. (This latter process was not in itself independent of economic success because to be able to lobby and influence policy-makers one has to be rich.)

As for labor, a transfer occurred from manufacturing activities into services (not unlike the transfer from agriculture into manufacturing that occurred during the first technological revolution). The service sector is more heterogeneous in terms of occupations and skills than is the manufacturing sector, and the wage dispersal is much greater. Figure 2.21 shows the ratio between the wages at the 90th percentile of the wage distribution and the wages at the 10th percentile of the distribution for US manufacturing and services

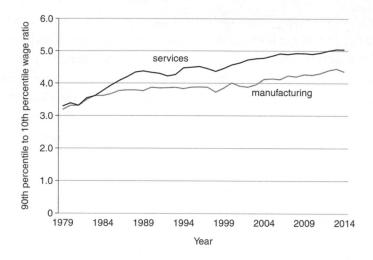

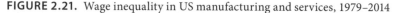

FIGURE 2.21. Wage inequality in US manufacturing and services, 1979–2014

This graph shows wage inequality among wage earners in manufacturing and services in the United States as measured by the ratio between the wage at the 90th percentile of the distribution and the wage at the 10th percentile of the distribution. It shows that wage inequality in services is greater than wage inequality in manufacturing and that the difference has been increasing. Data source: Unpublished tabulation of data from the CPS ORG (Current Population Survey Outgoing Rotation Group) kindly provided by Larry Mishel of the Economic Policy Institute. Details on the data in appendix B of http://stateofworkingamerica.org/files/book/Appendices.pdf.

from 1979 to 2014. In 1979–80, the gaps were almost the same in both sectors. But since then, while wage inequality has increased in both sectors, the increase has been much greater for services; in 2014, the 90–10 wage gap was 5.0 in services and 4.4 in manufacturing. Thus the shift of labor from manufacturing into services will tend to increase wage inequality, and ultimately, income inequality.

The service sector involves greater physical dispersal of activity than does manufacturing and has units of much smaller size. These two features have made organization of workers more difficult or of less relevance. In an era where common interests among various groups of employees are less clear and workers are physically more dispersed, syndicalist organizations have less appeal than they did in the past, resulting in an almost universal decline in trade union densities in the rich countries. This decline is illustrated in Figure 2.22, where, together with the United States and the United Kingdom, I show data for Austria and Germany, long considered examples of the corporatist "world of welfare capitalism" (Esping-Andersen 1990), where strong unionization was supposed to be a key characteristic of the system. The level of unionization declined in all four countries from 1999 through 2013, especially strongly in the two corporatist states. The unweighted average share of unionized labor among employees in all OECD countries went down from 21 percent in 1999 to 17 percent about a decade and half later.[46] The decline of trade union

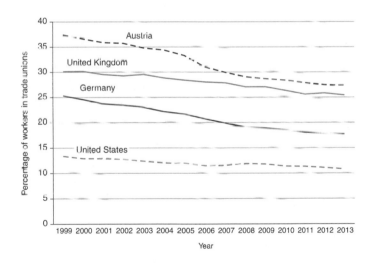

FIGURE 2.22. Trade union density in selected OECD countries, 1999–2013

This graph shows the percentage of workers who belong to trade unions in Austria, the United Kingdom, Germany, and the United States. It shows that the percentage has been decreasing since 1999. Data source: Based on OECD data available at https://stats.oecd .org/Index.aspx?DataSetCode=UN_DEN.

density was especially strong in the private sector. In the public education and health sectors, commonality of interests among workers has remained as strong as in the past, and union density has declined less.[47]

The decline in trade union density underpins a more general process of the weakening of the bargaining position of labor vis-à-vis capital. In a recent revisiting of his own contribution to the theory of growth, Robert Solow looked at the possibility that the declining labor share in rich countries is due to a renegotiation of rents in favor of capital owners.[48] Solow considers an economy-wide model of imperfect competition where value added is distributed between labor and capital, paid according to their marginal products plus a rent, which is the object of negotiation between the two. These rents could be monopoly rents, patent rents, rents arising from obstacles to entry, and the like. The essential point is that the distribution of the rents at the level of each enterprise, sector, and ultimately the whole economy depends on the relative bargaining power of capital and labor. The current era of globalization has witnessed a huge increase in available labor, both because world population has increased by two-thirds since 1980 and because China and the former communist countries have entered the global labor market. This growth in the availability of labor, according to Solow, has weakened labor's position worldwide and allowed capital owners to take most of the rent for themselves. A similar idea is expressed by Chau and Kanbur (2013), who model it as a Nash equilibrium game where the fallback position of capital, because of its ability to move from one country to another in search of lower taxes, is much stronger than that of labor.

The reasons for the increase in inequality in OECD countries have been extensively studied in the last two decades, since the increase became apparent. Originally, lots of attention was paid to wage-stretching, especially, in the United States, with two main contenders as explanatory factors being skill-biased technological change and globalization.[49] After the publication of Piketty's *Capital in the Twenty-First Century,* the role of capital income (both its rate of return and the increasing capital-income ratio) has attracted more attention. Policy changes, in particular reduced marginal tax rates on the highest incomes and lower taxes on capital, have also been found (somewhat obviously) to have contributed to the increase in inequality. In other words, the redistributive function of the modern developed state has either become weaker or remained more or less the same as in the 1980s. And even in the rare instances where redistribution increased, it was not sufficient to check the increase in market income inequality (inequality in primary labor and capital incomes, that is, before social transfers and direct taxes are included). This underlying increase in market income inequality—reflecting higher wage dispersion, greater concentration of income from capital, and association of high incomes from both capital and labor in the same individuals—is crucial for understanding the upward portion of the second Kuznets wave.

Figure 2.23 illustrates the significant increase in inequality of market income that occurred in both the United States and Germany between 1970 and 2010. Consider the United States first: the graph shows that when we add social transfers to market income (to get gross income) and then deduct direct taxes (to get disposable income), the level of inequality is reduced each time; that is, both social transfers and taxes do indeed reduce inequality. However, the trend in the increase of disposable income inequality is almost the same as the trend in the increase of market income inequality. Market income inequality went up from 42 to just over 50 Gini points (an eight-point increase), while disposable income inequality rose from about 36 to 41 Gini points (a five-point increase). Redistribution became slightly more important, or more progressive, but it failed to offset the underlying increase in market income inequality.

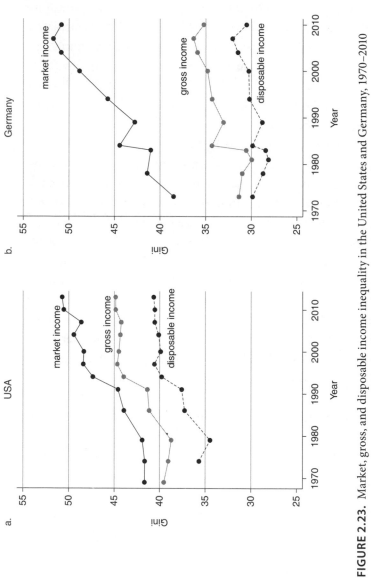

FIGURE 2.23. Market, gross, and disposable income inequality in the United States and Germany, 1970–2010.

This graph compares inequality in market, gross, and disposable income in the United States (a) and Germany (b) between 1970 and 2013. Market, or factor, income includes labor and capital incomes before taxes but does not include any government (social) transfers. Gross income is equal to market income plus social transfers (public pensions, unemployment and child and family allowances, and social assistance). Disposable income is equal to gross income minus all (federal and state) direct taxes. All calculations are done on a per capita basis (that is, Ginis are calculated across household per capita incomes). Data source: Calculated from Luxembourg Income Study (http://www.lisdatacenter.org/).

Looking at the data for Germany, we see that government policies, especially through greater social transfers, have had a powerful effect on reducing inequality—in Germany as compared with the United States as well as within Germany over time. These policies failed, however, to fully offset the increase in German market income inequality: disposable income inequality still went up, even if by only 1 to 2 Gini points.

Some other factors have also been adduced as "culprits" for increased inequality. One of these concerns behavioral changes, such as the greater prevalence of assortative mating, or homogamy; marriages between partners who both have high skills and high incomes have become more common than they were in the 1950s and 1960s (Greenwood et al. 2014). Another suggested cause involves vaguely defined changes in ethical or pay norms, which allow for much wider gaps between the pay of top managers and average workers (Levy and Temin 2007; Piketty 2014, chap. 9).

It is not my objective here to adjudicate between all the likely factors. I believe that because of the complexity of the process, the explanation is overdetermined in the sense that piling all these explanations up on top of each other and assigning relative importances to them would lead us to explain more than 100 percent of the change. This complexity is perhaps best seen when we contrast the two dominant explanations for the increase in US wage inequality: skill-biased technological change and globalization. It could be, as Ebenstein, Harrison, and McMillan (2015) argue, that in a head-to-head competition between these two explanations, the lower price of capital goods leading to the replacement of routine labor and greater complementarity between capital and high-skilled workers wins—namely, explains most of the rising inequality in wages. But that particular causal chain (lower price of capital goods ⇒ technological change ⇒ replacement of routine labor) could have occurred only under the conditions of globalization, where reduced prices of capital goods were made possible thanks to the existence of cheap labor in China and the rest of Asia.[50]

In simple language, it could be that SAP software, Lenovo computers, and Apple iPhones did replace the jobs or reduce the wages of travel agents, hotel clerks, accountants, and shop assistants, but what we may interpret as skill-biased technological change happened because cheap hardware for these products was produced in low-wage Asian countries. This is exactly the interpretation that we can give to the reclining S curve from Chapter 1 (Figure 1.1): these interrelated developments in Asia and the West helped increase the incomes of relatively poor people in Asia (the emerging global middle class) while slowing down to practically zero the growth of incomes of the lower middle class in advanced economies. (Those who like models can think of the world economy as composed of three sectors—one that builds capital goods in low-wage economies, another that uses those machines to get rid of the low-skilled labor in rich countries, and a third that uses only skilled labor to produce luxury goods and services.)

Technological change and globalization are thus wrapped around each other, and trying to disentangle their individual effects is futile. Removing either of them would do away with almost all of the increased wage inequality. And conversely, adding either of them to the existing level of the other (e.g., "adding" globalization to the existing computerization) would on its own explain almost the entire increase in wage inequality. If, in addition, we regard policy changes as endogenous with respect to globalization (as I think we should), it becomes very clear that all three elements of the TOP (technology, openness, and policy), are mutually dependent and cannot be separated in any meaningful sense.

This type of endogenous technological change, where inventions do not fall from the sky but are made to replace relatively more expensive factors of production (such as labor in rich countries), is precisely the same type of technological change that, according to Robert Allen, was responsible for the first technological revolution, which ushered in the first (modern) Kuznets cycle. In a series of papers and a book, Allen (2003, 2005, 2011) argued that it was not British property rights (which were weaker than in France), or low taxation (which was actually higher than in France) that were crucial for the British take-off, but rather the high cost of labor. High wages made it profitable to try to find ways to replace labor with capital. Going further back into the past, the same mechanism was adduced by Aldo Schiavone (2002), following Marx (1965), as an explanation for why capital-intensive production never took place in the ancient world, specifically in Rome. Labor, often consisting of people who had been enslaved as the result of conquests, was too cheap for the Romans to think seriously about replacing it with machines—even if the steam engine was discovered, and used as a toy, in second-century Alexandria. Thus, today's technological progress does not "behave" differently, or respond to different incentives, than in the past, except that the scope of operations is global.

Accounting explanations for the increased inequality in rich countries, as presented in several OECD reports (OECD 2008, 2011), are more modest, since their aim is not a causal explanation of the increase in inequality. They may be preferable in some ways, because they avoid the issue of overdetermination and are noncontentious in the sense that the factors they list can be shown to have been responsible for higher inequality (to be sure, in an accounting sense only). But their drawback is that they do not provide an analytic explanation (e.g., for what caused wages to become more unequally distributed), and they also leave a large chunk of the increase in inequality unexplained. For inequality among households, OECD (2011), using household survey data from some twenty rich economies between the mid-1980s and 2008, found that 60 percent of the increase was due to the widening disparity among men's earnings along with the greater labor participation of men (with the former factor accounting for two-thirds of this total). But we cannot tell whether this wage-stretching was a result of skill-biased technological change or globalization (in the form of displacement of domestic labor by cheaper imports and outsourcing). Assortative mating and change in family structure (e.g., more young people deciding to live alone) explained another 22 percent of the change. Women's increased participation in the labor force, however, reduced inequality by some 19 percent. In the end, about 40 percent of the increase in income inequality remained as a residual. (It is interesting to speculate whether the increased participation of women in the labor force is related to the rising importance of assortative mating, and whether the net effect of these two phenomena on income inequality may be close to zero [22 minus 19, in this case].)

One can, with some effort and simplification, allocate all these "accounting" elements to one of three groups of factors: technology, openness/globalization, and policy (our TOP). But one could argue that TOP, in turn, is directly related to the second technological revolution: technological progress and movement of labor into services are part of this revolution almost by definition; globalization has been an indispensable companion to the development of broader production networks and reduction in the costs of production; and policy, most clearly in the case of lower taxation of capital, has been an "endogenous" response to globalization, that is, to the mobility of capital.

Forces offsetting the increase in inequality. There is no doubt that the Kuznets curve started rising from the early 1980s to the second decade of the twenty-first century, and that this rise has been the key reason for the disenchantment with Kuznets's hypothesis—which predicted only a single curve, with inequality rising up and then going down. On more speculative grounds, we can now ask how long the rich countries can continue on this upward trajectory and what might ultimately check and then reverse the increase in income inequality.

I will argue in Chapter 4 that the forces pushing for a continuation of the increase in inequality seem overwhelming in the United States. They include not only the existing, and well-studied, forces of TOP, but new ones too. Especially important are the combination of high labor and capital incomes received by the same individuals or households (which increases inequality) and the greater influence of the rich on the political process and thus on rule-setting favorable to themselves. The benign economic forces that can curb increasing inequality appear to be scarce. Malign forces, which, as we have argued, set income inequality on a downward path in the early twentieth century, are impossible to predict. However, we should note that very often in history, it has been precisely the malign forces of war, strife, conquest, or epidemics that have reduced inequality. Their influence and role cannot be excluded in the future.

Here, however, I want to discuss not the prospects for any particular country but, at a very abstract level, what benign forces could hypothetically push rich countries onto the downward portion of the second Kuznets wave. They are five. The first involves political changes that may produce higher and more progressive taxation. In democracies with full franchise, this change should come "naturally," in the sense that one would expect increased inequality to result in greater demand for government redistribution. This is, for example, the implication of the median voter hypothesis, which states that in more unequal settings voters will choose a higher tax rate, but its empirical relevance is unclear (Milanovic 2000, 2010a). But we ought to be skeptical of the likelihood of such changes. If anything, globalization has been accompanied by reduced taxation; and political solutions to higher inequality are limited by the mobility of capital as well as by the ability of people to change their jurisdictions to avoid taxation (see Zucman 2013). The increased role of money in politics is similarly pro-rich. Also, those who would benefit from greater redistribution may not be aware of it because they suffer from "false consciousness." (I will return to these themes, within the US context, in Chapter 4.)

The second force is the race between education and skills. Some of the rising skill premium, especially in the United States, could be closed by the rising supply of highly skilled workers. But here, too, we face a natural limit: the number of years of education is bounded from above because it is unrealistic to increase the average number above thirteen years. Even the fact that the US average education level is no longer the highest in the world, according to UNESCO data, is an unsatisfactory or at least an exaggerated explanation for the increase in the wage premium: the gap between the countries with the highest number of years of schooling (Switzerland and the United Kingdom) and the United States is 0.7 years (13.7 vs. 13 years). Moreover, it is not even certain that the United States has slipped from the top position. The Barro-Lee data set, which is the key source of comparative education data and measures the same thing as the UNESCO data, still shows the United States as number one in 2010, just ahead of Switzerland.[51] So, to believe that much can be accomplished by increasing the average level of schooling by about half a year or that it is a significant cause for the rise in the education premium is, I think, unrealistic.

Of course, the quality of education could be improved, but there too it seems that we face natural limits, given by the aptitude and interest of students to excel in whatever they choose to do. It cannot be expected, even if opportunities were fully equalized, that everyone would be both interested in becoming an Einstein and having the aptitude to be one.

The third force for reduced inequality is the dissipation of rents accrued in the early stages of the technological revolution. As the revolution progresses, other people and companies catch up with the early innovators, rents are reduced or eliminated, and income inequality shrinks. Indeed, lots of current wealth has been accumulated in the new technological sectors, best exemplified by Silicon Valley. James Galbraith (2012, 144) shows that one-half of the increase in US personal income inequality between 1994 and 2006 is explained by the exceptionally high income growth in five (out of more than 3,000) US counties: New York County (comprising the borough of Manhattan), Santa Clara, San Francisco, and San Mateo Counties in California, and King County in Washington State. From what we know about these counties, it is not difficult to conclude that people working, or owning stocks, in financial, insurance, and IT sectors were the main beneficiaries. They earned huge rents. But these rents are not going to last forever: their dissipation will reduce inequality.

The fourth element that may check the increase in inequality in the rich world is income convergence at the global level, with wages in China and India rising to come close to those in today's rich countries. This movement, which is opposite to the one that we have witnessed in the past twenty-five years of globalization (see Chapter 1), would put an end to the hollowing out of the rich countries' middle classes and could set the stage for a reduction in within-nation inequalities. That of course assumes—a big and perhaps unwarranted assumption—that other poor countries like Indonesia, Vietnam, and Ethiopia do not come up and take the place vacated by China and India and maintain the pressure on US and other rich countries' wages.

The fifth and final force is more speculative: low-skill-biased technological progress, that is, technologies that would increase the productivity of unskilled workers more than that of skilled workers. Bringing this idea up now, when it is taken as almost axiomatic that technological progress is high-skill-biased or is (at least) inimical to the position of workers performing routinized tasks, sounds somewhat quixotic. But, as implied by the theory of endogenous technological change (whereby technology adapts so as to increase the use of the less costly factor of production), it is pro-low-skill inventions that we should expect if the wage gap between high-skilled and low-skilled labor continues to rise. As high-skilled labor gets relatively more expensive, there must come a point where production conducted with less-skilled labor becomes more efficient. That in turn should provide incentives to inventors to look for low-skill-biased technological innovations. (Note that this process works through incentive effects which are similar to the ones that make the acquisition of higher education advantageous when the skill premium is high. So, the Tinbergen race and endogenous innovations have the same root cause.)

Low-skill-biased technological change would run against the grain of technological innovations that have historically been anti-low-skilled labor and have been a feature of capitalism since its beginnings. It could be argued, however, that, at least in part, the reason why technological change tended to be labor-replacing was that it was used as a labor-disciplining device, and during periods of class conflict, capitalists found it convenient to depend less on labor. A machine will always be more docile than a worker. To the extent that the power of organized labor declines and class conflict recedes, capitalists may become less fearful of stimulating pro-low-skilled labor innovations. This suggestion is, however, speculative, and I am not sure how much hope one can put in it.[52]

These, then, are the forces that we may hypothesize would lead rich countries onto the downward portion of the second Kuznets wave. One should also keep in mind that the peak level of inequality in this wave (which most countries have not yet reached as of this writing, in 2015) is very probably going to be less than the peak of the first Kuznets wave. The reason lies in the number of automatic inequality "reducers," in the form of extensive social programs and state-funded free health and education, that have been established since the latter part of the nineteenth century. If the peak of the second Kuznets cycle is less than the peak of the first, we may perhaps expect also that the downward slide (when it occurs) may not be as steep as it was in the first part of the twentieth century. Consequently, the Kuznets cycles may become less dramatic. But this is just a conjecture. The future often likes to throw curve balls.

3

Inequality among Countries

From Karl Marx to Frantz Fanon, and Then Back to Marx?

Your Honors should know by experience that trade in Asia must be driven and maintained under the protection of Your Honors' own weapons, and that the weapons must be paid for by the profits from the trade, so that we cannot carry on trade without war nor war without trade.

—JAN PIETERSZOON COEN, Dutch East India Company (1614)

Changing Level and Composition of Global Inequality

Having explored patterns of within-nation inequality in Chapter 2, we turn in this chapter to differences in inequality among nations. First, recall what we saw in Chapter 1 about recent changes in global inequality. The reclining S curve (Figure 1.1) showed that the top 1 percent grew much richer between 1988 and 2008, thus adding to global inequality, but inequality was reduced by strong growth among wide sections of the world population situated between the 40th and 60th percentile. The graph thus suggests that overall, global inequality may have decreased. And indeed, we find that the global Gini value decreased from 72.2 in 1988 to 70.5 in 2008 and then to around 67 in 2011 (with some caveats that will be mentioned below). This represents the first time since the Industrial Revolution that global inequality has ceased to increase.[1] We shall look now at the long-term trend in global inequality and how inequalities in different countries have contributed to it.

Global inequality from 1820 to 2011.   Estimates of global inequality for the period 1820–1992 use the very approximate data produced by Bourguignon and Morrisson (2002). Not having household surveys for the period from 1820 to the late 1960s, Bourguignon and Morrisson made some broad assumptions about the evolution of inequalities within nations and used Angus Maddison's estimates of GDP per capita for countries' mean incomes.[2] They found that global inequality increased consistently throughout the nineteenth century, driven by increases in mean incomes in western Europe, North America, and Australia, while countries in the rest of the world, especially India and China, were either stagnant or in decline (see Figure 3.1).[3] Thus, for example, British GDP per capita, according to Maddison, increased from $2,000 in 1820 to almost $5,000 on the eve of the First World War; in contrast, Chinese GDP per capita went down from $600 to $550 during this period, and the figure for India barely edged up, from $600 to $700 (all values are in 1990 international dollars). To use an analogy, the Industrial Revolution (or what we call in this book the first technological revolution) was similar to a big bang that launched a part of mankind onto the path of higher incomes and sustained growth, while the majority stayed where they were, and some even went down. This divergence of paths widened global inequality.

In addition to this divergence among nations, within-nation inequality was increasing in leading countries in the nineteenth century, too, as we saw in Chapter 2. Thus, during the nineteenth century, both among- and within-nation inequalities widened, together pushing

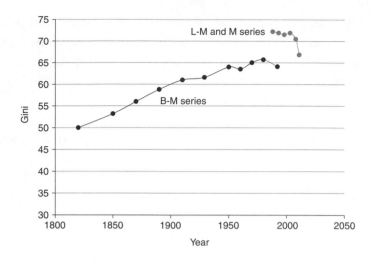

FIGURE 3.1. Global inequality, 1820–2011

This graph shows estimated income inequality (measured by Gini values) between all citizens of the world in the past two centuries, based on three different but related sources. We see that inequality kept increasing until the end of the twentieth century and that it has been on a decline since then. The B-M series uses 1990 international dollars and the L-M and M series use 2005 international dollars; hence the break in the graph. Data sources: B-M series is from Bourguignon and Morrisson (2002); L-M series is from Lakner and Milanovic (2013); M refers to author's (unpublished) results for 2011.

global inequality up. The process, as can be seen in Figure 3.1, slowed down in the post–World War I period, where the movement of global inequality displays a concave shape (increasing more slowly over time) until the level peaks in the last quarter of the twentieth century. Given the scarcity of data, we cannot be sure about the exact date when global inequality reached its maximum; it could have been any time between 1970 and the mid-1990s.[4]

For estimates of global inequality from the late 1980s to the present, we can use the much more detailed and precise household survey data that are available (see Excursus 1.1). From 1988 onward, I rely on figures from Milanovic (2002a, 2005, 2012b) and especially

Lakner and Milanovic (2013), who have created income data by decile for more than 100 countries. Estimates of the level of global inequality from these sources are higher than estimates by Bourguignon and Morrisson (2002) (see Figure 3.1) because the new data include many more countries (some 120 countries vs. 33 geographical areas in Bourguignon and Morrisson) and many more income groups within each country (often 100 percentiles or at least ventiles [20 groups of 5 percent each] obtained from microdata vs. 11 income fractiles in Bourguignon and Morrisson).

In addition, the underlying purchasing power parity exchange rates (PPPs) are different. The availability of PPP exchange rates, which adjust for the differences in price levels between countries, is absolutely indispensable for the calculation of global inequality (see Excursus 1.1). Without PPPs, we would be assuming that people in India face the same prices as people who live in the United States. But PPPs themselves are not stable from year to year, particularly for Asian countries. This instability introduces another unfortunate element of variability into our estimates of global inequality. If the price level of China is estimated (based on surveys of hundreds, and in some cases thousands, of prices) to be relatively low, as was the case with 1990 PPPs used by Bourguignon and Morrisson, then Chinese incomes will be estimated to be relatively high, and global inequality will be less. When the Chinese price level is found to be relatively high, as in the 2005 PPPs used by Lakner and Milanovic, the result will be the opposite. This variation in PPPs is the second element, in addition to the greater availability of data, which results in a higher estimate of the global Gini coefficient by Lakner and Milanovic than by Bourguignon and Morrisson. It is important to keep in mind, however, that this difference in estimates of the overall level of global inequality does not affect, in any substantial way, conclusions about changes in global inequality. Variation in PPPs imparts a one-off upward or downward shift to the level of global inequality but leaves yearly movements practically the same.[5]

From the late 1980s to approximately the turn of the twenty-first century, the level of global inequality was relatively constant, oscillating at slightly above 70 Gini points. A detailed analysis shows that this stability depended on China: if China is excluded from the calculations, the global Gini value increases over time (Milanovic 2012b). Up to 2000, China was the great income equalizer; after 2000, India joined it in playing this role. These countries first kept the increase in global inequality in check and then contributed to reducing the overall level of inequality. Since approximately 2000, there have been unmistakable signs of a decrease in global inequality: each successive year for which we have the data—broadly the same household surveys from the same set of countries—exhibits a slight decline in the Gini coefficient (as shown in Figure 3.1). This slight downward tendency is present for the 1988–2008 period, studied by Lakner and Milanovic (2013). Data for 2011 show an even greater decrease in the global Gini value, driven this time by the stagnation of incomes in the rich world and continued growth in the rest, particularly in Asia.[6] So the decrease in global inequality seems well-established. However, a number of caveats are in order.

First, these results showing a decline in global inequality cover a relatively short period of just a decade. Second, they are the product of progress in Asia coupled with a slowdown in the West. Although there are good reasons at this point (2015) to think that growth rates in Asia will remain high, even if growth decelerates in China, we cannot be absolutely sure of this; a reversal of these tendencies is possible, and the current drop in global inequality may, in the longer term, appear simply as a blip in an otherwise upward trend.

The third caveat, which is even more serious, has to do with our inability to estimate accurately the highest incomes. In Chapter 1, I explained that the share of the global top 1 percent goes up if we make sensible and rather moderate assumptions regarding the omission of high incomes from national household surveys. The same thing happens to the global Gini value: it goes up when we incorporate assumptions to correct for the underestimation of top incomes. What appeared before as a sizable decline of almost 2 Gini points between 1988 and 2008 becomes a slight drop of just half a Gini point (Lakner and Milanovic 2013). Thus, our very conclusion that global inequality is on the decline ought to be taken with a grain of salt. Even though the 2011 data show the decline to be rather steep, if one wishes to be on the conservative side (and in such matters one should be), the most accurate statement would be that the evidence suggests that global income inequality is either stable or on a decline. A stronger statement would be to say that there is no evidence of rising global income inequality (and the difference in income between the Western and Asian middle classes has clearly been shrinking).

Calculating global inequality is a relatively recent exercise that began to be undertaken only at the close of the twentieth century. Even the very concept of global inequality is new. Investigations of the topic have been stimulated by two related developments: globalization, which brought to our attention the problem of large differences in incomes between people living in different countries, and, for the first time in history, the availability of detailed household survey data for most of the world. Crucial events leading to the second development were the opening of China (with household surveys, after the hiatus during the Cultural Revolution, restarting in 1982); the fall of communism in the Soviet Union, which opened to researchers the data on income distribution that had previously been treated as a state secret; and, finally, the expansion of survey methodology and data gathering to cover many African countries (thanks largely to the World Bank).

Let us contrast now the two long-run estimates of inequality that have only recently become available: those for the United States and those for the world as a whole (Figure 3.2).[7] Several interesting conclusions can be made from this comparison. At the turn of the

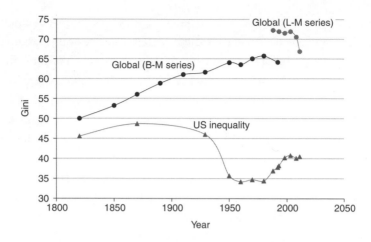

FIGURE 3.2. Global and US inequality, 1820–2011

This graph shows global and US income inequalities (calculated across world and US citizens, respectively). We see that in the recent period, global inequality is decreasing while US inequality is going up. US inequality is, however, much lower than global inequality. Data sources: For US data, see sources listed for Figure 2.10; for global data, see sources listed for Figure 3.1.

nineteenth century, global and US inequality were not very different, as measured by Gini values. Compared to today, the world was then much more equal, and the United States was much more unequal. Until the Civil War, US inequality increased almost in step with global inequality (there is no claim of causality or relationship there, just a recording of the facts). The rise in the global Gini value was driven by the success of western Europe and its offshoots, including the United States, and by lack of growth elsewhere. US inequality went up as land rents increased relative to wages (with continued migration, the land/labor ratio was going down) (Peter Lindert, pers. comm.). But after the First World War, and especially after the Depression and the New Deal in the United States, the two inequalities went their separate ways: while global inequality continued to increase, albeit at a slower pace, American inequality decreased substantially, particularly during the post–World War II period, widely thought today to have been the golden age of capitalism. The parting of the ways continued, but in a reverse direction. After another turning point in the 1980s, global inequality turned stagnant and then, mostly thanks to China's growth, began to decrease, while US inequality began to rise. As Figure 3.2 shows, the gap between the two, while still enormous, has narrowed.

This short overview of US and global inequalities provides us with the key theme that we shall treat in Chapter 4 when we try to predict (or rather divine) the evolution of inequalities in this century and perhaps the next. The United States and the world are to some extent emblematic, because it could very well turn out that current trends, namely a downward movement for the world and an upward movement for the United States, will continue, and that in a half century we will return to the starting point of the early nineteenth century, with the two inequality levels being very similar.

"Location" versus "class" in global inequality.   But is this comparison of global and national inequalities, and their different courses, of anything more than passing interest? In fact it is much more than that: the way that global inequality is shaped, what its most important component is, and what drives it up or down—these questions contain fundamental implications for how we view the world and our place in it. Investigating them is where the political importance of global inequality emerges. It is important to determine whether the key cleavage is the one between individuals (poor and rich) who live in the same country or the one between individuals who live in different countries. For simplicity, we shall call the first "class-based inequality" and the second "location-based inequality." In other words, we are asking whether most global inequality results from the fact that there are poor and rich people more or less equally distributed among countries, or whether, on the contrary, global inequality is mostly explained by a concentration of the rich in one set

EXCURSUS 3.1. Global Inequality Decomposed into "Location" and "Class"

In very general terms, we can write the following equation:

Global inequality = inequality among nations + inequality within nations

= (sum of) differences in mean incomes *among* nations + (sum of) inequalities of personal incomes *within* nations

= "location" component + "class" component.

The exact definition of the "sum" will depend on what measure of inequality we use (Gini or Theil, another popular measure of inequality, or yet a third one), and it will always be a weighted sum, where weights can be the shares of each country in total world population or in total world income or both. The Gini coefficient is special because it does not decompose exactly into these two components but includes an additional term (called "overlap"), which moves up or down together with the "within" component and can be treated as part of it (Milanovic 2002a, 82–84). Theil measures of inequality are, however, exactly decomposable into "among" and "within" components.

Some intuition may help to explain what the location and class components stand for. Consider a group of countries with approximately the same mean income levels, like the early European Union members, known as the EU15.[8] If we calculate overall inequality of personal incomes across the EU15, little of that inequality is explained by the differences in mean country incomes, or by what we call "location," simply because the mean incomes of Germany, France, the Netherlands, and so on, are very similar. Most of the inequality is due to inequalities within nations, or what we call, with some poetic license, "class": it reflects inequalities among individuals belonging to the same nation.

But now let the EU expand, mostly to the east, to reach its current size of 28 countries (the EU28).[9] Since the expansion includes poorer countries, we expect that overall inequality will go up, but also that the share of total inequality due to the differences in mean incomes (the among-nations component, or location) will become greater. The reason is simply that there are large gaps in mean incomes between Bulgaria and Germany, Romania and France, and so on. It should then be obvious that when we look at global inequality and take into account the fact that differences in mean incomes among countries of the world are very large (think of the gap between Luxembourg and Congo), the among-nations component can be expected to be very large too.

A final point, which we have left aside so far in order not to complicate the exposition: in all of these calculations, more populous countries matter more—in effect, they matter in proportion to their population size.

of countries and the poor in a different set. These two distributions correspond to the two components of global inequality—respectively, inequality within nations and inequality among nations. Inequality in the United States, as shown in Figure 3.2, is obviously just one, albeit an important, part of the total inequalities within nations. To determine the overall importance of these inequalities, we have to add them up for all countries. If all such within-nation inequalities increase, then (everything else being the same), global inequality will tend to go up too.

How did global inequality increase over the past two centuries? The dominant force, invoked in our simile of a big bang, was the divergence of mean country incomes. Schematically speaking, it is because Great Britain, western Europe, and the United States became rich while China and India remained poor that global inequality increased in the nineteenth century and then continued to rise throughout most of the twentieth.

We can calculate exactly the importance of location (differences in mean country incomes) in global inequality. Figure 3.3 shows the between-country component in percentage terms, using a different measure of inequality (Theil (0) or Theil entropy index), whose advantage over the Gini measure is that it is fully decomposable between class and location.[10] (Gini decomposition yields very similar results.) As Figure 3.3 shows, the location element was almost negligible in 1820: only 20 percent of global inequality was due to difference among countries. Most of global inequality (80 percent) resulted from differences within countries; that is, the fact that there were rich and poor people in England, China, Russia, and so on. It was class that mattered. Being "well-born" in this world (as we also see in the literature of the time) meant being born into a high income group rather than being born in England, or China, or Russia. But as the upwardly rising line in the figure shows, that changed completely over the next century. The proportions reversed: by the mid-twentieth century, 80 percent of global inequality depended on where one was born (or lived, in the case of migration), and only 20 percent on one's social class. This world is best exemplified by European colonialism in Africa and Asia, where small groups of Europeans disposed of incomes a couple of hundred times greater than those of the native people.[11] The key point is not just to compare the incomes of Europeans in Africa with those of Africans, but to realize that these were *typical* incomes for such classes of people in western Europe.[12] It is by juxtaposing Europeans living in close physical proximity with Africans or Asians that we can see how stark the differences were.

The situation in the world was then (and still is) such that being born in a rich country mattered much more than being born "well" (in a rich family). The contrast drawn by Frantz Fanon between the

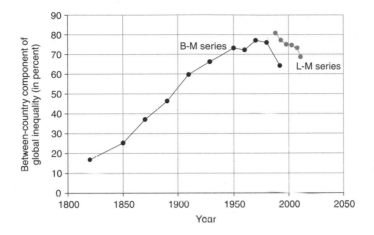

FIGURE 3.3. Share of the between-country component in global inequality, 1820–2011

This graph shows what percentage of global inequality (measured by the Theil (0) or Theil entropy index) is accounted for by between-country inequality, that is, by the gaps between national per capita incomes. When that share increases, it means that national mean income, as opposed to a person's individual circumstances, is becoming more important. Data sources: See sources listed for Figure 3.1.

colonizers and the colonized represents that type of world best—as opposed to the world with which Marx dealt, for practically his entire life, which was the world of class.[13] The situation started to change toward the end of Marx's life and after his death, as can be seen in Engels's writings (1895) on how the British "labor aristocracy" was pulling ahead of the rest of the world's workers. Engels attributed this shift to the British exploitation of the colonies: "As long as England's industrial monopoly [in the world] was maintained, the English working class to a certain extent shared in the advantages of this monopoly. These advantages were distributed among the workers very unevenly; the lion's share was snatched by a privileged minority, though something was left over from time to time for the broad masses."[14] By 1915, when Bukharin wrote *Imperialism and World Economy*, there was no more doubt that even workers in rich countries enjoyed a higher standard of living than most of the population in colonies. The labor aristocracy that was created in the rich countries thanks to colonial exploitation, among other factors, was the reason why the Second International broke down and supported the war: as Bukharin (1929, 165) wrote, "the exploitation of third persons (pre-capitalist producers) and colonial labor led to the rise in the wages of the European and American workers." This is exactly the phenomenon we see reflected in Figure 3.3: the rising importance of location meant that, say, British workers' standard of living outpaced the standard of living of the middle classes and even of many rich people in Africa and Asia (that is, people who were rich within their own countries' distributions). Indeed, this period saw the creation of the Third World. In the words of the economic historian Peer Vries (2013, 46), "what occurred in the nineteenth century with Western industrialisation and imperialism was not simply a changing of the guard. What emerged was a gap between rich and poor nations, powerful and powerless nations, that was unprecedented in world history."

The inequality gap among nations probably reached its highest point around 1970, as shown in Figure 3.4, where we contrast GDP per capita in international dollars for the United States, China, and India. (These three countries decisively influence the movement of global inequality because of their large populations and income shares.) Around 1970, China and India had about the same GDP per capita, and their relative distance with respect to the United States was greater than at any point since the early nineteenth century. From the 1950s to the mid-1970s, US GDP per capita, expressed in international dollars, exceeded the Chinese GDP by a ratio of around 20 to 1. By the end of the first decade of the twenty-first century, the ratio was less than 4 to 1. It had become the same as the ratio in 1870.

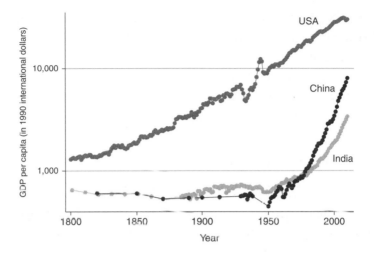

FIGURE 3.4. GDP per capita in the United States, China, and India, 1820–2010

This graph shows the long-run evolution of American, Chinese, and Indian real GDP per capita (measured in 1990 international dollars). Vertical axis is in logs. Real GDPs per capita are comparable across time for the same country as well as across countries. Data source: Calculated from Maddison Project (2013).

The world where location has the most influence on one's lifetime income is still the world we live in. It is the world that gives rise to what we might call a "citizenship premium" for those who are born in the right places (countries), and a "citizenship penalty" for those born in the wrong places (countries). This topic, which is of both economic importance (relating, for example, to migration) and philosophical import (in considering whether this premium can be defended on the grounds of "justice") is what we shall deal with in the next section. But in the background, we need to keep in mind that slight downward kink in Figure 3.3, which shows a decreasing importance of the locational element during the past decade. If we extend it into the future, we can ask: Could the people living a century hence be living in a world where class, as in the early nineteenth century, will be the dominant cleavage rather than location? Indeed, if we assume that there will be faster growth in poor and emerging market economies than in rich countries (economic convergence) and increased inequalities within nations in all three types of countries (thus a hollowing out of national middle classes), this is exactly what will happen. But we are not there yet.

The Citizenship Premium

It is hardly necessary to point out that the world is unequal in terms of individuals' incomes. The global Gini value of slightly under 70 is significantly greater than the national Gini value in even the most unequal countries in the world, such as South Africa and Colombia. But as we have just seen, the world is unequal in a very particular way: most of the inequality, when we break it down into inequality within countries and inequality among countries, is due to the latter. When income differences among countries are large, then a person's income depends significantly on where they live, or indeed where they were born, since 97 percent of the world's population live in the countries where they were born.[15] The citizenship premium that one gets from being born in a richer country is in essence a rent, or if we use the terminology introduced by John Roemer in his *Equality of Opportunity* (2000), it is an "exogenous circumstance" (as is the citizenship penalty) that is independent of a person's individual effort and their episodic (that is, not birth-related) luck.

I would now like to address three questions: How big is the citizenship rent? How does it vary with one's position in the income distribution? and What does it imply for global inequality of opportunity and migration?

Can we empirically estimate the citizenship rent? Yes, we can, and I have done so by using the data from household surveys conducted in 118 countries in and around the year 2008 (Milanovic 2015). For each country, I use microdata (at the household level) which are ordered into 100 percentiles, with people ranked by their household per capita income. This gives 11,800 country-percentiles, with the mean per capita income of people in each percentile expressed in dollars of equal purchasing power. Next, we can try to "explain" these incomes by only one variable: the country where people live. People living in the United States tend to have higher incomes, at any given percentile of the national distribution, than people living in poor countries. This means that a person at the 10th (or 50th or 70th) percentile of American income distribution is better off than a person at the 10th (or 50th or 70th) percentile of, say, Kenyan income distribution: there is a "premium" to being an American compared with being a Kenyan at any point of the income distribution. But how do these premiums look for the world as a whole? In a regression, I use Congo, the poorest country in the world, as the "omitted country," so that the citizenship premium is expressed in terms of the income gain compared to Congo. The average national premium for the United States is 9,200 percent; for Sweden, 7,100 percent; for Brazil, 1,300 percent; but for Yemen, only 300 percent.[16] It turns out that we can "explain" (in a regression sense) more than two-thirds of the variability in incomes across country-percentiles by only one variable: the country where people live. We now have an answer to the first question: a lot of our income depends on where we live. Just by being born in the United States rather than in Congo, a person would multiply her income by 93 times.

The citizenship rent, or premium, thus calculated is an average premium, country against country, and calculated across all citizens; but now we can ask, turning to the second question, whether it varies along the income distribution. In other words, if we were to take into consideration only people belonging to the lowest parts of income distributions everywhere, would the premium still be the same? What about if we were to compare only rich people within each nation, say, top one-percenters from Congo, Sweden, the United States, and Brazil? Intuition may help here. Suppose we focus only on the incomes of the lowest deciles in all countries and assume that incomes are more equally distributed in rich countries than in poor countries (which is generally true). Then the gap between rich and poor countries would be especially great for the nationally poor people, that is, people in the lower parts of their countries' income distributions. This is indeed what we find: Sweden's citizenship premium (when compared with Congo) for the lowest decile is 10,400 percent (vs. 7,100 percent on average), but Brazil's is "only" 900 percent (vs. 1,300 percent on average). In other words, the poor in Sweden are doing even better relative to the poor in Congo than the average Swede is doing compared with the average Congolese. But in Brazil this is not the case.

The situation at the top is exactly the opposite: Sweden's advantage at the 90th percentile of income distribution is "only" 4,600 percent, whereas Brazil's advantage is 1,700 percent. While at every point of an income distribution it is better to be Swedish than Congolese, that advantage is especially great at the bottom of the distribution and is less at the top. And similarly, while at every point of an income distribution it is better to be Brazilian than Congolese, that advantage is especially great at the top of the distribution and is less at the bottom.

Citizenship premium and migration. Let us now address the third question posed above. The existence of the citizenship premium has important implications for migration: people from poor countries have the opportunity to double or triple or increase ten-fold their real incomes by moving to a rich country. But the fact that the premium varies as a function of one's position in the income distribution carries additional implications. If a person considers two countries with the same average income as his possible migration destination, his decision (based on economic criteria alone) about where to migrate will also be influenced by the expectation regarding where he may end up in the recipient country's income distribution, and thus about how unequal the recipient country's distribution is. Suppose that Sweden and the United States have the same mean income. If a potential migrant expects to end up in the bottom part of the recipient country's distribution, then he should migrate to Sweden rather than to the United States: poor people in Sweden are better off compared to the mean than they are in the United States, and the citizenship premium, evaluated at lower parts of the distribution, is greater. The opposite conclusion follows if he expects to end up in the upper part of the recipient country's distribution: he should then migrate to the United States.

This last result has unpleasant implications for rich countries that are more egalitarian: they will tend to attract lower-skilled migrants who generally expect to end up in the bottom parts of the recipient countries' income distributions.[17] Thus, having a more developed national welfare state could have the perverse effect of attracting migrants who are less skilled and can contribute less. Another element, however, has to be taken into account, even in this admittedly very rough sketch: how much social mobility there is in the recipient country. More unequal countries with strong social mobility will, everything else being the same, tend to appeal to more-skilled migrants who expect to end up in the upper part of the recipient countries' income distributions. The ability to move up the ladder was precisely the image, and might also have been the reality, of the United States in the nineteenth century and perhaps most of the twentieth. But this third attractive feature of the United States (in addition to higher mean income and more unequal income distribution) may be losing some of its luster, since, according to some studies, intergenerational mobility is now lower in the United States than in northern Europe (see, e.g., Corak 2013).

Some countries with highly developed welfare states may try to isolate themselves from the "negative" effects of disproportionately attracting low-skilled migrants. One way to do it, as in Canada, the United Kingdom, and Australia, is by accepting only "qualified" migrants. These are migrants with high levels of education or some special characteristics which make them attractive to the recipient country (say, high athletic or artistic ability). Other countries try to attract rich migrants. In this case, residency permits and ultimately citizenships are bought: a person needs to invest a certain amount of money (which may range from a couple of hundred thousand to several million dollars) into a company or real estate. The United States is one of the countries that takes this approach, allowing migrants who invest $1 million in US companies (or $500,000 in companies located in rural or high-unemployment areas) to receive a green card. A number of countries in Europe allow foreigners to reside there, and thus to travel visa-free within the Schengen zone (an area of free movement within most of the European Union), in exchange for a real estate investment. Both such filters, education and money, are supposed to improve the pool of immigrants a country receives, and thus ultimately to contribute to the country's economic output and enable the maintenance of its welfare state by minimizing the number of migrants who depend on social transfers. From the point of view of individual countries, these are intelligent strategies. The problem is that from the global perspective, this approach to migration is heavily discriminatory. To one set of "discriminations," the citizenship rent, we add another set of discriminations whereby this rent may also be enjoyed by those who were not lucky enough to have been born in a rich country but have exceptional abilities or wealth. We run the risk that such policies will result in the poor world, and I am thinking especially of Africa here, becoming even poorer as its most educated and wealthiest members leave.

All of these problems illustrate both the complexity of the issues in the era of globalization and the need to think of the problems from a global perspective rather than solely from the point of view of individual nations and their populations. We shall return to this point at the end of the chapter, where I discuss some rules for migration policy.

The Coase Theorem and the rule of law in the era of globalization. Differences in income among nations have many policy implications of which we are only beginning to be vaguely aware because most of our economic tools were developed to be used within nation-states. Inequality of opportunity is a good example: we almost never think of it as extending beyond the confines of a nation-state. Global inequality of opportunity, which we discuss in the next section, is so little mentioned that even the expression represents a terminological novelty. But there are other cases, too, many of them linked to migration. Consider the privatization process in the former communist countries, particularly in Russia, where this process was the most extensive and probably the most corrupt. At the time, a key argument for the benefit of fast privatization, even if unjust or corrupt, was that, from the point of view of efficiency, it does not really matter to whom assets are sold and at what prices. Surely, the argument went, there will be distributional consequences regarding who benefits from cheap assets (some people will become immensely rich, while many others will get nothing), but there will not be longer-term implications for economic efficiency. Why not? Because if assets are given practically for free to people who do not know what to do with them, those people will have an incentive to sell the assets quickly to "real" entrepreneurs who know how to manage them. This argument was consistent with the Coase Theorem, which states that we can separate matters of economic efficiency from matters of distributional justice, essentially by relegating the latter to an area outside economic policy.

Moreover, even before the new tycoons sell the assets—that is, as soon as they have been gifted with them—they will have an incentive to push hard for the rule of law. This conclusion seemed self-evident. Even if privatization was done in the most lawless and nontransparent fashion, the new millionaires would, like the robber barons in the United States, demand the rule of law and property rights in order to protect their newly acquired wealth. Thus, however badly the first round of privatization went, neither economic efficiency nor the property rights needed for dynamic efficiency (that is, for economic efficiency over a longer period of time) would suffer. Everything would work out as in the best of all possible worlds. This view informed the policy-makers and liberal economists in Russia, Ukraine, and the West in the mid-1990s.

But it was wrong in at least two important ways. First, it disregarded distributional issues by simply assuming they were political or social matters that could be neatly separated from economics. Once rules are broken in such an egregious and unjust manner, however, the effects endure both politically and economically. The temptation is there to break the rules again and to seize the assets that were once stolen, or to give them to other people. So believing that one can leave distribution out of economics was wrong.

But there is a second problem that interests us here, and which arises because economists and policy-makers failed to take globalization into account. The view that robber barons may demand the rule of law and the protection of property rights once they have acquired property seems reasonable—so long as we assume that there is no globalization. But with globalization, it is not necessary to fight for the rule of law in one's own country. A much easier course of action is to take all the money and run away to London or New York, where the rule of law already exists and where nobody will ask where the money came from. A number of plutocrats from Russia, and increasingly from China, are taking this route. It makes complete sense from the individual point of view. And it also shows how our economic thinking has not caught up with the economic reality. In the nineteenth century, families like the Rockefellers championed property rights in the United States because there were few other places where they could go and squirrel away their money. The lesson here is that theories that might in principle work when we take the nation-state as our framework, as we often tacitly do, may not be applicable to a world where capital movements are almost entirely free and difficult to control, and where the rich can easily move from one jurisdiction to another—in particular, to a jurisdiction where the rules for migration favor the wealthy.

Global inequality of opportunity. The very existence of a large citizenship premium indicates that there is currently no such thing as global equality of opportunity: a lot of our income depends on the accident of birth. Should we strive to remedy this situation? Or should we concede that the quest for equality of opportunity ends at national borders? The *ne plus ultra* of the nation-state? This is a question that political philosophers have thought about more than economists. Some, following John Rawls and his *Law of Peoples* (1999), believe that global equality of opportunity is not a significant issue and that every argument for it conflicts with the right of national self-determination. Differences in wealth and opportunity between countries are viewed as the product of the differences in choices made by nations: people in some nations, according to Rawls, decide to work and save more; those in other nations decide to work and save less: "if [a people] is not satisfied [with its wealth] it can continue to increase savings or ... borrow from other members of the Society of Peoples" (p. 114).[18] Those who are poorer have no claim on the income or wealth of the richer. Their claims cannot be a matter of justice (according to Rawls and other statists). If they really could lay a claim on richer societies' income, whether in terms of redistribution or through a right to move there, we would run into a moral hazard problem, where some people would make irresponsible collective choices and then ask to share income acquired by those who were much more prudent or made better decisions. National self-determination, that is, decisions taken by a group of people who share a citizenship, would be meaningless in this case.[19]

It could additionally be argued that effort (which we cannot observe) is not the same across countries (that is, across individuals living in different countries). If people who live in rich countries expend greater effort than people in poor countries, then the observed gap in incomes is not entirely (or perhaps not at all) due to the differences in their circumstances and thus cannot be considered a rent.

The effort argument does not carry much empirical weight, though, for at least two reasons. First, we know that the number of hours worked is, if anything, greater in poor countries, and second, when we compare the same occupations that involve the same amount of effort, we still find very large differences in real wages in different countries.[20] Using detailed data from the UBS (2009) survey of occupational wages in capital cities of the world, we can easily compare the wages of workers in various occupations (both nominal [dollar] and real [adjusted for domestic price level] wages). Consider three occupations with increasing levels of skill—construction worker, skilled industrial worker, and engineer—in five cities, two rich (New York and London) and three poor (Beijing, Lagos, and Delhi). The real hourly (that is, per unit of effort) wage gap between the rich and poor cities is 11 to 1 for the construction worker, 6 to 1 for the skilled worker, and 3 to 1 for the engineer (Milanovic 2012a). So the argument that people in rich countries are paid more because they work more can, I think, be soundly rejected.[21]

But what about the national self-determination argument, which is indeed more serious? Shifting this argument back from the level of nations within the world to that of individual families within the nation-state, this argument looks very similar to the arguments that are used against redistribution within nations. There is a symmetry between (A) families versus the nation in discussions of equality of opportunity within a nation-state, and (B) nations versus the world in discussions of global equality of opportunity. A conservative position holds that in the case of both (A) and (B), intergenerational transfers of collectively acquired wealth are a good thing even though they reduce equality of opportunity: it is acceptable for families to transfer their wealth and advantages intergenerationally, and it is also acceptable for nations to transfer wealth within the nation and not redistribute it to poorer nations. "Cosmopolitans" also maintain a consistent position: they reject claims to allow the transmission of wealth within families (case A) and within nations (case B), holding that it is more important, at both levels, to guarantee equality of opportunity. Others, such as Rawls, maintain the difficult "intermediate" position that in case (A) the transmission of *family*-acquired advantages across generations is not desirable (that's why Rawls and most liberals argue for high inheritance taxes) but in case (B) the transmission of *nationally* acquired advantage across generations is acceptable.

In the intermediate position, it is necessary to argue that there is something fundamentally unique about a nation (in relation to the rest of the world) that is lacking in a family (in relation to other families of the same nation-state). The arguments against global equality of opportunity have to be very carefully calibrated to make the case that equality of opportunity is a good thing as long as we are talking of a single nation-state but becomes a bad thing once we cross borders. Simon Caney (2002) presents such an argument in terms of Rawls's implicit "domain restriction": civil and political rights and distributive justice apply to the domestic realm, but not to international affairs. It is not self-evident why this would be the case, though. Almost a century ago, the British economist Edwin Cannan, in his discussion of Adam Smith's invisible hand, asked this question: "if . . . indeed, it [is] true that there is a natural coincidence between self-interest and the general good, why . . . does not this coincidence extend, as economic processes do, across national borders?"[22]

To maintain Rawls's position, one must also show that national self-determination plays a fundamentally different role than individual "self-determination" does, that is, a person's free will. For indeed the claim that redistribution within the nation-state may create a moral hazard problem because the poor may choose not to work is found wanting by Rawls in his *Theory of Justice,* but then in *The Law of Peoples* he invokes approvingly an almost identical claim to dismiss the argument for redistribution among nations. There is an unresolved tension between Rawls's *Theory of Justice,* where, within a nation-state, the arguments against equality of opportunity are rejected through the ingenious invention of the veil of ignorance, and his *Law of Peoples,* where very similar arguments against equality of opportunity among global citizens are considered valid. To quote Rawls from *Theory of Justice* (1971, 100–101): "the principle [is] that undeserved inequalities call for redress, and since inequalities of birth and natural endowments are undeserved, these inequalities are to be compensated for." But obviously, for Rawls, this principle does not hold globally.

Other political philosophers, such as Thomas Pogge (1994), Charles Beitz (1999), Peter Singer (2004), and Darrel Moellendorf (2009), believe that in an interdependent world, large differences in life chances between nations should not be accepted lightly. If nations are interconnected, and the relationships between individuals from different nations are not simply mediated by their states but are entered into by individuals themselves, then an implicit social compact exists between citizens of the world. It may not be as clear as the compact that exists between the citizens of a single country who elect and share a government, but this is just a difference of degree, not of kind.

A possibly different way to look at global distributive justice is through a much more flexible and open definition of citizenship proposed by the legal scholar Ayelet Shachar in *The Birthright Lottery* (2009). If citizenship were defined in broader terms, as in Shachar's concept of *jus nexi,* the idea that citizenship should be granted to all those who can demonstrate genuine social connectedness with a polity, and/or if migration from poor to rich countries became easier, then the citizenship premium would gradually erode and lose the salience that it currently has.[23]

But this erosion could also happen through the process of globalization if continued high growth rates among poor, populous countries result in a reduction of the differences in mean incomes between poor and rich nations, thus diminishing the importance of the location component of global inequality. If China, India, the United States, Europe, Brazil, Russia, and Nigeria all end up having about the same mean income, not only will global inequality decline, but the location element will also be less important, and the citizenship rent will become much lower. As we shall see in Chapter 4, this process may happen in the twenty-first century.

Fundamentally, if the forces of economic convergence and migration are strong enough, the citizenship rent will diminish. But can we expect migration to play a significant role if the obstacles to migration are becoming ever higher?

Migration and Walls

There is a fundamental contradiction at the heart of globalization as it exists today. In its broadest terms, globalization implies the seamless movement of the factors of production, goods, technology, and ideas across the world. But while this is true for capital, merchandise exports and imports, and increasingly even for the trade in services, it is not true for labor. The stock of migrants globally, measured as a share of world population, did not increase between 1980 and 2000 (Özden et al. 2011). We do not yet have full data on the recent increase in migration and do not know if the migration flows will subside or if the higher numbers represent a new normal. But we are often under the impression that migration has increased dramatically partly because the world is becoming more closed or inimical to migration. Thus, a given number of migrants simply attracts more attention. At the same time, the potential number of migrants has risen owing to better knowledge about the differences in incomes between nations. This tension is most visible in Europe, which has a very hard time absorbing more migrants and yet is exposed to relentless pressure from the poorer areas that surround it, both from the east (the former Soviet republics and the Balkans) and the south (Arab countries and sub-Saharan Africa).

Figure 3.5 highlights the places in the world where there are physical barriers to the movement of people: walls, fences, and minefields. (The map was completed just before the upsurge of immigration into Europe in the summer of 2015 and the erection of several new border fences.) In almost all cases, the barriers correspond to the places where the poor and the rich world are in close physical proximity. In other words, when we look at countries that are contiguous (by land or across water) and have large differences in income, we find the places with the greatest barriers to migration.

Consider the eight locations shown in Figure 3.5. The fence between the United States and Mexico runs for 650 miles out of a total land border of almost 2,000 miles. The Mediterranean flank of southern Europe is "defended" by a quasi-military operation called Frontex, consisting of a fleet of small patrol boats that are supposed to intercept and return migrants to Africa, or if they refuse to return, to place them in camps where the would-be migrants often live under (to put it mildly) very difficult conditions. The wall between Israel and Palestine was erected for political, but also economic reasons: the

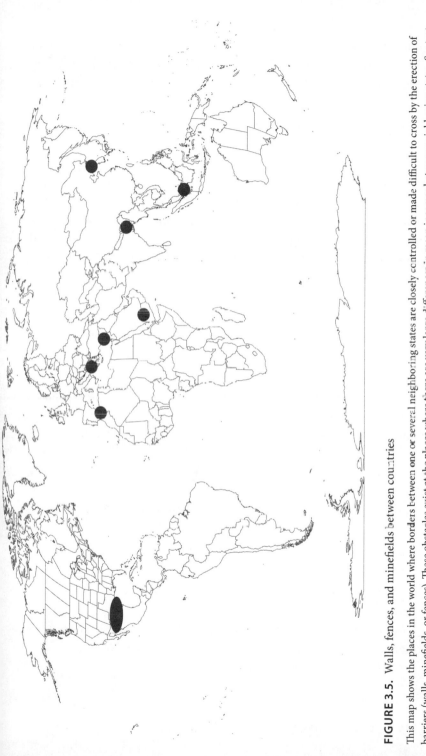

FIGURE 3.5. Walls, fences, and minefields between countries

This map shows the places in the world where borders between one or several neighboring states are closely controlled or made difficult to cross by the erection of barriers (walls, minefields, or fences). These obstacles exist at the places where there are very large differences in mean incomes between neighboring states. See text for discussion of locations.

ratio in the average income between an Israeli and a Palestinian (inhabitant of the West Bank or Gaza) is, according to household surveys, 10 to 1.[24] The same combination of reasons (political and economic) motivates Saudi Arabia's wall on the border with Yemen. North and South Korea are divided by minefields, for political reasons. But gaps that were originally political have ended up creating enormous economic gaps. We do not know what the mean income in North Korea is, but it is unlikely to be greater than one-tenth of South Korea's income. The Strait of Malacca, where Indonesia and Malaysia come closest to each other, is patrolled by boats whose objective is to prevent movement of Indonesian labor to Malaysia—still, some 400,000 Indonesians are working in Malaysia. Yet another wall or fence in our melancholy series is the one being built between India and Bangladesh (stretching for more than 2,000 kilometers, and in part going over the water). Although the income gap between these two countries is not as wide as in the other cases, the gap does exist (amounting to some 50 percent, according to household surveys, or two to one, according to GDP per capita); in addition, the ethnic and religious similarity between Bangladesh (formerly East Bengal) and West Bengal in India helps to feed a constant stream of migrants into India. The wall was built with the express purpose of blocking this stream.

Bulgaria has recently started building a wall on its Turkish border. Its main motivation is to stop the influx of Syrian migrants into the European Union. Although Bulgaria is not a member of the Schengen zone, it is a member of the EU, and once Syrian refugees are inside the EU, they can hope to migrate from Bulgaria to other parts of Europe.[25] Thus, like Spain and Italy in the south, Bulgaria and Greece in the southeast represent the "soft underbelly" of Europe, where the need for border controls is the greatest.

As the crudest ways to physically stop migration are becoming more common by the day, we must ask whether this problem can be solved, or at least addressed in a better way than the world is doing now.

How to Reconcile Migration with Unwillingness to Open Borders

There are four elementary features of migration that must be stated at the outset, each of which involves a tension of some kind. First, there is a tension between the right of citizens to leave their own country and the lack of the right of people to move wherever they see fit. Second, there is a tension between two aspects of globalization: one that encourages free movement of all factors of production, goods, technology, and ideas, and another that severely limits the right of movement of labor. Third, there is a tension between the economic principle of maximization of income, which presupposes the ability of individuals to make free decisions about where and how to use their labor and capital, and the application of that principle within individual nation states only, not globally. On an abstract level, we know that the maximization of income in each individual nation-state cannot lead to the maximization of global income, any more than the maximization of income within each individual city (with fixed population) would lead to the maximization of overall national income. We thus have to provide a justification for believing that a departure from maximum global income is justifiable. Fourth, there is a tension between the concept of development that stresses the development of people within their own countries and a broader concept of development that focuses on the betterment of an individual's position regardless of where he or she lives.

We need to dispose of one fallacy, however, before we move on to discuss these four tensions. The fallacy is the view that the reduction of absolute poverty worldwide would somehow alleviate or even eliminate these tensions. Simon Kuznets dismissed this idea long ago (in 1954). Huge gaps in income and standard of living between, for example, a New Yorker and a member of a tribe in the Amazon render any meaningful contact and comparison of ways of life between them impossible. But large income gaps, that is income gaps smaller than what we called "huge" in the previous sentence, between peoples who belong to the same civilizational circle and interact with each other—which today includes practically everybody in the world—make political tensions worse: "Since it is only by contact that recognition and tension are created . . . the reduction of physical misery [in underdeveloped countries] . . . permit[s] an increase rather than a diminution of political tensions" (Kuznets [1958] 1965, 173–174). In other words, the point where the four tensions are most acute was not in the past, when income differences were the greatest, and will probably not be in the future, when we expect that they may diminish, but precisely . . . now.

I will only briefly discuss the four tensions. The first one (the human right to migration) belongs properly to political philosophy, so we shall not consider it further here.[26] For economists, it is only important to be aware that it exists. The second tension (globalization and migration) goes to the core of how we define globalization and whether certain features that naturally belong to it can be excised or excluded from it.

The third tension (maximization of income and migration) has been very well addressed by Pritchett (2006, 95) and Hanson (2010). Pritchett makes a helpful analogy between trade in goods and movement of people. The standard approach in economics is not to ban trade for fear that it might have deleterious consequences for a group of workers, but to allow free trade on the grounds that it will lead to the maximization of overall income, and then in a second, remedial, step, to consider transfers to mitigate any negative effects of trade on some workers. Pritchett rightly asks why the same approach is not applied to labor: allow migration in the first place and then address its possible negative effects (e.g., on native workers whose wages are reduced by the inflow of migrants). There is clearly an inconsistency between trade and migration policies which is possible to explain only if there is an unstated prior assumption that maximization of income takes place under the constraint that a group of people (i.e., a nation-state) is a given and cannot be altered by external inflows.[27]

The fourth tension, relating to concepts of development, is rarely addressed by economists. The exceptions that I know of are Frenkel (1942), who might have been one of the originators of this line of thought, and more recently Pritchett (2006), who writes: "there are two possible ways to reduce global poverty: migration, and increasing peoples' wages while in their home countries. Why should only one of them count as 'development'?" (p. 87).

Let us now consider some numbers. It is estimated that the world-wide stock, or number, of migrants (defined as people who were not born in the country where they reside) is currently around 230 million people, or just over 3 percent of world population.[28] This number is between the populations of Indonesia and Brazil, respectively the fourth and fifth most populous countries in the world. (So if the migrants created their own country, say, Migratia, it would be the fifth most populous country in the world.) About one-tenth of that number, however, are a particular type of migrant who, after the breakup of the Soviet Union, happened to be living in a republic—now an independent nation—different from the one in which they were born. Internal migration thus turned into international migration.

The stock of migrants grew at an average annual rate of 1.2 percent between 1990 and 2000 and then accelerated to 2.2 percent annually in the period since 2000 (up to 2013, the last year for which the UN data are available). This last number is about twice the world population growth rate; thus, the number of migrants as a share of world population has been increasing (indeed, it went up from 2.8 percent in 2000 to 3.2 percent in 2013). The pent-up demand for migration is many times greater than the actual rate. According to Gallup surveys conducted since 2008, some 700 million people (10 percent of the world population, or 13 percent of adults) would like to move to another country.[29] Therefore, the potential stock of migrants is 16 percent of the world population, in comparison with the actual stock of 3 percent (I assume that these actual migrants would like to stay in the countries to which they have migrated). To get a better idea of what this means, consider that the overall proportion of migrants in the world as a whole is currently similar to the proportion in Finland (less than 3 percent); but if all potential migrants were to move, the world would look more like the United States or Spain (with about 15 percent of migrants in the population). Obviously the gap between the two situations is huge.

The current international climate, especially in the rich countries that would be the main recipients of the new migration flows, is not favorable to serious consideration of how to bridge the gap between the actual and potential numbers of migrants. But short of the removal of all barriers to migration, there are practical methods for advancing toward greater freedom of migration and reducing the "culture shock" experienced by recipient countries. A key problem is domain exclusion, that is, the rights and privileges one can enjoy only if one is part of a well-defined community (domain). Under current conditions, people in rich countries and their governments are very concerned with providing (at least, legally) equal treatment to all people living within the country's borders. At the same time, they are largely indifferent to the treatment of workers outside their borders. Discrimination based on a difference in citizenship or residency is considered acceptable, but once a person has become a resident, discrimination within a nation-state is unacceptable. For example, the inhumane treatment of foreign workers in the Gulf countries is often criticized; less frequently noted is the inhumane treatment these workers face in their own countries (chiefly Sri Lanka, India,

Nepal, and Pakistan). The fact that they continue to migrate to the Gulf countries suggests that they find the conditions there, including the wages they receive, preferable to conditions at home. I am aware that there may be issues of intentional misinformation and human trafficking, and that once the workers have migrated, they may be exposed to unexpected mistreatment, such as the seizure of passports, which converts them into virtual slaves. However, it is unlikely that, if such practices were common and extremely harmful to the migrants, information would not spread and deter future migrants.

But however discriminatory such practices are, it could be argued that the Gulf countries by welcoming foreign workers en masse are actually contributing effectively to the reduction in world poverty and world inequality (see Posner and Weyl 2014). I use this example not to show that I personally approve of how, say, Qatar, in preparing to host the 2022 World Cup of soccer, treats its foreign workers (scores of whom have died at the construction sites), but to show that even such admittedly very harsh treatment has another side: improving economic conditions for the majority of such foreign workers and their families at home, and reducing global poverty.

By extension, less harsh and yet still discriminatory treatment of migrants in the rich countries could have even more beneficial global effects. But to take that step, one would have to accept what seems like a huge shift in policy: discriminatory treatment of migrants in the recipient countries, and de jure introduction of two or three levels of "citizenship" rights, at least for a while. Currently, citizenship is in theory often viewed as a binary variable: one is either in or out. If one is "in," all rights (and duties) follow. But this is already not exactly true; there are gray areas. In the United States and a number of EU countries, legal residents cannot vote, but they pay taxes. The balance between rights and duties is less favorable for them than for citizens. Still, many of them do not object, and they stay in their new countries even though they remain noncitizens. One could go further and create new types of residents for whom the balance of rights and duties would be even less favorable—if doing so were the price one needed to pay for increased migration.

There are many schemes whereby this could be done. Since migrants are, almost by definition, the greatest beneficiaries of migration, and it is conceivable and even probable that because of migration the incomes of some classes of individuals might go down in both the sending and the recipient countries, migrants might be required to pay higher taxes (Freeman 2006). Proceeds could be used to help those who have lost out from migration. Migrants might be assessed taxes to recoup the cost of their education incurred by the sending countries (with taxes remitted to the sending countries). Or they might be required to spend, at regular intervals and until a certain age, a given number of years working in their countries of origin (Milanovic 2005). Another alternative might be to allow many more temporary workers, a practice followed by Switzerland (Pritchett 2006). The most radical view is advocated by Posner and Weyl (2014), who argue that allowing in migrants who then face discrimination, both at the workplace and in terms of civic rights, as in Qatar, does more to benefit the poor people in the world than do the exclusionary policies of rich countries, which are justified by the countries' inability to give the same set of formal rights to all would-be migrants. There is a sharp trade-off, in Posner and Weyl's view, between openness and civic rights: a more open migration policy requires withholding some civic rights. We can debate the sharpness of the trade-off, but we cannot deny its existence.

The common feature of all these schemes is that native-born populations and migrants are not treated equally (according to the rules of the recipient country) for at least one period of the migrants' lives. Many of these scenarios are currently happening informally, as in the case of some 10 million undocumented immigrants in the United States who, because of their unsettled status, have to accept lower-paying jobs. But such discrimination is not codified. In the eyes of many people, it therefore does not exist. The question, then, is whether it is better (1) to accept de facto but not de jure a difference in treatment between the native-born population and a portion of the migrants while limiting the flow of migration, or (2) to allow for a larger inflow of migrants while introducing a legal difference of treatment between migrants and natives.

From an economic point of view, (2) seems preferable for two reasons. First, it has been documented that an increase in migration contributes to the increase of global GDP and incomes of migrants (World Bank 2006). The negative economic effects on some groups in both the country of origin and the country of reception are minimal, and they can be, as Pritchett (2006) suggests, dealt with separately. (We should also not forget that a complementarity in skills exists between some migrants and the local population in the recipient country, resulting in higher incomes for the local population.)[30] Second, we can be quite sure that migrants would consider mild discrimination or unevenness in treatment in recipient countries to be preferable to remaining in their countries of origin by looking at their revealed preference (to use Paul Samuelson's term): their very willingness to migrate reveals their belief that migration would increase their welfare.

The arguments against unevenness in treatment therefore seem weak. It is indeed true that if we lived in a different world where there was much greater willingness of the populations and governments in the rich countries to accept the idea of free migration of labor, the first-best solution would be precisely to allow such migration and to treat all residents equally, regardless of their origin. But this is not the world we inhabit. We confront three options:

(1) Allow unrestricted movement of labor and enforce nondiscrimination between domestic and foreign labor in all countries (the countries themselves may, however, differ in labor regulations).

(2) Allow for a limited but higher level of migration than what currently exists, with legally defined relatively mild differences in treatment of local and foreign labor.

(3) Keep the flow of migrants at the current level or an even lower level and maintain the fiction of equal treatment of all residents while allowing for de facto differential treatment of the "illegals."

The first option seems to me unattainable, and the third—the present solution—inferior in terms of both efficiency (maximization of output) and equity (reduction of global poverty and inequality). Moving toward option 2, however, would require the willingness of rich countries to redefine what citizenship is and to overcome current anti-immigrant, and in some cases xenophobic, public opinion, a topic which I discuss at the end of Chapter 4.[31]

4

Global Inequality in This Century and the Next

> In my view every economic fact, whether or not it is of such a
> nature as to be expressed in numbers, stands in relation as cause
> and effect to many other facts; and since it never happens that all
> of them can be expressed in numbers, the application of exact
> mathematical methods to those which can is nearly always a waste
> of time, while in the large majority of cases it is positively
> misleading.
>
> —ALFRED MARSHALL (1901)

A Cautionary Introduction

In preparation for writing this chapter I read or reread several books, popular in their time, that tried to visualize or predict future economic and political developments. Reading those books today (when very few people still read them) provides us with a cautionary tale. We know that purely economic forecasts tend to be very wrong.[1] But I thought that less formal discussions of the political and economic forces that were considered most important for shaping the future would provide more accurate insights and projections. I discovered that was not the case. I looked at books written during three different time periods: the late 1960s and early 1970s, the period during and just after the oil crisis of 1973, and the 1990s. The overwhelming impression is not only that they failed to predict or even imagine the most important future developments, but that they were strongly anchored in the popular beliefs of their age. Their predictions generally consisted of simple extensions of current trends, some of which had been in existence for only five or ten years and quickly disappeared.

The books of the late 1960s and early 1970s see the world of the future as being ever more dominated by behemoth companies and expanding monopolies, and they predict a widening gulf between shareholders and managers, with the latter having the upper hand (examples are John Kenneth Galbraith's *The New Industrial State* [1967], Lester Brown's *The World Without Borders* [1972], and Daniel Bell's *The Coming of Post-Industrial Society* [1973]). They all note similarities in the primacy of technology in both the United States and the Soviet Union. Gigantism in the USSR seemed to be a response to the same technological requirements that were observed in the United States: management of complex systems needed to be left in the hands of the best and the brightest, with help from the state. Large companies would prevail over small ones because technological progress was seen as involving increased returns to scale and requiring a more educated population, which could only be ensured through a more active state. This view of the requirements imposed by technology (which is quite Marxist in its essence) leads the authors to postulate a process of convergence between socialism and capitalism. And indeed the spread of limited market-based forms of economic organization in Eastern Europe (e.g., Yugoslav market socialism, the Soviet *khozrashchet* [cost-accounting] reform of 1965, and the Hungarian reforms of 1968) gave such a view a dose of plausibility. At the same time, in the West, the role of the state in ownership, management, and acting as an honest broker between employers and labor had never been greater. Thus, it seemed as though socialism was moving toward freer markets, and capitalism toward a greater role for the state. This view on the convergence of the two systems was articulated in works by such renowned thinkers as Jan Tinbergen (1961) and Andrei Sakharov (1968). We now know, however, that the real change that occurred over the subsequent twenty years was entirely different. The second technological revolution made irrelevant many of the behemoths that were thought to be indestructible: socialism collapsed, and the capitalism that triumphed was of a very different type than was envisaged in the late 1960s. No one predicted the rise of China. Indeed, China is remarkable by its absence in these books.[2]

The 1970s, following the oil shock and the quadrupling of real oil prices, generated an entire literature concerned with the depletion of national resources and limits to growth (*The Limits to Growth,* by Donella Meadows et al., was one of the most famous books of that time).[3] A period of slower, almost zero, economic growth in the West suggested a much less optimistic view of the future.[4] Endless growth driven by technology was no longer envisaged. Unlike the preceding period, it was a time when people contended that "small is beautiful" (to quote the title of another influential book, by Ernest F. Schumacher, published in 1973). The future no longer seemed to belong to industrial giants like IBM, Boeing, Ford, and Westinghouse. It was a time to celebrate the flexibility and small scale of the German *Mittelstand* (mid-sized manufacturers) and the family enterprises in Emilia-Romagna, Italy. Japan's rise began to look unstoppable. No one took notice of China yet. And of course the end of communism was not foreseen at all.

A final wave of literature that I want to mention here is from the 1990s. It was dominated by the Washington Consensus (a set of policy prescriptions that emphasized deregulation and privatization) and the forecasting of the "end of history" (the title of an influential 1989 article by Francis Fukuyama, leading to the book *The End of History and the Last Man* [1992]). Japan still appeared to be ascendant, but China made a cameo appearance. Many of the books celebrated neoliberalism and predicted its speedy extension to the rest of the world, including the Middle East. Later, the US invasion of Iraq would be justified by, among other things, an appeal to the "end of history."[5] The war was supposed to bring democracy to Iraq and indirectly to the rest of the Arab world, resulting in an end to the intractable conflict between Israelis and Palestinians in negotiations between the now democratic parties. Encomiums to American power make a frequent appearance in these books. (Interestingly, many of them were published less than a decade after the United States was supposed to be on a path of long-term decline.) Those who were unhappy with globalization and the triumph of Anglo-American individualistic capitalism and "short-termism" (focus on short-term business profits) used Japan and Germany as alternative models (Todd 1998). No financial crises were predicted, nor was the rise of the group of emerging economies now known as BRICS (Brazil, Russia, India, China, and South Africa).

To generalize, all of these works share three types of mistakes: the belief that the trends that appear to be most relevant at a particular time will continue into the future, the inability to predict dramatic single events, and an exaggerated focus on key global players, especially the United States. All three problems, even if accurately diagnosed, seem to be very difficult to solve.

The first mistake is common to all forecasting, whether formal and quantitative or impressionistic. *Natura non facit saltum* is the epigraph to Alfred Marshall's *Principles of Economics*. Economists and social scientists see the future as being composed of fundamentally the same substance as what makes up the present and the very recent past. We just extend into the future the most salient trends of today. What seems salient to us today, however, may turn out later to be inconsequential. But even correctly identifying the important trends does not solve the problem of prediction because of the second issue, our inability to foresee game-changers—big events that cause major shifts.

This second mistake is in some ways an extension of the first. When we focus on incremental change, we lose sight of singular events that can significantly influence further events but cannot be predicted well. Thus, the Reagan-Thatcher revolution was impossible to predict; the same is true of Deng Xiaoping's ascendency and Chinese reforms, the breakup of the Soviet Union and the fall of communism, and the global financial crisis. We can see with hindsight that in all of these cases the individuals (or phenomena, in the case of the financial crises) behind such momentous changes were responding to deeper socioeconomic forces. But while we see that in retrospect, we cannot do so in advance. Moreover, predicting important discrete events may be a form of charlatanism. In perhaps 99 out of 100 cases, we are likely to be wrong. And even in the 1 case out of 100 where we happen to be right, the value of that guess will be considered to result more from pure chance than from any genuine ability to extract from the past and predict the future. These singular events will remain totally outside our predictive ability, just like the appearance of black swans, as popularized in Nassim Taleb's recent book *The Black Swan* (2007). And since we cannot believe that they will cease to occur in the future, it simply means that all our predictions will largely be faulty.

Although we cannot predict any particular event that might occur in the next century, we can consider some possible scenarios that could change the economic composition of entire continents or even the world:

1. Nuclear war between the United States and Russia or China that could lead to massive destruction and long-lasting radioactive contamination.
2. A nuclear bomb detonation by terrorists.

3. War between China and Japan.
4. Political revolution and/or civil war in China, leading to breakup of the country.
5. Civil war between Muslims and Hindus in India.
6. Revolution in Saudi Arabia.
7. Growing irrelevance of Europe as a result of decreasing population and inability to absorb migrants and refugees from the Middle East and Africa.
8. Conflict between Muslims and Christians that could engulf the Middle East and spread to Europe.

This list does not include any events centered in Latin America and Africa. This omission reflects the fact that in recorded world history these two continents, probably because of their distance from centers of civilization in the Mediterranean, India, China, and the North Atlantic, have never played an important autonomous role. But that itself may change in the coming decades, with the rising importance of Brazil, Nigeria, and South Africa.

The third mistake, an exaggerated focus on key players, is perhaps the only one we could avoid, but doing so remains difficult. We tend to simplify the world by focusing on what happens in the key countries that seem to shape the evolution of things to come. It is not surprising that the United States figures prominently in the literature I have reviewed here, as it probably does in all similar literature over the past seventy years. The United States is always contrasted with another country that, at a given point in time, represents its antipode or seems to be its chief competitor. The literature of the 1960s portrayed the world in terms of the communist-capitalist rivalry or convergence. Then, as the importance of the USSR dwindled and that of Japan increased, two different capitalisms came face to face: American and Japanese (with German capitalism playing a somewhat subsidiary role). China has now totally eclipsed other competitors, so much so that today's books—and this one is no exception—tend to be structured around that antinomy.

The approach of zooming in on several key countries is justifiable to the extent that powerful countries, through their example and soft power (and hard power, at times), and also through their position at the forefront of technological progress, have a preponderant effect on how the rest of the world evolves. Big countries are also important in purely arithmetic terms because their populations and economies are so large. But this approach essentially regards one-half or two-thirds of the world as mostly passive, which is unlikely to be true. Events in small countries sometimes have disproportionate political and economic repercussions, be it the Sarajevo assassination in 1914, the military coup in Afghanistan in 1973, or the 2014 crisis in Ukraine. Moreover, from a global or cosmopolitan perspective, the experiences of people in all parts of the world are just as important as the experiences of people living in key nation-states.

The reader should keep in mind the fundamental problems with our attempts to see into the future. Although we may be aware of these problems, and possibly of a few more, awareness of them alone is not sufficient to allow us to devise an alternative approach to avoid the mistakes that others have made. In the rest of this chapter I will try to avoid some of these pitfalls, but I am aware that if this book is read twenty years from now (that is, in the mid-2030s) many of its forecasts may be found wanting no less than the ones that I found wanting in the earlier literature.

Outline of the Main Forces: Economic Convergence and Kuznets Waves

Our thinking about the evolution of global inequality in the next few decades is informed by two powerful economic theories. The first is that with globalization there should be greater income convergence, that is, that incomes in poor countries should be catching up with those in rich countries because poor or emerging economies are expected to have higher growth rates on a per capita basis than rich countries. This prediction is not invalidated by the decline in the growth rate of some emerging economies (such as China); the process of convergence continues as long as poor and emerging countries have *higher* growth rates than rich countries. Two caveats are, however, in order. First, we are talking of a broad pattern, which does not mean that all poor countries will participate in the catch-up. Actually, one of the surprises of the current globalization process has been precisely how many countries have fallen even farther behind, let alone failed to catch up. The same thing cannot be ruled out in the future. The second caveat is that when we are dealing with the welfare of individuals, as we do here, income convergence in the most populous countries is what matters the most. This perspective puts a special emphasis on the importance of countries like China, India, Indonesia, Bangladesh, and Vietnam continuing with the catch-up process.

The second powerful theory has to do with the movement of inequalities within nations, which, as argued in Chapter 2, is characterized by movement along different portions of either the first or the second Kuznets wave (depending on where an economy finds itself). Individual countries may be going through different Kuznets waves and different parts of each wave, depending on their income level and structural features. Thus, inequality in China may begin to go down, sliding along the downward portion of the first Kuznets wave, while some very poor countries may witness increases in inequality as they start climbing up their first Kuznets wave. The richest economies, which are well advanced in the process of the second technological revolution, may go further up the rising portion of the second Kuznets wave (as I think the United States will; see below) or may soon start on its downward portion. So we may find a variety of experiences; but the most important patterns will be determined by what happens in the United States and China because of the size of the countries and their emblematic character.

There are two additional things to worry about as we consider the evolution of global inequality. The first is the balance between the benign and malign ways in which economic inequality can be reduced. We may be used to emphasizing the first set—rising education, declining skilled wage premiums, and greater demand for social security—but the second set, as in the run-up to World War I, is also compatible with globalization. Powerful national political interests may, as they did a century ago, combine to produce several dispersed wars, which then, following their own logic, could bring the world to the brink of, or to an actual, third world war. The Iraq war provides a good illustration of how economic interests are never far below the surface of wars that are ostensibly fought for another reason, whether it be antiterrorism or the spread of democracy (see Bilmes and Stiglitz 2008). James Galbraith, in *Inequality and Instability* (2012), shows that the profits earned by the economic beneficiaries of government outlays for the Iraq war (lobbyists, private security firms, military companies) were so significant that they were evident in income distribution statistics for the Washington, DC, area. One need only to open a copy of *Politico*, a free Washington, DC, daily that is targeted at Capitol Hill, to notice that most of the advertisements are for military hardware, from helicopters to fighter jets. The financial interests of people who benefit from destruction—the famed military-industrial complex—is a huge and unexplored area, and one hopes that the type of empirical analysis that Page, Bartels, and Seawright (2013) recently undertook to shed light on the influence of money in US politics will be done about those who have manifest financial interest in wars. At the risk of simplification, it could be said that in the United States today, wars are fought by the poor (including many who are not even US citizens), are financed by the middle class, and benefit the rich. This situation is unlikely to be different in countries such as Russia and China.[6]

The second thing to worry about is a set of factors that are almost by definition impossible for an economist to account for, even though they could have huge economic effects. These are political, social, or ideological developments that lead to dramatic events like civil wars or the breakup of countries. Note the difference between, on the one hand, the malign effects of inequality that may lead to wars and, on the other, autonomous political developments. The former are political developments induced by economic factors; the latter are entirely "pure" political developments (to the extent that any event could be said to be purely political) with possibly tremendous economic consequences. One such important event could be a political transition to democracy in China, or, to be less teleological, its political evolution. Nothing guarantees that such a transition would be peaceful. A violent turn of events would have a huge impact on the Chinese growth rate, global economic convergence, the rise of the global middle classes, and practically every other globalization-related phenomenon—so influential is China. Yet a transition like this is outside economics proper. A similar example is the rise of violent fundamentalist Islam, a force that can only in part be explained by economic causes, but which has huge economic consequences. One of these consequences is the destruction of the middle classes and reasonably well-educated modern, secular societies in Iraq and Syria. Europe is not exempt from such political developments: anti-immigration and right-wing nativist politics may yet reduce Europe's commitment to globalization. There would be economic costs, but politics or ideology might matter more to people than income growth. We shall return to some of these imponderables at the end of this chapter. For now, however, we stay within the economic framework sketched earlier, turning first to the prospects for income convergence and what it would mean for global inequality.

Income Convergence: Will Poor Countries Grow Faster Than Rich Countries?

Are income levels in poor countries converging toward those in rich countries? The answer appears to be obvious. Globalization is supposed to make access to technology, including the best economic policy, much easier and faster for poor countries.[7] It is also supposed to make it easier for them to get capital and to buy the goods they need in order to develop. So even without the movement of labor (that is, even in an era of incomplete globalization), poor countries should have higher growth rates of income than rich countries. But as Figure 4.1 shows, this was not the case until at least the year 2000. The dashed line in Figure 4.1 shows the Gini coefficient calculated across mean GDPs per capita for practically all countries in the world, with each country's weight being the same.[8] When this line rises, it means that the gap in mean income among countries is getting bigger; when it declines, the gap is getting smaller. This measure of inequality increased between 1980 and 2000, the era of "high globalization," because Latin America and Eastern Europe (parts of the world that are around the middle of international distribution by GDP per capita) experienced large recessions or depressions. Russia's per capita GDP went down by more than 40 percent between 1989 and 1998, and although the extent of the decline was larger in Russia than almost anywhere else, the decline itself was not uncommon. Brazil's GDP per capita in 2000 was only 1 percent above its 1980 level. Africa, the poorest continent, had practically ceased growing in the 1990s and even went into reverse: African real GDP per capita in 2000 was 20 percent below its 1980 level. Meanwhile, rich countries continued to grow, not at spectacular rates, but at a steady rate of approximately 2 percent per year, which resulted in their GDP per capita being some 50 percent higher in 2000 than in 1980.

Thus, contrary to expectations, income convergence failed to materialize between 1980 and 2000. But after 2000, as all three regions

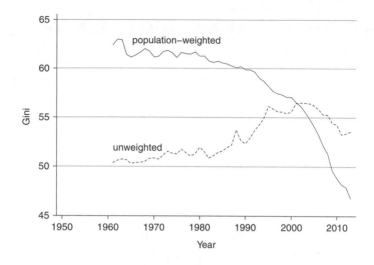

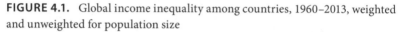

FIGURE 4.1. Global income inequality among countries, 1960–2013, weighted and unweighted for population size

This graph shows inequality (measured by Gini values) among countries' real GDPs per capita for most countries in the world, using two different measures: the unweighted Gini, where each country counts equally (dashed line), and the population-weighted Gini, where each country's importance reflects its total population (solid line). The strong increase in GDP per capita in China and India significantly reduced the population-weighted Gini, especially after 2000. GDPs per capita are in 2005 international dollars (based on 2011 International Comparison Project). Data source: Calculated from the World Bank's World Development Indicators (WDI) database (http://data.worldbank.org /data-catalog/world-development-indicators, version September 2014).

(Latin America, Eastern Europe, and Africa) picked up growth, and the rich world was struck by the financial crisis, convergence did happen. So the current era of globalization has a rather mixed record on convergence, and it is possible that another slowdown in, say, demand for raw materials, which largely underwrote the growth in Latin America and Africa in the first decade of the twenty-first century, may again put a halt to convergence.

But we get a different result if we weight countries by the size of their populations (rather than giving each country the same weight), as indeed we should do in a work concerned with people. Using this measure of inequality, income convergence did indeed occur: population-weighted intercountry inequality, shown by the solid line in Figure 4.1, has been uniformly decreasing since the late 1970s, since about the time when China introduced the "responsibility system" (de facto private ownership of land) in rural areas and growth picked up. Moreover, convergence (the decrease in intercountry, population-weighted Gini values) has been remarkable and has accelerated in the first decade of the twenty-first century. We have already seen that this movement was the key factor behind the decrease in global inequality and the broadening of the global middle class. Moreover even when China is excluded from the analysis, convergence is still evident beginning in around 2000 (not shown in the graph). This result is very important because it shows that population-weighted convergence no longer depends on economic and social evolution in just one large country; convergence could continue even if China's growth were to sputter. Nevertheless, it is true that the future of global income convergence is very strongly influenced by the per capita growth rates of China and India on the one hand, and the United States on the other. But other populous countries matter too.

To show the rising importance of fast-growing populous countries other than China for the process of convergence, we contrast in Figure 4.2 the average combined (population-weighted) annual per capita growth rate of the principal emerging economies *excluding* China (India, Brazil, South Africa, Indonesia, and Vietnam) and the combined per capita growth rate of the rich world (the United States, the European Union, and Japan). The figure shows the gap between the two. The emergence of a growth gap in favor of the emerging economies after 1980, and especially strongly after 2000, is quite clear. Since 2000, the average per capita growth rate of the emerging economies has consistently been greater than the average per capita growth rate of the rich world, and the gap was large: emerging

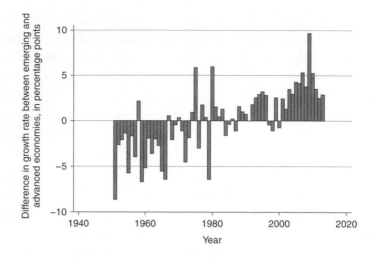

FIGURE 4.2. Difference in the combined (population-weighted) growth rates between the principal emerging economies (excluding China) and the advanced economies, 1951–2013

This graph shows the difference in population-weighted GDP per capita growth rates between emerging economies other than China (India, Brazil, Indonesia, South Africa, and Vietnam) and advanced economies (United States, European Union, and Japan). When the bar is above 0, the emerging economies have grown faster than the advanced economies. Since the mid-1980s, this has been true in all years but three. GDPs per capita are in 2005 international dollars (based on 2011 International Comparison Project). Data source: Calculated from the World Bank's World Development Indicators (WDI) database (http://data.worldbank.org/data-catalog/world-development-indicators, version September 2014).

economies had a growth rate of 4.7 percent per annum, compared with only 1 percent for the rich countries.[9] This gap was the key force behind the decline in global inequality, resulting in a decrease of the global Gini value starting in around 2000 (as discussed in Chapter 3). Between 1980 and 2000, the gap in growth rates was not as large: it was, on average, 1 percentage point (2.9 percent vs. 1.9 percent), but the emerging economies were still growing faster. We have to go back to the period before the 1970s to find a gap that was mostly in the other direction, when Europe, North America, and Japan were growing faster than what were then called "developing countries." During the past thirty-five years, there is only one year (1998) when the key emerging economies (excluding China) grew at a perceptibly lower rate than the rich world. This was the year of the Asian financial crisis, when Indonesia's economy shrank by 15 percent and the contagion affected Brazil and South Africa too, leading to modest negative growth rates (minus 1 percent) in those countries.

To argue that the growth of the emerging global middle class, which is "fed" by these countries and by China, will slow down, we would need to argue that there would be a significant reversal in the growth pattern that has characterized the past thirty-five years. Even if China were to slow down, these other large economies may be expected to continue growing at approximately the same rates as in the past decades. What is needed for income convergence to continue, and for the global middle class to grow, is for this rate to continue to be greater than the growth rate of the rich countries. It seems more likely that this tendency will continue than that it will reverse.[10]

Is Convergence an Asian Phenomenon?

A convergence in per capita incomes (or GDPs per capita), when they are population-weighted, is evident from the data and is, as we have seen, the main factor behind the recent decline in global inequality among citizens of the world. However, recall that convergence does not appear (except in the first decade of the twenty-first century) when we look at unweighted GDPs per capita among countries (that is, conventionally defined unconditional convergence). This contrast suggests that the main factor behind the population-weighted convergence is the fast economic growth of populous Asian countries. This conjecture is confirmed when we plot countries' average growth rates during the 1970–2013 period against their GDPs per capita in the 1970s. Figure 4.3a shows such a plot for all countries in the world except Asia. The long-term growth rates are neither increasing nor decreasing with 1970 GDP per capita levels. If we were to draw a regression line it would be flat at less than 2 percent per capita per year, suggesting that both rich and poor countries grew at the same rate. Figure 4.3b shows only Asian and Western countries, with Western countries defined as Western Europe, North America, and Oceania (Australia and New Zealand), or WENAO. The regression line now displays a very clear downward slope. The poorer countries, and they are invariably Asian, have grown faster over this forty-three-year period than the rich Western nations.[11] Not only is population-weighted convergence an Asian phenomenon, so is unweighted convergence: it is only Asian countries that have been catching up with the rich world.

This conclusion has implications for what we may expect regarding income inequality among countries in this century and the next. First, it provides us with a more cautionary tale about the power of economic convergence because large parts of the globe are not achieving it. Second, it introduces additional caution in our estimates because it is precisely in the "left-out" regions of Africa where we expect the largest demographic increases. Thus, nonconvergence, from being manifest in population-unweighted data, might "spread" to the population-weighted data too, and in turn check the projected decline in global inequality. In other words, as population numbers in Africa grow, the lack of convergence of African incomes with those of the rest of the world might begin to make a strong appearance not only in data comparing poor and rich countries, but also in data comparing poor and rich individuals.

Let us consider the position of Africa in more detail. In 2013, population-unweighted (that is, calculated simply across countries) GDP per capita in Africa was 1.9 times higher than in 1970 (see Table 4.1, column 2). This is the lowest ratio of the five regions. GDP per capita in Asia was multiplied by a factor of almost 5 during the

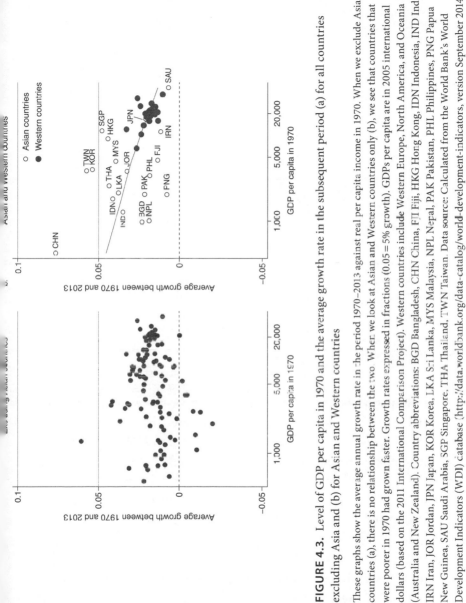

FIGURE 4.3. Level of GDP per capita in 1970 and the average growth rate in the subsequent period (a) for all countries excluding Asia and (b) for Asian and Western countries

These graphs show the average annual growth rate in the period 1970–2013 against real per capita income in 1970. When we exclude Asian countries (a), there is no relationship between the two. When we look at Asian and Western countries only (b), we see that countries that were poorer in 1970 had grown faster. Growth rates expressed in fractions (0.05 = 5% growth). GDPs per capita are in 2005 international dollars (based on the 2011 International Comparison Project). Western countries include Western Europe, North America, and Oceania (Australia and New Zealand). Country abbreviations: BGD Bangladesh, CHN China, FJI Fiji, HKG Hong Kong, IDN Indonesia, IND India, IRN Iran, JOR Jordan, JPN Japan, KOR Korea, LKA Sri Lanka, MYS Malaysia, NPL Nepal, PAK Pakistan, PHL Philippines, PNG Papua New Guinea, SAU Saudi Arabia, SGP Singapore, THA Thailand, TWN Taiwan. Data source: Calculated from the World Bank's World Development Indicators (WDI) database ⟨http://data.worldbank.org/data-catalog/world-development-indicators, version September 2014⟩.

TABLE 4.1. Growth record of various regions of the world between 1970 and 2013

Region	(1) Average 1970 GDP per capita (population-weighted)	(2) Ratio of 2013 GDP per capita to 1970 GDP per capita (across countries)	(3) Average percentage shortfall in 2013 from the historical peak (across countries)
Africa	2,900	1.9	10.2
Asia	2,200	4.9	0.6
Latin America	7,000	2.0	1.8
Postcommunist transition countries	8,300	2.4	5.3
WENAO	19,700	2.3	2.5
World	6,400	2.6	2.8

Note: GDP per capita in 2005 international dollars (based on 2011 International Comparison Project results). WENAO = Western Europe, North America, and Oceania.
Source: World Development Indicators (http://data.worldbank.org/data-catalog/world-development-indicators), various annual versions.

same period, but even Latin America and the postcommunist transition countries had ratios equal to or greater than 2. Rich Western countries (WENAO) were 2.3 times better off in 2013 than in 1970. If income convergence were occurring we would have expected Africa, which in 1970 was poorer than any region except Asia, to have grown faster than most other regions and its 2013-to-1970 ratio to be close to that of Asia. But this is far from being the case: African countries grew the slowest.

The divergence of Africa was not caused only by slower per capita growth than in the rest of the world, as would be one way to interpret the figures here: for example, Africa's ratio of 1.9 implies an average per capita growth rate of 1.5 percent per annum, while WENAO's ratio of 2.3 implies 2 percent per year. The problems in Africa are more complex than these numbers suggest. African countries have often had spurts of growth followed by swift declines, and it is the inability to sustain even modest rates of growth for long periods that seems to be the major problem. The fluctuations in growth are driven by political conflicts, civil wars, and cyclical price trends that affect the natural resources on which much of Africa's output and exports are based. To illustrate these fluctuations in growth, let us denote the highest GDP per capita ever reached by a country as 1, and then look at how the actual 2013 GDPs per capita compare with that historical maximum. In WENAO, the average ratio of 2013 GDP per capita to the peak value across countries was 0.975, so the shortfall (the difference between 1 and 0.975) was 2.5 percentage points (entirely caused by the Atlantic recession) (see Table 4.1, column 3).[12] Latin America and Asia were, on average, less than 2 percent below their historical peaks, and the post-communist transition economies were 5 percent below. But this pales in comparison with Africa, where the shortfall from the historical peak was over 10 percent. African countries can and do grow, but they also have sudden and sharp income declines. The final outcome is absence of income convergence with the rich world, and even with other regions.

In some extreme cases, the failures are so overwhelming that our data are insufficient to illustrate them fully. Thus, the GDPs per capita of Madagascar and the Democratic Republic of Congo are lower today than they are estimated to have been before independence (around 1950). It is reasonable to suppose that incomes in the 1930s and 1940s were below those in 1950 (that is, we assume some growth during these decades). It follows that Madagascar and Congo first reached the income levels they have today some eighty or even ninety years ago. In terms of development and catch-up with the richer countries, an entire century has been wasted.[13] We don't have any

EXCURSUS 4.1. Forecasts of Global Inequality

How will the level of inequality among all citizens in the world change during the next several decades? If Asia's income convergence with the West continues, this will be a very strong force for the overall convergence of individual incomes. However, once China's mean income is at a level such that more than half of the world population, when ranked by their countries' mean incomes, are behind China, continued growth in China will lead to global incomes becoming less equal (especially given high interpersonal inequality within China itself).[14]

In an interesting exercise, Hellebrandt and Mauro (2015) have tried to predict the evolution of global inequality from 2015 to 2035. They estimate that global inequality will, in the most likely scenario, decrease by almost 4 Gini points. This exercise rests on three building blocks: GDP per capita growth rates, population growth rates, and within-nation inequalities. For countries' growth rates, Hellebrandt and Mauro use forecasts from the OECD, the IMF, and Consensus Forecasts (a private forecaster); for population growth rates, they use the United Nations' median forecast; and for inequalities within nations, they assume no change. Although I am very skeptical about forecasts in general, and the authors themselves point out that such forecasts almost always turn out to be overly optimistic and that the error increases dramatically with the time-horizon, their three conclusions are worth considering.

First, the forecast shows that in a growth scenario based on reversion to the mean (a slowdown of poorer countries' growth rates as they get richer), the reduction in global inequality would be minimal (less than 1 Gini point).

Second, the projections underscore the huge importance of India's economic growth for reducing global inequality. The reason is that

China's role as the main engine driving the reduction in global inequality becomes less important as the country gets richer. In 2011, China's mean per capita income, calculated from household surveys and expressed in international dollars, was 22 percent below the global mean and was greater than the mean incomes of 49 percent of the people in the world (assumed to have the mean incomes of their countries).[15] The world will very soon be in the position where China's high growth rate begins to add to global inequality, not detract from it.[16] India's mean income is currently ahead of only 7 percent of the world population, and India cannot be expected to "turn the corner," that is, to become, in average per capita terms, richer than more than 50 percent of the world population, in the next twenty years. Thus it will, if it grows fast, take over from China as the main engine of global income equalization.

Third, Hellebrandt and Mauro find that only very substantial increases in inequalities within nations (a Gini increase of more than 6 points for all countries in the world) would overturn the equalizing impact of mean income convergence from the most likely scenario. If the convergence of mean incomes is slower, the offsetting increase in within-nation inequalities need not be as high. Nevertheless, this result illustrates that even as inequalities within nations become more important, they will not, at least in the next twenty years, play as much of a role in global inequality as the catch-up of poor countries.

During the next twenty years, absent any of the dramatic negative events which we listed at the beginning of this chapter, the prospects for continued reduction in global inequality are good but not extraordinary. One cannot expect global inequality to be reduced by more than one-fifteenth of its current level. While such a reduction would be remarkable in historical terms, we are hardly likely to live in a world of an egalitarian global utopia any time soon.

guarantee that the same thing will not occur in this century. If it does, the convergence story takes on an entirely different hue: convergence might still happen, but the odds are longer.

The Other Side of the Equation: Inequalities in China and the United States

The other side of the global inequality equation, in addition to the change in inequalities *between* nations, is the change in inequalities *within* nations, and especially in China and the United States. These two countries are important not solely on account on their size but also because they provide the prime examples of the changes in inequality in emerging and rich economies. If the tendency toward mean income convergence continues, the prospects for the reduction of global inequality could still be derailed by what happens to inequality within individual countries. We cannot look at the evolution of inequality in most of them. But expectations or educated guesses regarding what might happen in China and the United States are worth making. Let us start with China.

Mr. Kuznets goes to Beijing? The facts regarding inequality in China since 2010 are murky because the Chinese National Bureau of Statistics (NBS), which has never been forthcoming with data and has never distributed microdata (at the household level), has become even more closed. For a quarter of a century, household surveys in China were organized differently for rural and urban areas (creating problems for researchers wishing to combine the two); they were reformed in 2013, and the NBS then ran the first unified all-China household survey. This survey was supposed to be an important marker for improving knowledge of changes in inequality and other social and demographic variables. As of January 2015, however, the NBS had not released any data. So instead of knowing more, we now know less. One can speculate that the reason for this sudden silence is that some results were unexpected or difficult to reconcile with the results obtained from earlier surveys.

Based on the evidence we do have, it looks as though income inequality did not rise in the five to six years before 2013 and may in fact have declined a little. The data from household surveys show that the all-China Gini coefficient has stayed relatively stable since 2000 (Figure 4.4). The NBS made the same claim in a press release. Income inequality calculated from urban household surveys has been stable since 2002 (Zhang 2014; not shown in the figure here). According to Zhang (2014), intersectoral wage inequality declined between 2008 and 2012. Intersectoral wage inequality measures inequality between wages

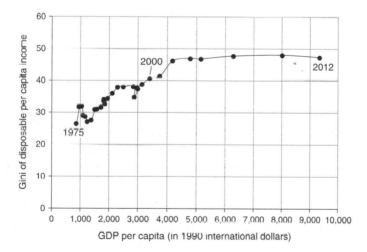

FIGURE 4.4. Income inequality in China, 1975–2012

This graph shows the evolution of income inequality across individuals (measured by Gini values) in China against China's real GDP per capita. We see that inequality in China has increased steadily since the reforms started (after 1975) but has recently been stable. Data sources: Ginis: All the Ginis database (http://www.gc.cuny.edu/branko -milanovic), calculated from the official Chinese household surveys. GDP per capita from Maddison Project (2013).

in different industrial sectors; it is not the same as wage inequality between individuals or income inequality among households, so it is at best a proxy of "real" interpersonal inequality.[17] Nevertheless, Zhang's results may reflect a similar trend in interpersonal inequality, especially because in the past, changes in intersectoral wage inequality closely paralleled those in overall income inequality.[18]

If evidence showing absence of a further increase in income inequality is confirmed, it may be that China's level of income inequality has reached a plateau and will soon begin moving downward, in line with Kuznets's theory. The pattern in China would then perfectly fit the shape of the first Kuznets wave, with increased inequality occurring during the period of structural transformation of the economy, combined, in China's case, with a transition from socialism to capitalism. The subsequent fall in inequality would be driven by the usual benign forces: equalization of levels of education (at a higher overall level), aging of the population and thus greater demand for old-age security and social transfers, and perhaps most importantly, the push for increased wages that comes at the end of a period of so-called Lewisian growth, during which the supply of low-wage (rural) labor is almost limitless. The theoretical support for the proposition that China might be turning the corner on increasing inequality comes from several sources. As mentioned, the usual Kuznets interpretation would lead us to expect China's level of inequality to decline, but so would Tinbergen's emphasis on the declining returns to education: as the supply of highly skilled workers expands, their relative wages should be reduced. And finally, so would Arthur Lewis's story of the low-skill wage-push coming from the exhaustion of cheap sources of labor. China could thus reach both the Kuznets and the Lewis turning points at the same time.

But other forces could work against this scenario. Pervasive corruption and a political system that generates it could counteract the purely economic forces of income equalization. Recent political moves, especially the targeting of corruption at all administrative levels and a vast government plan of regional "rebalancing" that is supposed to lower inequality between the maritime and inland provinces (in itself a major contributor to all-China inequality), seem to be motivated by the leadership's realization that inequality poses dangers for the maintenance of their own power. Another element that could work in the direction of rising inequality is the country's rapidly increasing wealth and the resulting increase in the share of net income that comes from the ownership of capital. Such shifts are usually associated with wider interpersonal inequality because ownership of capital is heavily concentrated. China is no exception to this rule. Using Chinese household surveys, Wei Chi (2012) showed that the share of capital income received by urban households is rising and that it is becoming very concentrated.

The question is then which set of forces will predominate. On balance, however, one can be optimistic that China's income inequality may have peaked.

But is the Chinese political system completely resilient, or does it contain internal features that could lead to its weakening or even collapse? The political system has a top-down structure much like that in imperial China, with the communist bureaucracy rather than the imperial bureaucracy at the apex (Xu 2015). The top bureaucracy controls the judiciary but allows some policy flexibility among regionally decentralized units, such as provinces and even counties. The combination of centralization with local flexibility has been used, with huge success, to motivate competition between lower-level units in achieving material targets (like GDP growth rates) and to spur experimentation with various economic policies and forms of ownership. The system has allowed experimentation ranging from the Special Economic Zones in the 1980s to the Shanghai bourse in recent years. But while this political structure has performed very well in the past half century, it contains a number of vulnerable points.

The first is illustrated by the greed of local authorities who, either because they are corrupt or because they need to compete with other local authorities, resort to brutal forms of exploitation, confiscating land at nominal prices from farmers or imposing unbearable working conditions on workers. Such instances of mistreatment have led to a veritable epidemic of strikes and local protests across China. According to official statistics, there were about five hundred thousand of these in 2013 (National Bureau of Statistics of China 2014, table 24-4). As long as the protests are localized and do not erupt at the same time in many places, and the center, which essentially means the leadership of the Chinese Communist Party, is sufficiently united, the strife does not pose a major threat to political stability.

But unity of purpose or interest at the center is far from being guaranteed in a system that lacks accepted legal rules about how people get to the top, what powers they hold, and how long they stay there. In a decentralized system where local "barons" wield significant power, any vacillation at the center is bound to produce even greater freedom of action at the provincial and local level, with the ultimate result being that the center becomes whatever the provinces decide that it is. This would lead to either formal or informal dissolution of the country and is, I think, the most serious danger China faces in the coming decades. After all, during its 2,800 years of well-documented history, China has been unified for fewer than 1,000 years (Ma 2011, appendix, 35).

The United States: A "perfect storm" of inequality? There are two substantive differences between the United States and China in terms of our predictions about changes in inequality. First, we have more complete data and a better understanding of the economic forces underlying recent changes in inequality for the United States than we do for China. Second, the forces that would tend to drive inequality down in China do not appear to exist in the United States.

There are a number of developments that may lead to a "perfect storm" of rising inequality in the United States. They can be divided into the five following themes, which I will discuss in turn:

- Higher elasticity of substitution between capital and labor, in the face of increased capital intensity of production, will keep the share of national income that accrues to capital owners high.
- Capital incomes will remain highly concentrated, thus leading to high interpersonal inequality of incomes.
- High labor and capital income earners may increasingly be the same people, thus further exacerbating overall income inequality.
- Highly skilled individuals who are both labor- and capital-rich will tend to marry each other.
- Concentration of income will reinforce the political power of the rich and make pro-poor policy changes in taxation, funding for public education, and infrastructure spending even less likely than before.

Let us go over each of these possible developments in greater detail. The very technical issue of the elasticity of substitution between capital and labor has to do with whether the share of capital in net income rises or not when the capital intensity of production (ratio of capital to labor) goes up. It has been a standard view in economics that factor shares tend to be constant, with some 70 percent of national income going to labor and some 30 percent to capital. This nostrum has been overturned in the past couple of decades as it has become clear that capital shares are increasing in all advanced economies. Karabarbounis and Neiman (2013), who document this trend, ascribe it mostly to the reduced prices of investment goods, which leads companies to substitute capital for workers. A continuation of this trend of machines (such as robots) becoming less expensive would be expected to lead to further declines in the labor share, and thus to the increase in the share of capital. In the United States, Elsby, Hobijn, and Şahin (2013, fig. 1) show that the share of capital in net income increased from 35 percent to more than 40 percent between 1980 and 2013. (Note that the timing of the increase in the capital share coincides with the increase in interpersonal income inequality in the United States, discussed in Chapter 2.) Will capital share continue to rise? In a world as envisioned by neoclassical economics, where factor earnings are determined by economic forces alone, a way for the share of capital to increase is if capital can gradually replace labor without its own return decreasing commensurately. Thus, if robots displaced labor without reducing the return to the robots' owners (that is, the shareholders in the companies that produce or own the robots), the share of capital in net income would rise. This is one of Piketty's points in *Capital in the Twenty-First Century*. If the rate of return is more or less fixed as capital replaces labor, we have exactly this outcome: the share of the national income from capital rises.

But the same outcome may be brought about by other factors besides marginal productivity. One of the most important of these is the relative power of labor versus capital, as reflected, for example, in the percentage of workers in trade unions and the percentage of the labor force employed in steady, open-ended jobs. A continued weakening of labor's relative power, as has been going on during the past three decades, can result in rising capital share too. There is not a strong likelihood that either of the two processes—namely, greater capital intensity of production and the institutional changes which weaken the bargaining position of labor—will be reversed in the decades to come, and so we can expect that the same forces will bring the same outcome: rising, or at least nondiminishing, capital share in net income.

Now, the increase in the share of capital does not by definition directly translate into greater interpersonal inequality. Suppose, for example, that all individuals in a country had the same share in national capital: then, clearly, a rise in capital share would benefit everybody equally, and there would be no increase in interpersonal inequality. But the reality is different. In all modern capitalist societies, capital ownership is heavily concentrated (that is, it is in the hands of the few). That, too, would not be a problem if the few were not also rich. To understand why, suppose that capital were held by the poor. (I know that this situation is hard to imagine, because we are simply used to the fact that rich people are capitalists; technically, capitalists could be poor.) In that case, too, an increase in the share of capital would not increase inequality. But, of course, neither of these hypothetical situations exists: capital ownership is heavily concentrated, and capital owners who get large profits or rents from their property also tend to be rich.[19] Thus, an increase in the share of capital *plus* the concentration of capital ownership among the rich will definitely increase interpersonal income inequality. This is the second part of the perfect storm scenario.

Note that in principle this element of the scenario could be reversed by means of a "deconcentration" of capital ownership. Such a deconcentration, however, is not even on the horizon in the United States. Data from Edward Wolff indicate, on the contrary, that net assets and equity ownership have become even more concentrated. In 2007, 38 percent of all stocks were owned by the wealthiest top 1 percent of individuals, and 81 percent were owned by the top 10 percent. Both figures are higher than in 2000 (Wolff 2010, 31–32). These shares are higher than the shares of the top 1 percent or top 10 percent in all net assets (which include housing) because the composition of wealth varies in such a way that the *share* of financial assets in the wealth portfolio increases with the level of wealth. The richest 1 percent (by wealth) hold three-quarters of their wealth in the form of corporate stocks, financial securities, and unincorporated business equity, while the middle three quintiles hold less than 13 percent of their wealth in that form (Wolff 2010, table 8). The poorest hold almost nothing at all in equity.[20] In other words, financial assets are the most concentrated form of capital ownership; they are the quintessence of capitalism.[21] Thus an increase in the share of capital incomes directly translates into a greater concentration of overall wealth and income.

Another impetus to the concentration of personal incomes comes from an increasing tendency, documented by Lakner and Atkinson (2014), for the same people to receive high incomes from both labor and capital. This situation creates a potentially new, seemingly more meritocratic, style of capitalism, but ironically, it is a style with a potential for greater income inequality. The best way to visualize this is to go back to a simplified notion of nineteenth-century capitalism, what we might call classical, or old, capitalism, where capital owners were all rich and workers were all poor (and the reverse: all rich people were capitalists and all poor people were workers). Both capitalists and workers had only one factor income: capitalists' income came from owning property, and workers' income came from wage-labor. Now, let inequality among workers increase, so that some of them receive salaries that place them among the rich. We no longer have the straightforward identity of rich = capitalist. Such a process has actually been going on for almost a century in the advanced countries and has changed the composition of income among the top income groups in favor of labor. As Piketty and Saez (2003, 16, fig. 4) and Piketty (2014, chap. 8) show, among the top 1 percent, labor income is far more important today than it was a century ago.[22] This shift need not exacerbate inequality as long as the top wage earners are different people from the top capitalists.

The problems of inequality become more acute, however, when rich capitalists are the same people as those who receive the highest labor incomes. Lakner and Atkinson (2014) show, using information from US fiscal records, that the likelihood that a person (more exactly, a tax unit) in the top 1 percent according to the distribution of labor incomes is also in the top decile by capital income has increased from under 50 percent in 1980 to 63 percent in 2010 (Figure 4.5). A person with a very high labor income (top 1 percent) is almost assured (80 percent probability) of being in the top quintile of capital owners. The reverse association—being among top wage earners while having a high income from capital—has increased over the

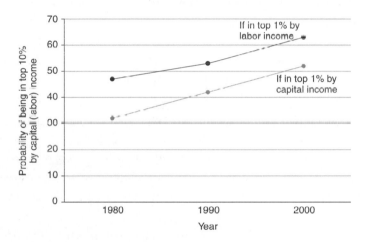

FIGURE 4.5. Probability (in percent) of being in top 10% by capital (labor) income if a person is in top 1% by labor (capital) income, 1980–2000

This graph shows the probability that a US tax unit (generally a household) that is in the top 1% according to labor (capital) income is also in the top 10% by capital (labor) income. Increased probability over time shows that more people are becoming both labor- and capital-rich, that is, they have both high wages and high income from property. Data source: Lakner and Atkinson (2014).

same period as well. To realize the importance of this association, note that in the extreme case of old capitalism, where all capital owners have only income from capital and all workers have only income from wages, the probability of overlap between capital and wage income would have been zero. The present-day association is also different from a situation where, say, the top 1 percent of workers had randomly drawn capital incomes; in that case, only 10 percent of them would be in the top decile by capital income. In reality, the top wage earners are over six times more likely to be in the top decile. Describing in statistical terms a much more complex reality, we can say that capitalism has moved from being a system with complete separation between capital and labor incomes to a variant where the correlation between the two was negative (those who had labor incomes had very little capital income) to the "new capitalism," where this correlation is positive.[23]

The same results are obtained from US household surveys, which have the advantage of covering the entire distribution (unlike fiscal data, which miss about 5–6 percent of the population). Figure 4.6 shows the increased correlation between income from labor and income from capital (which includes interest and dividends, rental income, and royalties) received by US households. The correlation, as in old capitalism, was close to zero in the 1980s; it then increased throughout the 1990s and early noughts, reaching a value of about 0.12, where it has stayed ever since.

One can speculate that the main mechanism by which this association operates is that people with very high labor incomes (e.g., CEOs of financial firms) save a sizeable portion of their income (or get paid in stock options) and become large capital owners. Thus, they increasingly draw high incomes from both labor and capital. If one projects this trend into the future and over at least two generations, with parents investing a lot in their children's education and children getting highly paid jobs while inheriting large capital assets,

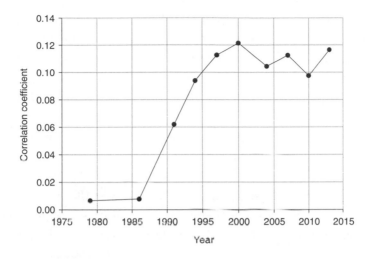

FIGURE 4.6. Correlation between labor and capital income received by US households, 1979–2013

This graph shows the correlation between income from labor and capital for US households. Greater correlation indicates that high incomes from labor and high incomes from capital are increasingly received by the same households. Data source: Calculated from Luxembourg Income Study database (http://www.lisdatacenter.org/) based on US Current Population Survey.

inequality becomes more entrenched within families and more stable (because it draws its source from both labor and capital), and it acquires an appearance of meritocracy that makes it politically more difficult to overturn.[24] A new capitalism, very different from the classical one based on the division between capital and labor embodied in different people, is thus born.

In the new capitalism, rich capitalists and rich workers are the same people. The social acceptability of the arrangement is enhanced by the fact that rich people work. It is moreover difficult or impossible for the outsider to tell what part of their income comes from ownership and what part from labor. While in the past, rentiers were commonly ridiculed and disliked for doing work that involved nothing more demanding than coupon-clipping, under the new capitalism, criticism of the top 1 percent is blunted by the fact that many of them are highly educated, hardworking, and successful in their careers. Inequality thus appears in a meritocratic garb. Inequalities generated by new capitalism are harder to tackle ideologically, and probably politically as well, because there is no popular groundswell of support to limit them. They appear—and to some extent they may also be—more justifiable and are therefore more difficult to uproot.

The next development promoting inequality in the United States is closely related to the one that we have just discussed. It may originate in the same social mores that favor high levels of education and hard work as desirable features that justify high incomes no matter how high they are. This development is the documented tendency of highly skilled, and thus generally rich, individuals, to increasingly marry people who share similar characteristics. Here again, a simplified contrast with the past allows us to best capture the difference. In the 1960s, when relatively few women worked (the participation rate in the labor force for women in the United States was 40 percent, vs. more than 90 percent for men),[25] it was common for well-off men to marry women who did not work outside the household and thus did not contribute a monetized income. This practice tends to diminish inequality, in comparison with a situation where highly paid men marry highly paid women. The latter has indeed been happening more often in the past quarter century. Greenwood et al. (2014) document the increasing trend of homogamy (assortative mating) among American couples and consider it one of the contributing factors to rising income inequality. It is paradoxical that increasing inequality has resulted from a change in social norms that has seen the labor participation rate of women almost catch up with that of men (73 percent for women, 84 percent for men in 2010) and has encouraged marriages that are based on a model of equal partnership between people with similarities of interests and backgrounds rather than a hierarchical model where the husband is the breadwinner and the wife a homemaker. This trend may continue in the future, as the gap in both educational achievement and labor force participation between men and women disappears. It will, however socially desirable in some ways, add to interpersonal income inequality.[26]

Finally, we come to the fifth element that makes the reversal of inequality in the United State particularly difficult: the growing importance of money in electoral politics. No political campaign can nowadays be run without huge amounts of money. The 2012 US presidential elections are estimated to have cost $2.6 billion.[27] While the amounts spent in state and local elections are smaller, money is no less indispensable for winning, or even participating. The major contributors who fund political campaigns are, by definition, rich (poor people cannot afford to do so), and they are not interested in throwing their money away. To believe that the rich do not use their money to buy influence and promote policies they like is not simply to be naïve. Such a stance contradicts the key principles of economics as well as the ways in which the rich people have amassed their wealth— surely not by throwing it around while expecting no return on it.

US senators and congresspeople are much more concerned with issues that affect their rich rather than their poor constituents, according to studies by Bartels (2010), Gilens (2012), and Gilens and Page (2014). Gilens (2012, 80, figs. 3.3, 3.4) shows in a striking graph that politicians' responsiveness to the concerns of the people at the 90th percentile of income distribution continuously increases as the issue becomes more pressing (to the rich). In other words, the greater the concern of the rich with an issue, the greater the responsiveness of the legislators. In contrast, for both the poor (people at the 10th percentile of the income distribution) and the middle class (people at the 50th percentile), legislators' responsiveness is a flat line: whether the poor or the middle class care a lot or not at all about a given issue has no influence on legislators. The findings illustrate that the gap in political influence is enormous not only between the rich and the poor, but between the rich and the middle class. The rich spend billions on funding political campaigns and, like the oil and pharmaceutical industries, in lobbying; as a result, the policies that are in their interests are implemented.[28]

In a positive feedback loop, pro-rich policies further increase the incomes of the rich, which in turn makes the rich practically the only people able to make significant donations to politicians, and thus the only ones who get a hearing from the politicians. The political importance of each individual becomes equivalent to his or her income level, and instead of a one-person one-vote system, we approach a system of one-dollar one-vote, which is nothing else but the projection on the political plane of the existing distribution of income. This system is evident in a perhaps unwitting quotation from George W. Bush, when he was speaking to a rich crowd in Washington, DC: "This is an impressive crowd—the haves and the have-mores. Some people call you the elites; I call you my base."[29] A plutocracy is thus born.

These five developments are all strongly pro-inequality, and it is hard to see where any forces might come from that could counter rising income inequality in the United States.[30] The economic logic of the rising share of capital in net income is reinforced by the way that high incomes from capital and labor are distributed (high concentration of capital income and the personal association between high labor and high capital incomes), by social norms (homogamy), and finally by economic policies. It is this unusual confluence of economic, social, and political factors that seems likely to keep inequality at a high level for the foreseeable future in the United States. Forces promoting offsetting policies such as more widespread education, a higher minimum wage, and more generous welfare benefits seem weak compared with the almost elemental forces that favor greater inequality.

Now that we have reviewed the recent fortunes of income inequality in both China and the United States, we can compare the two countries in terms of the methodology developed in Chapter 2. Looking schematically at changes in income inequality, we can conclude that income inequality in China may be on the descending portion of the first Kuznets wave, whereas inequality in the United States is either still rising or is about to reach the peak of the second Kuznets wave (Figure 4.7).

One of the most pernicious consequences of the rise in inequality in the rich countries as they slide up the second Kuznets wave has been the hollowing out of the middle class and the rising political importance of the rich. This danger, however, is coupled with its nemesis, a popular class rebellion, which tends to morph into populism or nativism. Neither populism nor plutocracy is compatible with the classical definition of democracy. So the question arises as to whether inequality is a threat to Western democratic capitalism. We address this question in the next section.

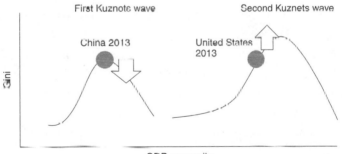

FIGURE 4.7. Kuznets waves for the United States and China

This graph presents a stylized estimate of the current position of China and the United States on the first and second Kuznets waves. The United States, being a more developed economy that went through the first technological revolution more than a century ago, is now approaching the peak of the second Kuznets wave. China may be around the peak of the first Kuznets wave, poised to become less unequal.

Perils of Inequality: Plutocracy and Populism

To answer the question "Does inequality threaten the sustainability of Western democratic capitalism?" we need to divide it into two parts. First, Does inequality threaten capitalism? And second, Does inequality threaten *democratic* capitalism?

The answer to the first question, at least in the medium-term, seems to be in the negative. For the first time in human history, a system that can be called capitalist, defined (conventionally) as consisting of legally free labor, privately owned capital, decentralized coordination, and pursuit of profit, is dominant over the entire globe. One does not need to go far back into the past, or to have a great knowledge of history, to realize how unique and novel this is. Not only was centrally planned socialism eliminated as a competitor only recently, but nowhere in the world do we now find unfree labor playing an important economic role, as it did until some 150 years ago.

Such is the hegemony of capitalism as a worldwide system that even those who are unhappy with it and with rising inequality, whether locally, nationally, or globally, have no realistic alternatives to propose. "Deglobalization" with a return to the "local" is impossible because it would do away with the division of labor, a key factor of economic growth. Surely, those who argue for localism do not wish to propose a major drop in living standards or a Khmer Rouge solution to inequality. Forms of state capitalism, as in Russia and China, do exist, but this is capitalism nevertheless: the private profit motive and private companies are dominant.

It is often stated that Islam is the only remaining ideological competitor to Western liberal capitalism. This is, I think, true in many respects as far as liberal society is concerned but not in the one that we address here, namely, the effects of inequality on *capitalism*. For Islam itself, not only as it exists in dominantly Muslim countries, but even in theory, is indeed a kind of capitalism, in its emphasis on private ownership of the means of production, the pursuit of gain, and the rejection of unfree labor.[31] The only area of economics where Western and Islamic capitalisms part ways is in the treatment of interest (as differentiated from profit, which, unlike interest, is a variable rather than a fixed source of income that depends on the success of the enterprise). But this is a relatively minor point which can be taken into account and made compatible with standard Western practice, as is done in Islamic banking. It could even be argued, and I believe that there is some truth in it, that rejecting a fixed and guaranteed interest on debt, as Islam does, allows the system to be much more flexible and not to get stuck in a situation, as happened in Greece and Argentina, where debtors cannot repay the entire debt but there is no mechanism to acknowledge this and move on.

Increasing inequality of income, however, undercuts some of capitalism's mainstream ideological dominance by showing its unpleasant sides: an exclusive focus on materialism, a winner-take-all ideology, and the disregard of nonpecuniary motives. But since no significant ideological alternatives currently exist, and since there are no powerful political parties or groups pushing for alternatives, the hegemony of capitalism looks almost unassailable. For sure, nothing guarantees that the situation will look the same in twenty or fifty years, for new ideologies can be invented, but this is how it looks to a reasonable observer today.

But is *democratic* capitalism sustainable? This is quite a different question. Note first that these two words (democracy and capitalism) have not often been combined in history. Capitalism has existed without democracy not only in Spain under Franco, Chile under Pinochet, and Congo under Mobutu, but also in Germany, France, and Japan, and even in the United States, when blacks were excluded from the body politic, and Britain, with its severely limited franchise. It does not thus take a huge leap of imagination to see that capitalism and democracy can be decoupled. And inequality can play an important role in this decoupling. It already does so by empowering the rich politically to a much greater extent than the middle class and the poor. The rich dictate the political agenda, finance the candidates who protect their interests, and make sure that the laws that are in their interest are passed. The American political scientist Larry Bartels, whose work I mentioned before, finds that US senators are five to six times more likely to respond to the interests of the rich than to the interests of the middle class. Moreover, Bartels (2005, 28) concludes, "there is no discernible evidence that the views of low-income constituents ha[ve] any effect on their senators' voting behavior." Not only is the middle class being hollowed out, as we shall see next, but democracy is becoming more hollow too.

It is not for nothing that since Aristotle, and more recently since Tocqueville, the middle class has been seen as the bulwark against nondemocratic forms of government. There is no special moral virtue embodied among the "middlemen" that causes a person who has, for example, ceased to be rich and become middle-class to suddenly prefer democracy. People in the middle class favored democracy because they had an interest in limiting the power of both the rich and the poor: to keep the rich from ruling over them and the poor from confiscating their property. The large numbers of people in the middle classes also means that a lot of people share similar material positions, develop similar tastes, and tend to eschew extremism of both the left and the right. Thus the middle class allows for both democracy and stability.

Decline of the middle class. The existence and function of the middle class is under attack by rising inequality. The middle class in Western democracies is today both less numerous and economically weaker vis-à-vis the rich than it was thirty years ago. In the United States, where the change has been the most dramatic, the share of the middle class, defined as people with disposable (after-tax) incomes around the median (more exactly, between 25 percent below and 25 percent above the median), decreased from one-third of the population in 1979 to 27 percent in 2010. In other words, one-fifth of the members of the middle class in 1979 are no longer there, most having been pushed below.[32] At the same time, the average income of the middle class, which was 80 percent of the US overall mean income in 1979, dropped to being 77 percent of the mean in 2010. The result of the decline in relative numbers and relative income is a sharp drop in the economic power of the middle class. In 1979, they accounted for 26 percent of total income (or consumption); in 2010, for only 21 percent.

The decline of the middle class is not limited to the United States. As with other indicators that deal with inequality, the changes in the United States have been more dramatic than elsewhere in the West, and the data to study them are more abundant. But often the United States simply displays in more extreme form the same changes that have occurred in all advanced economies. Figure 4.8 shows the decline in the share of the middle class in selected Western democracies between the early 1980s and 2010. In all countries shown here, and probably in all but a couple of OECD members, the share of the middle class today is less than it was thirty-five years ago. The figure illustrates a slight difference in the process of the hollowing-out of the middle between northern European countries (Germany, the Netherlands, and Sweden), where the declines were smaller, and the United States and the United Kingdom, where they were larger. However, we are dealing everywhere with the same phenomenon. The figure also shows that while the United States often regards itself as a middle-class society, its share of the middle class was much smaller than in the northern European countries, even in the early 1980s.

The decline of the economic power of the middle class means that the goods and services consumed by the middle class (that is, middle-class patterns of consumption) become of much less importance to

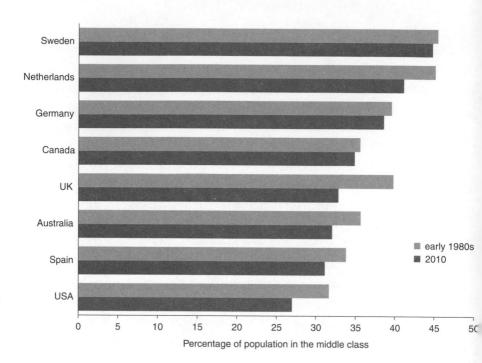

FIGURE 4.8. Decline in the share of the middle-class population in selected Western democracies, early 1980s to 2010

This graph shows the share of the population that can be considered middle class, defined as the percentage of people who have disposable per capita incomes within the range of 25% below and 25% above the national median, for selected Western democracies. We see that in all the countries listed here, the share of the middle class declined between the early 1980s and 2010. Countries are ranked by the share of the middle class in 2010. Data source: Calculated from Luxembourg Income Study database (http://www.lisdatacenter .org/).

producers. From the same data used to produce Figure 4.8, we can also calculate the income (and thus approximately, consumption) share of the middle class. We have seen that in the United States this share fell by 5 percentage points between the early 1980s and 2010. But the situation elsewhere was not much different. In Sweden, Australia, and the Netherlands, the decline was 4 percentage points; in Spain, 3; in Germany, 1.

The obverse of the decline of the middle class is the rising income share of the top of the income distribution, shown in Figure 4.9. The top 5 percent in the United States have almost as much income as the entire US middle class, as we define it here. (We are always dealing with disposable, or after-tax, income, unless otherwise indicated.) The share of the top 5 percent increased everywhere. An interesting case is Sweden, where the share of the middle class declined by very little but the top 5 percent became much richer and saw their income share grow by 3 percentage points. The shift in economic power away from the middle and in favor of the top has implications for overall consumption patterns. The rich are consuming more luxury goods, like expensive cars, vacations, restaurant meals, and jewelry than the middle class. This in turn means that producers are better off focusing on the type of goods and services consumed by the rich.

The decline of the middle class and its diminished economic power trigger a number of social and political effects. One of these effects is that support for the public provision of social services, principally education and health, declines. The rich may prefer to opt out and move toward private funding and consumption of these services (as they often do in emerging market economies), guaranteeing them higher quality. The countervailing power of the middle class is no longer sufficiently strong to oblige them to finance public health and education and participate in it. Rather than financing public education, the rich might prefer to use public funds on increased policing and what Marx called guard labor. In an influential article, Bowles and Jayadev (2005) showed that the percentage of labor involved in private and public security services and arms production had dramatically increased in the United States in the last three decades of the twentieth century. The use of guard labor was already the highest in the United States of all Western countries in 1970, with some 1.6 security workers per each 100 workers, but it shot up to more than 2 percent in 2000. Bowles and Jayadev estimate that more than

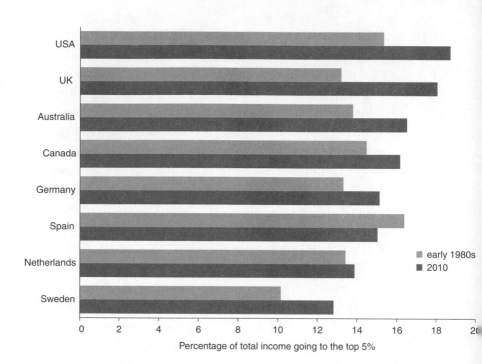

FIGURE 4.9. The rising income share of the top 5% in selected Western democracies, early 1980s–2010

This graph shows the share of total disposable income received by the richest 5% of people in each country, for selected Western democracies. We see that everywhere (except in Spain) the share of income received by the top 5% increased between the early 1980s and 2010. Countries are ranked by the share of the top 5% in 2010. Data source: Calculated from Luxembourg Income Study database (http://www.lisdatacenter.org/).

5 million workers in the United States are employed as guard labor. In addition, they argue that guard labor is more prevalent in more unequal countries.[33]

All of this leads us to one conclusion regarding the changes that have occurred during the past three decades: social separatism. This class bifurcation has many implications: politically, the middle class becomes increasingly irrelevant; production shifts toward luxuries, and social expenditures change from being directed toward education and infrastructure to policing.

As the political importance of the middle class continues to dwindle, it is not difficult to project into the future the current trends, most vividly seen in the United States, where financial support from rich individuals and companies is indispensable for political success. While the political system remains democratic in form because the freedom of speech and the right of association have been preserved and elections are free, the system is increasingly coming to resemble a plutocracy. In Marxist terms, it is a "dictatorship of the propertied class" even if it seems, formally, to be a democracy. The government becomes nothing else but, in Marx's words from the *Communist Manifesto*, "the committee for managing the common affairs of the bourgeoisie."

And indeed, a gap between ideology and reality will not be anything new to a student of politics and history. Rome seamlessly grew to be an autocratic empire while masquerading as a republic ruled by a senate. A bureaucratic class ruled Eastern Europe while claiming that both economic and political power were in the hands of the people. Every dictator today argues that he embodies the will of the people—that is, believes himself to be a democrat.

The slide away from democracy can take two forms. One of these may be called American and resembles a plutocracy; the other may be called European and is characterized by populism or nativism.

Plutocracy. Consider the march toward plutocracy first. Exhibit A in the case for plutocracy consists of the studies mentioned earlier, that show that elected officials are responsive almost solely to the concerns of the rich. Money plays an unprecedented role in US politics, and the Supreme Court decision to treat corporations as individuals (*Citizens United v. Federal Election Commission*) has opened the doors, legally and formally, to an ever-increasing influence of money on political decision-making. Figure 4.10 shows total election costs in inflation-adjusted dollar amounts since 2000, for each year in which there were both presidential and congressional elections. The costs have grown both in real amounts and as a share of GDP (the latter not shown in the graph).

Since it is in the interest of the rich to promote the current process of globalization, from which they are, as we saw in Chapters 1 and 2, strong beneficiaries, and since the middle class and the poor can at least formally derail that process, the focus of the rich is on democracy suppression (even though some of the measures are not consciously implemented as such). This suppression involves a two-pronged approach that includes (1) suppressing the vote of the poor, and (2) creating what I will refer to as false consciousness among the lower middle class and the poor.

Consider direct or indirect suppression of the vote. The United States is a country with a very skewed participation in elections, where 80 percent of people in the top income decile vote, compared with only 40 percent in the bottom decile.[34] Note that according to any economic theory, these numbers should be reversed: since no individual vote can influence electoral outcome, it is rational not to vote; and it is especially rational not to vote for people whose time is very valuable, that is for the rich. The fact that the situation is the reverse could result from several factors—greater civic consciousness of the rich, discouragement among the poor ("why bother to vote?"), or specific policies intended to keep the poor from voting, including holding elections on a workday and closing the polling booths by 8 pm, just a couple of hours after most people have left work and are rushing to get home.

Large groups of people are disenfranchised either because they are felons or are incarcerated (with the United States having one of the highest rates of incarceration in the world). Human Rights Watch estimates that about 2 percent of the US voting-age population is disenfranchised, one-third of whom are African American (Deaton

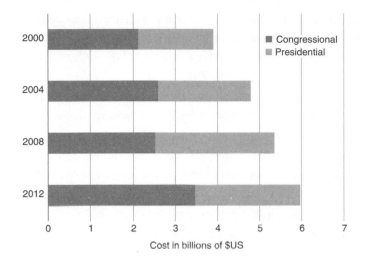

FIGURE 4.10. Cost of US congressional and presidential elections, 2000–2012

This graph shows the cost of US congressional and presidential elections (in the years when both were held) in billions of US dollars (constant 2000 prices). We see that the cost has steadily increased from 2000 to 2012. Data source: Calculated from the data provided in Open Secrets: Center for Responsive Politics, available at https://www.opensecrets.org /bigpicture/index.php?cycle=2012.

2013, 198). Finally, there is a rising tide of gerrymandering, whose objective is to redefine electoral districts in order to dilute the vote of the poor and minorities. These processes, like rising income inequality, have been going on for decades, and some of them date back to the very origins of American democracy, a political system created as a peculiar form of slave-owning democracy. They are more apparent now, however, because they have become stronger and because we have better data for documenting them.

The second part of rich people's strategy to suppress democracy is similar to what in Marxian terminology is called the creation of false consciousness or, to use Antonio Gramsci's terminology, hegemony. I do not like the term "false consciousness" because it seems to imply that there is an "authentic consciousness," which I do not believe exists. I use it because I lack a better term. What I mean by it is that middle class and poor people are being diverted, largely by design, from looking after their own economic interests into caring about other concerns, especially social or religious ones that are often divisive. This diversion does not necessarily arise from any sort of backroom conspiracy, but rather from a collectively manufactured elite consensus. It is, to some extent, an understandable (and acceptable) strategy because voting decisions are multidimensional: people do not vote solely on economic issues and may care deeply about such matters as migration, religion, and abortion. But given the enormous amount of private money that is used in politics and media, one cannot but think that the aim of these investments is very similar. In one case (politics), influence is sought directly; in the other case (the media), influence is created through shaping public opinion so that it agrees with the opinion of the funders. The creation of false consciousness takes place through ideological *matraquage* (a French term that means a brain-beating as if by a nightstick), where newspaper readers, TV viewers, and Internet surfers are bombarded with issues—running from abortion and gun control to the threat of Islamic fundamentalism—that distract popular attention from basic economic and social problems like unemployment, the incarceration rate, war profits, and billion-dollar tax loopholes for the rich. In other words, the culture war has a function, and that function is to mask the real shift of economic power toward the rich.

An important part of false consciousness is the belief that social mobility is more feasible than it really is. I will not enter here into a discussion of the hugely influential (and much discussed) belief that the doors of success are open to practically everybody in the United States, except to point out that now that we are able for the first time in history to measure both actual intergenerational income mobility and people's subjective perceptions of mobility, we find that the latter vastly outstrips the former. People with lower incomes are especially prone to overestimate overall upward mobility (Kraus and Tan 2015).[35] This finding is comforting for social stability. But it goes against the grain of what we would normally expect, namely, that people at the bottom would believe that there are some systemic features which keep them there. Unless we believe that poor people blame themselves for their own poverty, the only explanation for the hugely optimistic view of social mobility held by the poor is that ideology plays a role in it. (Note that Kraus and Tan did not ask about people's view regarding the likelihood of their own upward mobility. One might expect the poor to believe that they themselves have more room to move up than the rich who are already at the top. The question asked was about their assessment of *overall* national upward mobility.)

The US political system, composed of two parties only, is particularly propitious for the spread of this kind of ideology because any candidates who break from the consensus of either party tend to return to the fold once the primaries are over, and the chance of a third-party contender is almost nil.[36] Even a third-party presidential candidate would face a huge number of technical and legal hurdles just to be listed on the ballot in all states. The emergence of alternatives to the dominant narrative is thus minimized, although the 2016 elections have thrown up unconventional candidates, at least in the primaries, from both the left and the right.

There is, I think, little doubt that the obsolescent and restrictive nature of the American political system and its slant in favor of the rich would have come under intense scrutiny had the United States only recently become a democracy. But since it has a venerable tradition of two centuries of (somewhat limited) democracy that has shown itself capable of solving problems peacefully (with the exception of the Civil War), the system is left unchanged. In reality, the system has led to a party duopoly, an economic and social establishment that is at the same time both Republican and Democratic (as reflected in many companies that support candidates from both political parties), and to brazen attempts to manipulate electoral outcomes.[37] The recent quasi-dynastic look of American politics, which the country shares with India, Greece, the Philippines, and Pakistan, but which is unknown in other rich democracies, is a symptom of a deeply rooted problem with the American political system. Because of these aspects of the political system, the development of a plutocracy is the most likely response to the dissatisfaction of the middle class in the United States.

Populism and nativism. The situation in Europe is different from that in the United States. On the one hand, European systems are multiparty (as opposed to two-party), more democratic, and less subject to the unmitigated influence of money; hence, it is more difficult to turn them into plutocracies. But on the other hand, the problem of immigration and absorption of migrants even after one or two generations is strongly affecting, even poisoning, political life. Problems with migration add to the "ordinary" pressures of globalization that are common to all rich countries and have led to the stagnation of lower-middle-class incomes in the past twenty-five or thirty years. Thus, the pressures of globalization in Europe take two distinct forms—one due to the movement of labor (immigration) and the other due to the movement of goods (imports) and capital (outflows). The response to these pressures leads to middle-class populism or nativism.[38]

The first point regarding migration is to acknowledge that migration is just an aspect of globalization. The movement of people is, in principle, no different from the movement of goods and technology, or the movement of capital. So it is wrong to discuss it as if it were somehow independent from the massive income gaps between nations that have been revealed and often exacerbated by globalization (especially with respect to Africa).

However (and this is the second point), migration takes on particular importance for Europe for several reasons that are absent in other rich Western countries. For one thing, Europe has long been a continent of emigrants and lacks the experience that the United States, Canada, and Australia have in dealing with immigration. For another, European nation-states have historically been either ethnically homogeneous (or have been rendered such through central governments' policies, as in France and Germany) or, when they were not (as in Spain), the diverse groups have lived next to each other for such a long time that the cultural and normative differences between them would seem rather small to an objective observer.[39] The migrants who come to Europe, however, generally have dissimilar religious beliefs, cultural norms, and outlook on life.

The third point, which follows directly from the first two, is that Europe has serious problems in assimilating migrants, not only those of the first generation but also those of the second and third. This problem is perhaps the most difficult of all because it cannot be dealt with, to a first approximation, by the government, and a lack of contact and relationships between the native-born population and immigrants (especially if it persists for a couple of generations) often leads, as we see in major European capitals, to the creation of ethnic ghettos. The irony of the situation is that the immigrant issue in Europe has come to resemble in many ways the racial problems faced by the United States in the 1960s—whose handling was strongly criticized in Europe at the time. But unlike in the United States with respect to racial disparities, much less research has been done in Europe on income gaps, differences in educational attainment, and the existence of social and family relationships between the immigrants and the native population. Lack of data makes it very difficult to formulate an assimilation policy. The extreme example of this obsolete and self-defeating approach is the French government's insistence, until very recently, that everyone is simply a French citizen and that statistics on ethnicity and religious affiliation may not be collected. In many areas, they still are not. For example, household surveys do not ask questions about the ethnic and religious background of the household, and there is thus no way to compare groups according to income distribution, mean family income, family composition, or other relevant statistics.[40]

I said that this problem cannot be dealt with by the government "to a first approximation" because no government can force people to make friends with immigrants or to marry them. But that does not mean that the government's role is nonexistent. By collecting information and then establishing affirmative policies in favor of minorities, one can gradually erase the income and education gap that exists between them and the native population. There is little doubt that this process would facilitate the assimilation of migrants as they move up the economic ladder and would lessen their own and natives' view of them as "others." In the future, Europe may indeed solve its immigrant problem in such a way—but at present, that day seems quite far off.

The fourth point is that migrants often bring different cultural norms which may undercut the sustainability of the welfare state. This issue is subject to misinformation, which tends to portray immigrants as disproportionate users of welfare services. Although this is not true, and indeed immigrants contribute more in taxes than they gain from social transfers and social services (partly because they are younger than the native population), popular perceptions may be distorted precisely because migrants are often "different" in their skin color, dress, speech, and behavior and thus are more visible.[41] But although the belief that migrants are "moochers" is inaccurate, we should remember that the European welfare state was built on the assumption of ethnic and cultural homogeneity of the population. Homogeneity not only increases affinity among different segments of the population but ensures that most people observe similar social norms. If no one pretends to be older in order to get a pension, or takes sick leave when not ill, the welfare state is self-sustaining. But if these norms are not observed by all, the welfare state tends to crumble (see Lindbeck 1994). Peter Lindert (2014) and, going back to much earlier work, Kristov, Lindert, and McClelland (1992), argued that the main reason for the greater development of the welfare state in Europe, as compared with the United States, lies precisely in the greater affinity that exists between different layers of the population, or to put it another way, in the greater probability that people who are young and employed can visualize a time in the future when they will need social help. In the United States, by contrast, argues Lindert, it was precisely the economic distance between whites and African Americans that led to a much more modest welfare state. A similar situation—loss of affinity—may be developing now in Europe.

This pressure on the functioning and sustainability of the European welfare states comes on top of the partly imagined, partly real, pressure being exerted on welfare states and labor from globalization, through cheaper imports and outsourcing. The numerous attacks on the welfare state—including cuts in national health services, cuts in public education, increased fees for government services, a higher retirement age, a "flexible" labor market with zero-hours jobs (jobs where workers must show up but are not guaranteed any work)—are in reality attacks on the middle class, because the middle class was the largest supporter and beneficiary of the welfare state. It is true that most studies have found that the poor, through unemployment benefits and social assistance, gain a lot from the welfare state (Milanovic 2000, 2010a). But the middle classes gain even more through free or subsidized health care and education, pensions, and, more than anything else, through the presence of a safety net to catch them were they ever to fall to a lower station in life.[42] The welfare state was thus an indispensable element in the strengthening of the European middle class and democratic capitalism.

The reaction of the middle and lower middle classes to the gradual loss of welfare-state protection and encroachment on their other acquired rights has been to shift politically to the right, toward populist and nativist parties. This trend has been facilitated, first, by the disappearance of alternatives on the left, which were discredited after the end of communism, second, by the co-optation of leftist parties (such as the Socialist Party in France and PSOE in Spain) by centrist or center-right parties from which they can hardly be distinguished any longer, and third, by the discrediting of the mainstream parties following their inept handling of the Great Recession. The crumbling of the left and of the mainstream parties has opened the way, in practically all Western and Central European countries, to the rise of mildly antisystemic populist parties. I use the term "mildly" because the objective of these parties, unlike that of true antisystemic parties such as fascist and communist parties, is not to destroy the existing political order. In appealing to voters, however, they do present themselves as antisystemic: Europeans' disenchantment with their political systems and parties is so huge that many of them perceive being "antisystem" as a plus.

Almost no country, from Greece with its Golden Dawn party to Finland with its True Finns, has been spared the populist upsurge. Figure 4.11 shows the most recent polling numbers for populist parties in national elections (where we can assume that the importance of a purely protest vote, from which these parties often benefit, is less than in the elections for a largely meaningless European Parliament). The most successful populist parties receive around 20 percent of the vote, a share which may become even higher in the next elections in France. In almost all the countries considered here, the popularity of the right-wing parties is higher than it was ten to fifteen years ago, when some of the parties did not even exist. The only exception is Belgium, where the Vlaams Belang party, formed after the Vlaams Blok party was banned on the grounds of racism, has failed to repeat its previous electoral results; many of its policy planks, however, have been absorbed by the ruling People's Flemish party.

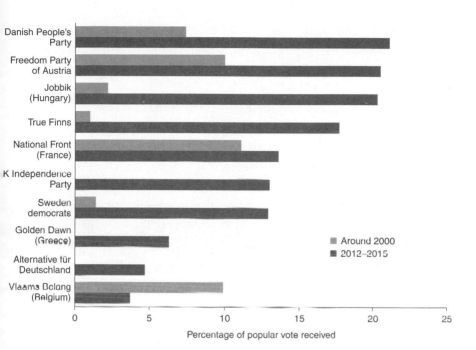

FIGURE 4.11. The share of the votes in legislative elections obtained by various European populist parties around the year 2000 and in the years 2012–2015

This graph shows the share of popular vote received in nationwide elections by right-wing nationalist or populist parties in various European countries. Popular vote is a better indicator of support than the seats the parties hold in national parliaments because the latter depend on countries' electoral rules. The graph shows, with the exception of Belgium, an increase in popular support for the right-wing populist parties since 2000. Legislative elections in 2012–2015 are the latest elections at the time of writing (August 2015): France (2012), Germany and Austria (2013), Belgium, Sweden, Hungary (2014), Greece, Finland, Denmark (2015). Parties are ranked from top to bottom according to their share in the most recent national election. Data source: Compiled by the author from various Internet sources.

The rise of such parties has had another effect: moving mainstream center-right parties more to the right. This shift is obvious in France, where the center-right party led by Nicolas Sarkozy is in many respects indistinguishable from the right-wing National Front (although Sarkozy's party attempts to highlight the differences and ignore the similarities). It is also obvious in the United Kingdom, where conservatives have in many instances moved closer to the positions held by the far-right United Kingdom Independence Party (UKIP).

It is unlikely that a populist party will come to power on its own or become the most important coalition member, not least because many other parties would refuse to govern with it. But, even without sharing power, these parties have already changed the European political landscape, and will continue to do so in the future. Ideas that only five years ago seemed unthinkable have become commonplace and almost mainstream: the UK leaving the European Union, Germany renegotiating its position within the Union, France stripping of citizenship naturalized citizens who get in trouble with the police, Denmark introducing extremely difficult citizenship and language tests, the Netherlands declaring itself "full" and thus closed to further immigration. Populism has thus entered fully into political life and has gradually moved toward displacing the mainstream—or rather, is becoming mainstream itself.

The populist and nativist movement undermines democracy by gradually revoking or redefining some fundamental rights of citizen, regarding them not as inviolable but as contingent on approval by national majorities. It also undercuts Europe's ability to fully and productively participate in globalization by rejecting the use of one obvious mechanism, the influx of migrants, through which Europe could stave off its demographic decline and open itself to talent from abroad. Populism represents a retreat both from globalization and democracy.[43]

These two reactions (American and European) address in different ways the problem of the trade-off between globalization and democracy. With a plutocratic government, as in the United States, there is an attempt to continue with globalization while ignoring the opinions and wishes of the people on the bottom and even in the middle of the national income distribution, in many ways rendering democracy meaningless. In the case of populism, as in Europe, the exposure to globalization is reduced both through obstacles to migration and through countries' attempts to protect themselves against unfettered flows of capital and trade while redefining citizenship and citizenship rights. To put it in an extreme form, plutocracy tries to maintain globalization while sacrificing key elements of democracy; populism tries to preserve a simulacrum of democracy while reducing exposure to globalization. Neither has so far succeeded—but what we have in mind here are their natural tendencies, which may become reality in the coming decades.

5

What Next?

Ten Short Reflections on the Future of Income Inequality and Globalization

> If you tender your advice with modesty and the opposition prevents its adoption, and, owing to someone else's advice being adopted, disaster follows, you will acquire very great glory. And, although you cannot rejoice in the glory that comes from disaster which befalls your city or your prince, it at any rate counts for something.
>
> —NICCOLÒ MACHIAVELLI, *Discourses on Livy*

In this concluding chapter I would like to go over some of the key themes and messages of the book. The chapter is part reminder of the book's main points, part prediction of future trends, and part agenda for change. It is organized around ten questions concerning matters of global income distribution that will be important in the years to come.

1. What Forces Will Shape Global Inequality in This Century?

The two forces that will shape global inequality are economic convergence and Kuznets waves. The prospect for convergence, or the economic catch-up of Asia with the West, seems strong. Even if China's growth were to sputter, the high economic growth rates of at least some of the very populous Asian countries such as India, Indonesia, Bangladesh, Thailand, and Vietnam will continue. It is unlikely that they would all slow down together. Until the turn of the twenty-first century, Chinese growth was largely responsible for the reduction of global poverty and inequality, but in the future, more Asian countries will be able to play that role, and consequently the chances that the process will continue will be greater—the eggs won't all be in one basket.

World economic power will shift much more toward Asia. In a nice exercise he has conducted for several years, Danny Quah has charted this gradual shift. In the 1980s, the center of gravity of world output was in the mid-Atlantic, located between Europe and North America. In his latest calculations, Quah locates the center in the middle of Iran, and notes that it has moved almost directly east over the past thirty-five years (Danny Quah, pers. comm.). By 2050, Quah expects it to lie between India and China, which will have thus taken on the roles previously played by Europe and North America (Quah 2011).

The catch-up of incomes in many Asian countries with incomes in Western European and North American nations will also reduce global inequality. However in this case, the role of China becomes ambiguous. Although China has been a great force for the reduction of global inequality over the past four decades, and until approximately 2000 was indeed the sole force because China alone made the difference between rising and declining global inequality, in the near future its fast growth will begin to add to global inequality. That effect will be small at first, but then, depending on what happens in Africa and whether the gap between China and populous poor countries increases, the effect may become greater. The bottom line is that for global inequality to go down, the world needs fast growth in other places besides China. That growth seems most likely to occur in Asia; it is doubtful that it will occur in Africa.

The role of the Kuznets waves is also not simple. Even if the waves were to be "well behaved," that is, if income inequality began to move along the downward portions of the Kuznets curves, first in China and later in the United States and the rest of the rich world, it still might take a decade for the reductions in national inequalities to become established and have an impact on a global level. Moreover, we cannot be sure if China and the United States are indeed at the peaks of their respective first and second Kuznets waves. In China, the main offsetting forces—that is, those that may keep inequality high—are the increased share of income coming from private capital, corruption, and regional income gaps. In the United States, those forces are the heavy concentration of capital in the hands of the rich, the unification of high capital and labor incomes in the same people (the "new capitalism"), and the political power of the rich.

Income inequality and political problems will remain closely linked. While one cannot expect high or even rising inequality to fundamentally alter the American political system other than by pushing it even further toward plutocracy, high inequality may end up undermining the Chinese political system and either transforming the rule of the Communist Party into a more nationalistic and autocratic regime or pushing it toward democracy. Either of these political changes would likely be accompanied by huge economic dislocation and a decline in the growth rate.

2. What Will Happen to Rich Countries' Middle Classes?

Rich countries' workers are squeezed between their own countries' top earners, who will continue to make money out of globalization, and emerging countries' workers, whose relatively cheap labor makes them more attractive for hiring. The great middle-class squeeze (which I discussed in Chapters 1 and 2), driven by the forces of automation and globalization, is not at an end. This squeeze will in turn further polarize Western societies into two groups: a very successful and rich class at the top, and a much larger group of people whose jobs will entail servicing the rich class in occupations where human labor cannot be replaced by robots. Education may not have much influence on what happens because many rich societies are already near the upper limit in terms of quantity of education (measured by the number of years of schooling) and possibly even in terms of quality of schooling that can be offered; in addition, many of those employed in service jobs are already overqualified for what they do.

We may have to adjust our thinking to a situation where the difference in skills and abilities between the top class and the service-sector workers is small. Chance and family background will play much more of a role than before. A person could become a Wall Street banker rather than a yoga instructor simply because of walking down the right street (and meeting the right person) one evening. Already, among the top 10 percent of wage-earners, we cannot identify differences in observable characteristics (education, experience) that could explain why salaries between the top 1 percent and the remaining 9 percent differ by a factor of ten or more (Piketty 2014, chap. 9). The reduced importance of education as an explanans of wages may spread down the wage ladder as educational attainments become more similar. Ironically, Tinbergen may turn out to have been right that the education premium would almost cease to exist in a society where everybody is well-educated, but that would not put a stop to large wage differences. In addition to blind chance, family endowments in wealth and, perhaps more importantly, connections, will matter more. One sees the effect of family money and networks in the United States very clearly in the occupations where lots of power and money accrue. Political dynasties are more common today than they were fifty years ago; people whose parents have been film actors or directors are almost ensured of a career in the same industry. The same is true in the financial sector. Are the children of politicians, actors, or stock traders the best qualified to do those jobs in the next generation? Assuredly not. It is just that previous success in these occupations breeds more success, including success for their offspring. Access to the people who make hiring decisions is crucial, and that access is helped by family background and connections.[1]

The new capitalism, where the contradiction between labor and capital will have been resolved at the top (in a peculiar way, since the richest people will be both the top labor earners and the top capitalists), will be more unequal. Success will depend on the chance of having been born well and having luck in life, more than it did in the past century (which was a century of major political and social upheavals). The new capitalism will resemble a big casino, with one important exception: those who have won a few rounds (often through being born into the right family) will be given much better odds to keep on winning. Those who have lost a few rounds will see the subsequent odds turn increasingly against them.

A child who has the luck of being born to the right (rich and educated) parents will benefit from heavy parental involvement and investment in education. Start with the ultimate objective parents set for their child: to get a good, high-paying job. To get such a job, one needs to go to the best university; to get to the best university, one needs to go to the best high school; to get to the best high school, one needs to go to the best elementary school; to get to the best elementary school, one needs to go to the best kindergarten. So a child's path is already determined by age five, provided his or her parents have enough knowledge, foresight, and indeed money. Very few poor or less educated parents have the resources or knowledge to make these choices so early on. If their child realizes later in life what is required to succeed, the path for him or her will be much harder. On the other hand, a child of rich parents is launched onto a path of success from the very beginning and may deviate from it only if he or she is uninterested in it or exhibits serious learning or behavioral problems.

It is hard to imagine that a system with such high inequality could be politically stable. But perhaps inequality will decline, and the problem of instability will disappear. What happens next depends on (1) the nature of technological progress, which might evolve in a pro-poor way, as by the replacement of people in some occupations that are very well paid now, say, professors, with lower-paid workers, and (2) the ability of the "losers" in this system to organize themselves politically. If the losers remain disorganized and subject to false consciousness, not much will change. If they do organize themselves and find political champions who could tap into their resentment and get their votes, then it might be possible for the rich countries to put into place policies that would set them on the downward path of the second Kuznets wave. How could this be achieved?

3. How Can Inequality in Rich Welfare States Be Reduced?

The short twentieth century is the only sustained period in history when rising mean incomes have been accompanied by decreasing income inequality. This happened not only in rich countries but also in many developmental states and in all communist countries. The second Kuznets curve will have to repeat the behavior of the first if inequality is to decline again. But it is doubtful whether this second decline will be accomplished by the same mechanisms as those that reduced inequality in the twentieth century: increased taxation and social transfers, hyperinflation, nationalization of property, and wars. Why not? Globalization makes increased taxation of the most significant contributor to inequality—namely, capital income—very difficult, and without a fully concerted action from most countries, which does not seem even remotely possible today, highly improbable.

Simply put, capital is hard to tax because it is so mobile, and the countries that benefit from this mobility have no incentive to help those that lose out. Tax havens exist not only in microstates, but in large countries like the United States and the United Kingdom. Think, for example, about the recent unwillingness of the United States to investigate and extradite Chinese citizens accused of embezzlement by their government (66 out of 100 of the "most wanted" people accused of economic crimes by the Chinese government are thought to be hiding in the United States and Canada),[2] or London brokers all too eager to accept Russian money regardless of its origin. Even high-income labor is becoming more difficult to tax because it can easily move from one country to another: there are no obvious reasons why a top executive may not be able to work in Singapore or Hong Kong rather than in London or New York. Hyperinflation and nationalization have fallen out of favor as a means of despoiling creditors and big proprietors. No more land will be nationalized. The balance of power has shifted to the side of the capitalists, with owners of assets and creditors holding political power. Finally, one hopes that major wars will be avoided, although no sensible person can, unfortunately, exclude that possibility.

Interventions done before taxes and transfers kick in are a much more promising approach for the twenty-first century. These include a reduction in the inequality of endowments, especially inequality in the ownership of assets and in education. If endowments (private wealth and skills) became less unequal, and assuming that the rates of return on wealth do not differ markedly between big and small fortunes, market incomes (that is, incomes before taxes and transfers) would be distributed much more equally than they are today. If market income inequality could be controlled, and over time curbed, government redistribution via transfers and taxes could be much less important. A smaller emphasis on redistribution would satisfy those who believe that high taxes have negative effects on growth and are in favor of a small state, as well as those who believe that lower disposable income inequality is valuable in itself or who support it because it promotes equality of opportunity and is good for economic growth. It will also eliminate one of the most pernicious aspects of family-transmitted inheritance that I discussed in the previous section.

Economic models that combine low inequality of market incomes and a relatively small state are not unheard of; indeed, they exist in several Asian countries. Figure 5.1 shows a comparison of selected Western countries and three rich Asian countries (South Korea, Taiwan, and Japan). The Gini coefficient for disposable income (after taxes and transfers) is shown on the vertical axis, and the Gini for market income on the horizontal axis. The three Asian countries have about the same level of disposable income inequality as rich Western countries, but their market income Ginis are much lower, by as much as 15 Gini points. Consequently, to achieve a given level of disposable income inequality, government redistribution in Asia can be much smaller, and the government can also be smaller. Consider Taiwan and Canada. Both countries have a disposable income Gini of 33 points. But to get to that point, Taiwan engages in almost no redistribution (that is, its market and disposable income Ginis are almost the same), and its social transfers are equal to only 12 percent of market income. Canada, on the other hand, has a large tax-and-transfer system (three times greater than Taiwan's in relative terms) that brings its inequality level down from 47 Gini points (at market income level) to 33 Gini points (at disposable income level).

Figure 5.1 also shows that in Western countries, differences in disposable income inequality are a result of differences in the amount of redistribution (e.g., the United States and Israel redistribute much less than Germany and France) rather than of differences in market income inequality. This is why a lot of scholarly attention has focused on the redistributive role of the state, as if redistribution were all that

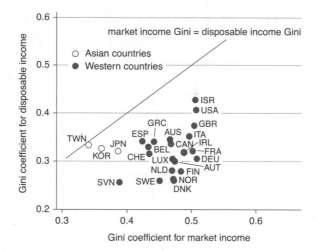

FIGURE 5.1. Inequality of market income and disposable income in selected rich Asian and Western countries (around 2010)

This graph shows the relationship between inequality of disposable income (income after social transfers and direct taxes) and inequality of market income (income before social transfers and direct taxes) for selected rich Asian and Western countries. The line shows the situation where disposable income inequality is equal to market income inequality. The distance between the line and the dots shows how much market income inequality is reduced as a result of government redistribution through social transfers and taxes. The three Asian countries have low market income inequality and low government redistribution (their dots lie close to the line). Country abbreviations: *Asia*: JPN Japan, KOR South Korea, TWN Taiwan; *Western countries*: AUS Australia, AUT Austria, BEL Belgium, CAN Canada, CHE Switzerland, DEU Germany, DNK Denmark, ESP Spain, FIN Finland, FRA France, GBR Great Britain, GRC Greece, IRL Ireland, ISR Israel, ITA Italy, LUX Luxembourg, NLD Netherlands, NOR Norway, SVN Slovenia, SWE Sweden, USA United States. Data source: Calculated from Luxembourg Income Study (www .lisdatacenter.org).

could be done to reduce inequality. The distribution of endowments is almost taken as a given. But as we see in the case of the rich Asian countries, this is not the case: endowments can be made more equal. So, the same level of inequality in disposable income can be achieved either through large taxes and transfers or through much more modest interventions by the government superimposed on a relatively equal structure of endowments.

How can the equalization of endowments be achieved? Here again, as in the past, the role of the government is crucial, although the government does not in this case work on current incomes (taxing and redistributing them) but rather works toward longer-term equalization of capital ownership and education. Policies that would work toward this long-term equalization include (1) high inheritance taxes (as Piketty calls for), which would keep parents from being able to transfer large assets to their children, (2) corporate tax policies that would stimulate companies to distribute shares to workers (moving toward a system of limited workers' capitalism), and (3) tax and administrative policies that would enable the poor and the middle classes to have and hold financial assets. Also fitting with this proposal is de Soto's (1989) call for much broader ownership of assets, along with the legalization of the assets the poor already possess, such as properties that in many countries are held without legal title and so cannot be used as collateral for loans.

But these policies would not be sufficient. The high volatility of returns from capital and the need for lots of information in order to make wise investment decisions, in addition to the problem of combining the risk of working for a company with the risk of owning shares in the same company, make a "people's capitalism" very difficult to realize. To reduce inequality in endowments, more widely spread ownership of capital needs to be combined with more equal distribution of education. By that I mean not only making sure that everyone has the same number of years of schooling, but equalizing *meaningful* access to education. Achieving this kind of access requires a reemphasis on state-funded education. The reason is as follows. If the objective is simply to make the number of years of education the same for all, we could conclude that four years at Harvard and four years at a small state college are of equal value, and the objective could easily be achieved. But if access to Harvard remains for all practical purposes limited to the children of the rich and the returns to four years of education at Harvard exceed manifold the returns to four years of education at a state college, nothing fundamental will have changed. There would be an apparent but not fundamental equality of education endowments. To attain fundamental equality, we need to equalize access to the schools that produce better returns to education and/or to equalize returns across schools. To equalize the returns by fiat is impossible in a market economy, since no one can dictate to firms that they must give equal pay to people who studied at different schools, regardless of the quality of those schools.[3] The only remaining sensible way to equalize educational endowments is to make access to the best schools more or less equal regardless of parental income and, more importantly, to equalize the quality of education across schools.[4] The latter can only be done by state investment and financial support.

In a system focused on equalization of endowments, the state has an extremely important role—but that role is quite different from the one it had during the Great Leveling. During the Great Leveling, the state worked on expanding access to education and on mechanisms of income redistribution consisting of insurance (e.g., Social Security in the United States) and assistance (e.g., food stamps in the United States). During the second Kuznets wave, it should work more on endowments and less on taxes and transfers.

But even if such policies are theoretically possible, and even if we have examples of countries that have used them, that does not mean they will be implemented. European welfare states, and to a lesser extent the United States, have been managed for almost a century on entirely different premises, and changing them now will not be easy. The anti-equality headwinds of globalization will make it even harder, as will the unevenness in returns to labor that often goes with globalization. To this we turn next.

4. Will Winner-Take-All Remain the Rule?

It is often said that winner-take-all is one of the characteristics of current globalization. For it is only thus that massive income differences between people with approximately the same abilities can be explained. As in tennis, a tiny difference in skill level is sufficient to make one person number one in the world, earning millions, and another person number 150, covering the costs out of his own (or more likely his parents') pocket in order to participate in tournaments. A useful way to visualize the winner-take-all rule is to think of the scalability of different jobs. As Nassim Taleb writes in *Black Swan,* scalable jobs are those where a person's same unit of labor can be sold many times over.[5] A typical example is that of a top pianist who in the past could sell her ability only to those who would come to listen to her. Then, with the invention of the record player, she could sell it to all who would buy the recordings; today, via the Internet, YouTube, and webcasting, she can sell it to practically the entire globe. Those who are just slightly less good pianists, or perhaps have not had as much luck, will hardly be listened to by anyone. Scalable jobs, then, create very large income differences within the same occupation. Moreover, these income differences are disproportionally large compared to any objective assessment of the differences in abilities.

Figure 5.2 is a schematic graph that shows the relationship between how many times a unit of labor can be sold (extent of scalability) and jobs' rankings according to scalability. Jobs on the far left side of the horizontal axis are jobs that cannot be scaled: a pedicure can be delivered only to the customer who is taking it; a spaghetti meal, after being cooked and prepared, can be sold only once; a taxi ride can be sold only to one person or one group of people at a time. Their value on the vertical axis is 1. A person has to produce more of these goods and services in order to earn more. Income from these jobs (compared to scalable jobs) is by necessity limited because the number of

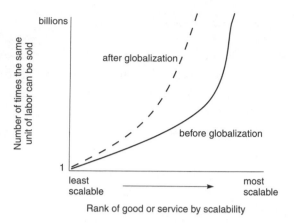

FIGURE 5.2. Scalability of goods and services

This graph shows how many times one can sell the same unit of labor in different types of activities. For activities on the left side of the horizontal axis, a unit of labor can be sold only once; for those on the right side, it can be sold many times over. The more times one can sell the same unit of labor, the more scalable is the activity. The dashed line shows the increase in the extent of scalability with technological change and globalization.

units one can produce is limited by the number of hours one can work. Advances in productivity may increase the number of units produced per day, but they do not change the lack of scalability of such products. (These can be characterized as private, excludable, and rival goods and services. The scalable goods and services, on the other hand, are private and excludable but nonrival; i.e., goods whose greater consumption by one person does not reduce possible consumption by another person.)

As we move to the right on the horizontal axis, we get to jobs that are increasingly scalable. Our examples of a tennis player or a pianist who can be watched (for a fee) by everyone on the planet are the extreme examples of scalability. Novak Djokovic and Rafael Nadal do not need to play a match for every spectator who watches them: they play once and get paid through millions of individual sales fees.

Their unit of labor is almost infinitely scalable (that is, up to 7 billion people in the world).

Now if the scalable activities employed a very small number of people, their impact on overall wage inequality would be limited. But with globalization, more jobs become scalable, and thus more people become employed in them. Further, the extent of scalability increases. This can be visualized by an upward movement of the curve in Figure 5.2. The new scalability curve is shown by the dashed curve that is higher for each individual job: a unit of labor can now be sold more times than before. Evidently, if there are more jobs with very high within-job inequalities, overall wage inequality will also tend to be greater. Thus, the massive wage differences that exist within the same types of jobs are a combination of (1) technological change, which makes jobs in principle scalable (without the ability to record sound, a pianist's performance would not be scalable) and (2) globalization, that is, the ability to reach every corner of the world. As I discussed in Chapter 2, we see here again that the effects of technological change and globalization cannot be readily separated: the two, while conceptually distinct, go together.

Perhaps the most important change will continue to be the increasing number of activities that are scalable. In *Black Swan*, Taleb gives the examples of a sex-worker and a cook as people whose activities are not scalable. But this is no longer necessarily the case. Entire industries have grown up on the Internet with people advertising their own nudity or teaching cooking, and doing this for thousands of fee-paying viewers simultaneously.[6] The point is: technology has tremendously expanded the ability of sex workers, cooks, personal trainers, teachers, and many others to sell their services: a rival good has become nonrival. Or take the example of people who have become famous on social media and are now paid by companies to mention (i.e., advertise) their products. In a recent interview, Josh Ostrovsky, who is famous under his Instagram name of Fat Jew, explains the advantage of scalability: "I want as many people as possible to know that I am very ... funny, ... but why would I fly around the world to do a stand-up show to hundreds, maybe thousands of people when I can reach far bigger numbers through my Instagram?"[7] There are some activities that, at least currently, we cannot imagine becoming scalable: a haircut is one; the same spaghetti cannot be eaten twice. But many things, and especially services, will increasingly become scalable.

It is important, however, not to confuse scalability of services with the ability to sell one's service more broadly. Surgery can now be performed remotely, with a surgeon in Houston controlling scalpel-wielding robots and operating on a patient in Chennai. This increases the income of the surgeon but still involves the sale of a discrete unit of labor only once. This is not the case with professors' ability to sell their teaching: they can sell it worldwide, many times over. I have to work only once to prepare my lecture but can (if there are any takers) sell it thousands or millions of times on the Internet to whoever wants to pay to listen to it. It is these types of occupations (professor, chef) that will continue to expand with the second technological revolution, and as more jobs combine scalability with wide reach, wage inequality will tend to rise.

5. Why Is It Wrong to Focus Exclusively on Horizontal Inequality?

In his book *The Killing Fields of Inequality*, Göran Therborn asks a puzzling question: Why have rich societies been so much more successful at reducing legal inequalities between various groups (blacks and whites, men and women, heterosexuals and homosexuals) than in reducing overall income and wealth inequalities? A focus on "existential," or "categorical," inequality was considered a radical position in nineteenth-century Europe, where it was associated with post-1789 developments. Once all formal distinctions of class between the clergy, the aristocracy, and the people were abolished, there would be, it was argued, no need to focus on income differences. As Piketty reminds us in *Capital in the Twenty-First Century*, this view reached its peak under the French Third Republic, when income inequality was going up by leaps and bounds but the existence of formal equality was used as an argument against trying to do anything about actual income inequality.

Therborn wonders if there is a trade-off between existential equality and income inequality. Will the achievement, or close achievement, of the former be regarded as such a success that we will forget about pursuing reduction in income or wealth inequalities? Or do we believe that the achievement of existential equality will ultimately translate, as it were automatically, into lower income inequality? Will equalization of the mean wages of women and men, for example, lead to a lower spread among wage-earners as a whole?

There have been substantial advances in the past thirty years in the equal legal treatment of different groups. For example, there is no official apartheid anywhere in the world, and gay rights are being accepted by an increasing number of countries. But until some thirty years ago, apartheid existed in South Africa, and until forty years ago, the World Health Organization listed homosexuality under the rubric of mental disorders. There has also been a strong push for "horizontal" equality, which is the term used in economics to indicate that on average there should be no wage difference between, for example, men and women, blacks and whites, heterosexuals and homosexuals. Or more exactly, if there are differences, they should be explained by measurable factors like better skills or greater experience. There has been significant progress in that area, too, although not as substantial as in legal equality. For example, in OECD countries, the gender wage gap has narrowed from an average of 20 percent in 2000 to 16 percent in 2010 (OECD 2012, 166).[8]

But an almost single-minded focus on existential inequality is not always helpful, and in some cases may be outright harmful to achieving a reduction of income and wealth inequalities. Note that success in reducing income inequality would also reduce income differences due to racial or gender discrimination. In other words, pushing for the reduction of overall income inequality may be preferable even if our primary objective is to reduce specific gender or racial income inequalities. But this is not the approach that has been taken. Rather, the focus has been on horizontal inequalities, while overall, general inequality has been left to its own devices.

The exclusive focus on existential inequality is wrong for at least three reasons.

First, an emphasis on group differences quickly spills into identity politics, splintering the groups that have an interest in fighting for change. The joint front crumbles, with different groups focusing only on their own situations; once their complaint has been addressed, they are indifferent to the plights of other groups.

Second, a focus on existential inequality leaves the basic problem unsolved because the way it poses the question is wrong. Take discussions regarding legalization of prostitution. To many feminists and others, prostitution is a reprehensible activity that they would like to either ban, discourage through education, or curb demand for by punishing clients, who are predominantly male. The issue is framed in gender terms. But this approach just drives the problem underground without solving it. It is also futile, because the root cause of prostitution is not addressed. The root cause today (and perhaps throughout history) is income and wealth inequality. There are many (mostly) men with high incomes and many (mostly young) women with poor job prospects and no money. This drives prostitution nationally and globally, as in sex tourism, where it is at its most obvious. The point is not to address gender inequality itself but rather its economic cause. Consider what would happen if horizontal income equality between men and women were achieved, something that may happen soon, given higher graduation rates among women than men and growing numbers of rich women. Prostitution might be transformed so that instead of 90 percent of customers being men and 90 percent of sex workers being women, there would be a "fair" and "gender-neutral" distribution of customers and workers, with 50 percent men and 50 percent women. Would anti-prostitution activists be content with this achievement? Obviously not: prostitution would merely have become gender-balanced. This hypothetical scenario reveals that the real cause of the problem lies elsewhere, in inequality of incomes and wealth, not solely in the income gap between men's and women's earnings.

Third, an emphasis on existential equality is politically relatively easy (and its pay-off is limited) because it does not go to the core of the problem. It faces no real opposition from right-wing politicians and conservatives because it does not affect the underlying structure of economic and political power. Instead of fighting for meaningful change, proponents of existential equality care only up to the point where legal equality is established. They give short shrift to issues on which progress in the past thirty years has often been minimal, especially in the United States, but which would move the wage-profit ratio in favor of labor and would thus face strong opposition from business (e.g., increased vacation time *for all,* a shorter work-week *for all,* longer maternity and paternity leave and better working conditions *for all* parents, a higher minimum wage *for all*). Strictly speaking, capitalists also know that existential equality is in their interest; discrimination is inefficient for the employers who practice it. On the other hand, general measures that improve the position of all workers do not please those who have economic power. Thus, the proponents of existential equality stop midway. Formal equality is surely a necessary condition for overall betterment. But it is not sufficient. A movement toward more generalized equalization of the human condition requires not only legal equality between the different groups that humans are divided into, but also substantively greater income and wealth equality.

Existential equality is equivalent to what John Rawls calls meritocratic equality—what he views as the lowest level of equality, where all participants are legally free to pursue whatever career they choose but where their starting positions are often vastly different. Those who care exclusively about "identities" aim to place everybody on the same starting line but do not care that some come to the starting line with Ferraris and others with bicycles. Their job is done once everybody is on the same starting line. Case closed: just when the real issues begin.

6. Will Labor Remain Different from Other Factors of Production?

When it comes to labor and migration, global governance of almost any kind is missing. By contrast, global institutions exist that deal with economic development (the World Bank), balance of payments and international debt (the International Monetary Fund), health (the World Health Organization), trade, including in intellectual property rights (the World Trade Organization), central banks (the Bank for International Settlements), and now regional trade (the Atlantic and Pacific trade agreements). When it comes to labor, the International Labor Organization, which is the oldest among the institutions mentioned here, has little power and deals mostly with national labor rules. The International Organization for Migration is a keeper of accounts and statistics, duly following all catastrophes, rather than a policy-setter. The reason for this lack of multilateral institutions regarding labor and migration is obvious: the rich and powerful countries have no interest in raising the issue. But ignoring the problem by following an ostrich policy is becoming more difficult as globalization makes people more aware of the glaring differences in national standards of living, and physical distance is much less of an obstacle than ever before. Europe, faced by an exodus from Africa, and more recently from the Middle East and the Indian subcontinent, will be perhaps the first to begin defining a multilateral policy on the movement of people. However, unlike what is envisaged now (multilateralism among EU members only), such a policy needs to include the sending countries as well. A world of more orderly migration, and of quotas at the level of both the sending and the recipient countries, should be the goal.

In order for such a change to become feasible, we need to change the binary character of the current rules for national citizenship (as argued in Chapter 3). With some exceptions, citizenship today confers on the person who obtains it the same rights and duties as are enjoyed by all other citizens. It is that binary nature of citizenship that makes current citizens reluctant to share their "citizenship rent" with migrants: in monetary terms, the citizenships of rich countries are very valuable. Physical walls between jurisdictions are being built, in part, because there is a huge financial wall between being and not being a citizen of a rich country. But citizens of rich countries might be more open to foreign migration if this financial wall could be lowered through the introduction of an intermediate level of citizenship that would be less valuable (because, for example, it might involve higher taxation, lower access to social services, or an obligation to return to work in one's country of origin at periodic intervals). A policy such as this would bring globalization to the forgotten factor of production, labor, and through migration would lower global poverty and inequality. For this to happen, two changes are essential: (1) the redefinition of citizenship, and (2) multilateralism involving sending and recipient countries.

But even if migration were to become more common than it is today, it is still extremely unlikely that the change would be so momentous as to lead to fully open borders and a situation whereby GDP growth rates of poor countries would become unimportant because people could just leave whenever they wanted to. Thus, the growth of poor nations will remain of crucial importance. We turn to this next.

7. Will Economic Growth Still Matter?

Economic growth will still matter a great deal in the coming century: it is the most powerful tool for reducing global poverty and inequality (as it is, also, for reducing national poverties). One can hardly over-estimate its importance in poorer countries as a means of making the lives of ordinary people better. The disparagement of growth that surfaces from time to time comes mostly from rich people in rich countries who believe that they can dispense with more economic growth. But these people either are deluding themselves or are hypo-critical: their own behavior—for example, when they negotiate their salaries and fees—shows that they do care about material incentives. Moreover, if growth were unnecessary, why wouldn't we celebrate the recession instead of trying to get rid of it? If growth did not matter, why would the referendum on Scotland's independence, or the possible future referendums on the United Kingdom staying in the European Union or Catalonia seceding from Spain, revolve around economic is-sues and often be decided by them? If rich people care about income and economic growth, why shouldn't poor people care even more?

Those who are calling for a slowdown in growth because of envi-ronmental concerns are themselves often the biggest contributors to environmental degradation and global warming. One need only think of the hypocrisy of conferences on carbon-neutrality where the organizers try to convince the well-heeled participants not to feel bad about flying for fifteen hours to get to the conference by paying the so-called carbon emission offsets—a practice similar to the erstwhile practice of buying indulgences for the expiation of sins in the Catholic Church. It suffices to look at the amounts of air conditioning, driving, and meat consumption that is being done by the global top 1 percent or global top 10 percent to realize that the rich are the main contributors to climate change. But they are often the ones calling for a reduction in growth (implicitly, in poor countries as well as rich countries) on the basis of the eventual ecological unsustainability of a world where today's poor would enjoy the standard of living of today's rich.

There is an unevenness in carbon emissions that is seldom recognized and on which empirical research is lacking, despite the availability of data. One could easily estimate the distribution of CO_2 emissions across the world population by income group and not, as is done today, by country. If income elasticity of carbon emissions is unitary (i.e., a 10 percent increase in real income entails a 10 percent increase in carbon emissions), then the Gini coefficient of global carbon emissions is around 70 points, which would mean that more than one half of all emissions are made by the global top 10 percent.[9] Almost all the people in the top world decile come, as we know, from rich countries. Not from Africa.

High rates of economic growth will remain crucial, especially for poor countries in Africa, and a few in Asia and Central America. Our main concern therefore should not be how to manage a slowdown in growth but how to raise the growth rates of the very poor countries. There is also a direct connection between the growth rates of poor countries and the migration pressure that was discussed previously. If the growth of poor countries picks up, we shall also more easily solve the problem of pent-up demand for migration as well as other political problems associated with migration in the recipient countries. That would mean less populist and often xenophobic politics in Europe, and less use of migration as a political football in the United States.

It is important to realize that a fine balancing act must be done between three variables: growth rates of poor (and populous) countries, migration, and environmental sustainability. Migration and the development of poor countries are, from the point of view of global poverty and inequality reduction, equivalent: poor people would become richer, either in their own countries or somewhere else. Politically, of course, they are not equivalent. But this worthwhile objective of increasing people's incomes has to be balanced by making sure that it is ecologically sustainable. That would, in principle, require the largest sacrifices from the rich. In other words, if, because of improvements in the standard of living of today's poor (whether through migration or faster growth in Africa and Asia), the ecological balance is upset, restraints on growth should be imposed on the rich. I know that this is an especially unpopular proposition to make while the Great Recession either still goes on or has barely ended, but the reasoning behind it seems to me incontrovertible.

8. Will Concern with Inequality Disappear from Economics?

It might have seemed until a couple of years ago that the concern with inequality was just a "flavor of the month," or at best, of the year, and that as the months and years passed, economists would move on to another topic. I do not think that this is a reasonable position to hold anymore.

First, there are methodological advances in economics, thanks to the reintroduction of inequality into economists' way of thinking, which will be difficult to forget about or ignore. Economics is moving from an almost single-minded concern with representative agents and averages to a concern with heterogeneity. And as soon as one enters the territory of heterogeneity, she is dealing with inequality. It need not be inequality only in wealth and income; it could be inequality in education, health status, IQ or SAT scores, trust, corruption, or anything. But once you no longer think only in terms of averages, your outlook on the world changes dramatically. It can be likened to going from a two-dimensional to a three-dimensional world. By now, these concerns are fairly deeply implanted among the new generations of economists and social scientists. Economists are including them in their dissertations, research projects, and empirical papers, and as these long-term projects become completed, and as the new generation begins to fill academic and research positions, the paradigm will gradually change. Replacing an old paradigm takes a long time; it sometimes requires an important economic event to reveal the discrepancy between what a paradigm teaches and how the world really functions. (This is precisely what the Great Recession did for the paradigm of the representative infinitely lived income-maximizing agent with perfect information.) The new heterogeneity- and inequality-based paradigm that is being created now will take some time to impose itself, but it, in turn, will not be easy to displace.

Increasing interest in inequality has also spurred an important ideological change whereby we look not only at the similarities among people but at the differences. We no longer try to cover up differences between economic agents or companies or individuals by the process of averaging, that is, by looking at group means; rather, we do exactly the opposite: we try to uncover dissimilarities. Once we start seeing the world through this new lens we cannot go back to the old ways.

9. Why Is Methodological Nationalism Becoming Less Relevant?

The concept of methodological nationalism is used to convey the idea that in social science research we often take the nation-state as a natural unit of analysis. Thus, income inequality, as we have seen in this book, is most often measured at the level of a country, the effects of economic policies are contrasted between different countries, government expenditures or exports and imports are calculated for countries, and so on. Indeed, for many economic variables it makes sense to use the country as the unit of observation not only because accounting is done in such a manner but because most policies are conducted by national governments—that is, neither by supranational bodies nor by local or provincial governments.

However, in many other instances, methodological nationalism is either becoming less relevant or may prove to be directly counterproductive for our understanding of new phenomena. Let us consider several examples where methodological nationalism is not useful or cannot be applied. Perhaps the best example is the introduction of the euro. Overnight, the monetary statistics of individual countries (the so-called base money, M0, or broader money supply, M2), which for decades were key national policy indicators, disappeared. There were no longer separate national monetary authorities or monetary series for France, Italy, or Spain. Nobody knows for sure how many euros in cash are held today in Spain as opposed to Germany. Another way that governments can lose all or a part of national monetary policy is by adopting another country's currency (as Panama and Peru have done with the US dollar). It is estimated by the US Federal Reserve System that about $1.3 trillion US dollars circulate outside the United States.[10] Anyone who has traveled to Russia must have noticed that despite twenty-five years of capitalism and the freely exchangeable ruble, many transactions are done, or prices are quoted, in US dollars. Since these dollars represent real purchasing power and are unlikely to return to the United States any time soon, Russian monetary policy must take into account their existence. In other words, they limit the ability of national authorities to conduct monetary policy.[11]

Or take the example of EU laws that supersede national laws or require harmonization between the laws of different nations. Methodological nationalism is clearly inappropriate in this situation. It is also unclear what relevance national exports and imports have in an integrated and globalized economy where large companies, through transfer pricing or internal "exports" and "imports" designed to minimize taxes, can strongly affect national trade statistics, showing a country's exports to be higher or lower without anything having been effectively changed. Similarly, if, for example, a high proportion of a country's exports comes from companies that belong to foreigners (as is the case with Ireland), export statistics may look high and Gross Domestic Product may increase, but Gross National Product (which includes only the earnings of citizens) may be much smaller or may move differently from the GDP. Indeed, in Ireland the gap between GDP and GNP is some 20 percent. With increased globalization, a discrepancy between GDP and GNP will become more common. The situation becomes even more unclear when we ask who these foreign citizens are. Many people have double nationalities, and many live in several different countries. As a result, net factor income (return on investments) that flows out of Ireland may appear to go to the citizens of the United States if a company is registered there, but it might turn out that these US residents are also Russian citizens who have a tax residence in the Bahamas. Has this income that has flowed out of Ireland gone to the United States, Russia, or the Bahamas? When the most important output is financial services, and net factor outflow is to individuals hiding under shell companies in the Cayman Islands (or in Luxemburg, where GNP is only two-thirds of GDP), the issue becomes even more intractable. As Gabriel Zucman (2015) points out, it is intentionally made intractable, so that incomes may be made untraceable and taxes evaded.

The gap between one's original citizenship, given generally by place of birth, and one's current citizenship or residency, although it affects only about 3 percent of the world's population, puts into doubt even our most venerable statistical indicators like GDP and GNP. Clemens and Pritchett (2008) have argued that "national" product should be calculated across people who were born in a given country and not, as it is now, across those who currently live in the country. For example, there may be a significant gap between the per capita income of people who were born in the Philippines and that of the current residents of the Philippines.

Transborder movements of people, income, and capital lead to statistical issues that were totally unknown even some twenty or thirty years ago. Mexican households report, among their social transfers, pensions received by Mexicans who have worked in the United States but have since returned and retired in Mexico. Should we treat these pensions as we treat "normal" Mexican pensions, thus giving the wrong impression about the size and distribution of Mexican social transfers? Or should we treat them as remittances, even though remittances are unrequited transfers between different individuals and not (like a pension) payment for past services to the same person? Mexico and the United States are just a representative pair here: the same problems appear in other parts of the world where a significant percentage of national population works or has worked abroad.

Studies of global inequality transcend the limits of methodological nationalism. But as we have seen in this book, the global level is best seen as a new, additional layer on top of national layers. The global level may in many instances be more useful to study, but the analysis still cannot dispense with the nation-state. For example, we have seen in Chapters 2 and 3 how inequalities within nations and among nations, respectively, enter into the calculation of global inequality, and how both of them still matter. But once we are willing to look at the world as a whole rather than as an agglomeration of nation-states, a number of issues appear under a new, and more revealing, light. We discussed in Chapter 3 two such examples: the rule of law and equality of opportunity. Believing that the rich always have an interest in fighting for the rule of law or property rights in their own countries might have made sense when transnational movements of capital were difficult or impossible. It does not make sense now.

Equality of opportunity cannot be a goal restricted to the level of the nation-state. We must pursue it globally.

As the world becomes more integrated, many more such revisions will affect the basic economic tools we use. I have already mentioned that national accounts will become less relevant and that monetary policy may no longer be conducted by states. (And one can think in addition of the role that private monies such as Bitcoin may play.) But even essential economic concepts like comparative advantage, which is based on an implicit assumption of methodological nationalism, that is, of national accounting and immobility of some factors of production, may have to be revised. In a single market both wine and cloth would be, as in David Ricardo's famous example, produced in Portugal because workers and machines would all move there (and none would stay in England). As the world changes and becomes more integrated, our ways of thinking and the tools we use to understand the world become obsolete. New ways to look at reality in the age of globalization are needed. This book is a modest step in that direction.

10. Will Inequality Disappear as Globalization Continues?

No. The gains from globalization will not be evenly distributed.

Notes

1. The Rise of the Global Middle Class and Global Plutocrats

Epigraph: Geminiano Montanari, *Della Moneta: trattato mercato* (1683), quoted in Marx (1973, 782).

1. Household per capita income is calculated by adding up the annual income made by all members of a household and dividing it by the number of household members.

2. A comparison with the period just before World War I is instructive. In 1913, exports as a share of world GDP were around 9 percent; almost exactly one hundred years later, in 2012, they were 30 percent. Foreign assets as a percentage of world GDP were 17.5 percent in 1914; they were 57 percent in 1995 and are probably even higher today (Crafts 2000, 26–27). Only labor is less mobile now; annual movements of workers between countries are, despite the recent upsurge in migrants and refugees, less than they were one hundred years ago.

3. It is remarkable (but is not our topic here) that, for any given decile, real income growth was greater in urban China and Indonesia than in rural China and Indonesia, meaning that the urban–rural gap, already large in both countries, further widened.

4. In all these countries, mean incomes increased even more than the median, resulting in increased inequality. (Income distributions are all skewed to the right; that is, they have a long tail on the right side, and in such distributions the mean is always greater than the median. When the mean increases more than the median, the distribution becomes more skewed and unequal.)

5. The OECD is an economic and political organization that includes rich countries of Western Europe, Japan, Oceania (Australia and New Zealand), and North America (what we call the "old-rich" OECD), as well as more recent members from Eastern Europe, and Chile, Mexico, and South Korea.

6. The calculation is as follows: the global top 1 percent consists of almost 70 million people, about 36 million of whom are Americans. Thirty-six million is 12 percent of the US population.

7. The literature is enormous. Suffice it to cite three comprehensive OECD reports: *Growing Unequal?* (2008), *Divided We Stand* (2011), and *In It Together* (2015). Notice the contrast between the second and third titles.

8. For the different testings of the "elephant curve," see Lakner and Milanovic (2013).

9. The number 100 on the horizontal axis refers to the top, 100th, percentile. The number 99 refers to the people between the previous value on the horizontal axis (95th percentile) and the 99th percentile. Hence, it includes the percentiles 96–99, or the top 2 to 5 percent.

10. The reader will recall that the global top 1 percent is almost entirely composed of rich people from the advanced economies.

11. Note that in the comparison of incomes from household surveys we speak of urban China, not all of China. Until 2013, China ran two separate household surveys, one for rural and another for urban areas, that researchers could only with difficulty, and using many assumptions, put together to represent China as a whole. In my work, I have tended to treat the two surveys separately, not only because they are not identical in their design, but also because price levels in rural and urban China are different and because China does not supply the individual household survey data that would be necessary for the combination of the two surveys to be conducted with anything resembling precision. The results of the 2013 all-China survey have not been released as of this writing (January 2015).

12. Based on Angus Maddison's estimates for 1890 (Maddison Project 2013).

13. Based on household surveys, Chinese average income in 2012 was about $4,300, compared with an EU average of $14,600 (all in 2011 international dollars based on 2011 ICP). Assuming a 1 percent average growth for the EU, and 5 percent for China, the two incomes will converge in 31–32 years.

14. Edward Gibbon described the first reversal of fortunes very well, when he wondered how bizarre it would seem to a person in Late Antiquity to envisage a situation where the entire subcontinent of India would be ruled by a company of merchants from a small, remote island in the North Sea: "Since the reign of Aurungzebe, their [Hindu] empire has been dissolved, their treasures of Delhi have been rifled by a Persian robber, and the richest of their kingdoms is now possessed by a company of Christian merchants, of a remote island in the Northern ocean" (Gibbon 1996, 3:853).

15. The super-wealthy are not included in household surveys for two reasons. The fact that they are so few in number (e.g., the United States has about 500 billionaires) makes it very unlikely that they will be included in national random surveys. Even the US Current Population Census, which has a relatively large sample size of 80,000 households (200,000 people), would have a negligible chance of interviewing a billionaire (3 in 10,000). Second, it is thought that rich and very rich people are less willing, even if selected, to agree to be interviewed (even though the data are anonymous). See also Excursus 1.1 on household survey data.

16. Just over 80 percent of people in the global top 1 percent come from WENAO countries (Western Europe, North America, and Oceania).

17. Both types of income data exclude capital gains and losses. WTID is available at http://topincomes.parisschoolofeconomics.eu/.

18. LIS data for 2010 (available at http://www.lisdatacenter.org/). The gap between 9.4 percent for the share of the top 1 percent in pre-transfer and pre-tax income for the United States, calculated from household surveys, and about 17 percent for the same year that Alvaredo et al. (2013, fig. 1) calculate from US fiscal sources can be explained by two factors: difference in recipient units (fiscal units vs. the per capita metric used here) and underestimate of the top income shares in household surveys.

19. For the United States, 19 percent of the population has negative or zero net wealth (Wolff 2010, 43, appendix B); for Germany, the percentage is 27 percent (Frick and Grabka 2009, 64, table 1).

20. For some rich people, changes in wealth could be negative (as when the stock market goes down), although they still may retain billions in net wealth.

21. There is no one metric (income, consumption, or wealth) that is better than the other. We must always weight accessibility and reliability of the data, and their meaning. Thus, when considering the political power of plutocracy, it is surely the wealth data that are more revealing. But if we are interested in the standard of living of 95 percent or 99 percent of people, using income or consumption makes much more sense.

22. The second and third estimates are based, respectively, on Lakner and Milanovic (2013) and Zucman (2013).

23. We need this assumption of the return on the assets to move from Zucman's (2013) estimate of hidden stock of wealth to an estimate of annual income received from these hidden assets.

24. In analyses of wealth, we use nominal (i.e., actual) rather than PPP dollars. The rationale, put forth by Davies et al. (2011) in the first study of global wealth inequality, is that for the "purchasing power" of wealth, and especially of the top wealth holders, it is only world, and not domestic, prices that matter. When one thinks of the super-wealthy this is rather obvious: they consume goods and services for which prices are broadly the same worldwide.

25. See http://www.forbes.com/sites/seankilachand/2012/03/21/forbes-history-the-original-1987-list-of-international-billionaires/. The estimate of $450 billion is arrived at by adding about $290 billion from the foreign list of billionaires and less than $220 billion for the United States (the total 1987 US list wealth is $220 billion, but it also includes people with wealth under $1 billion).

26. From nominal $450 billion out of $16.4 trillion of world GDP (2.7 percent) to $4.5 trillion out of world GDP of $73 trillion (6.1 percent).

2. Inequality within Countries

Epigraph: Kuznets (1955, 21).

1. Simon Kuznets first stated this hypothesis in his 1955 presidential address to the American Economic Association; he later restated and

expanded it (Kuznets 1966). An important precursor to Kuznets is Sergey N. Prokopovitch, whose 1926 *Economic Journal* article compared income inequalities in the United States (1910, 1918), Australia (1914–15), and Prussia and Saxony (1913). He wrote, "there exists some definite [negative] connection between [mean level of income of a country] and the degrees of inequality" (p. 78), thus describing the downward-sloping segment of the Kuznets curve. Kuznets mentioned Prokopovitch's article in his address (1955, 5). There is a voluminous literature on the Kuznets curve; I will not engage with it except when it deals very narrowly with the issue at hand.

2. In a review of Tinbergen's book, Sahota (1977, 726) wrote: "Tinbergen's projections to 1990 indicate that due to sheer [long-run] supply and demand forces, the rents that have been earned by university-educated workers will come to an end."

3. The Gini coefficient is the most popular measure of income inequality. It takes into account the entire distribution (that is, the incomes of everyone), unlike, for example, measures based on top income shares, which ignore all of the distribution except the top. The Gini coefficient ranges from a value of 0, for the theoretical case where everyone has the same income, to a value of 1, for the equally theoretical case where one individual possesses the entire income of a country. The Gini coefficient is often expressed as a percentage (e.g., as 41 rather than 0.41) and referred to simply as the Gini. When the Gini has increased from, say, 30 to 33, we say that it has increased by 3 Gini points. In the real world, Gini values range from the high 20s (in Scandinavian and Central European countries) to the mid-60s (in South Africa, Namibia, and Colombia).

4. Piketty does not in fact claim that inequality must increase under capitalism, but to infer such a claim is understandable because he pays little attention to the autonomous economic forces that may curb inequality. Some commentators, then, assume that Piketty believes they do not exist. But this is not true: we can in effect estimate what maximum steady-state inequality would be in Piketty's system. Suppose that the steady-state capital-output ratio in the United States were around 10 (with the savings ratio out of GDP 10 percent and GDP growth rate of 1 percent). This is about twice the current US capital-output ratio. With Piketty's standard real rate of return of 5 percent, capital income would take one-half of total net income. Further, with the current concentration coefficients of capital and labor income, respectively about 0.8 and 0.4, the Gini coefficient would be 60

$(0.5 \times 80 + 0.5 \times 40)$. This is the level of inequality existing today in Brazil and South Africa.

5. The same is true in modern societies (as we shall see below) but for different reasons.

6. The formula for the maximum feasible Gini is $\frac{\alpha-1}{\alpha}$ where α is how many times mean income is greater than subsistence. For $\alpha = 2$, maximum Gini is 0.5; for $\alpha = 10$, maximum Gini is 0.9. If we use the standard figure for subsistence level of about 400 international dollars per person per year, today's US mean income would be some 100 times greater, so the maximum Gini would be 0.99, or almost equal to 1.

7. Kuznets stated, "It is even more plausible to argue that the recent narrowing in income inequality observed in the developed countries was due to a combination of the narrowing inter-sectoral inequalities in product per worker, the decline in the share of property incomes in total incomes of households, and the institutional changes that reflect decisions concerning social security and full employment" (1966, 217).

8. Malign and benign forces were brought together as explanations for the emergence of the modern welfare state by Max Beloff (1984) in an influential book entitled, not surprisingly, *Wars and Welfare: Britain 1941–1945*.

9. Our very use of the term "service" or "tertiary" sector is problematic precisely because it conceals under one name an incredible variety of jobs and skills, with vastly different pay scales. But we seem unable to come up with a better classification.

10. In both the United Kingdom and the United States, government expenditures as a share of GDP are at about the same levels now as in the late 1970s to early 1980s.

11. The difficulty of taxing mobile capital was already known to Adam Smith: "The proprietor of stock is properly a citizen of the world and is not necessarily attached to any particular country. He would be apt to abandon the country in which he was exposed to a vexatious inquisition, in order to be assessed to a burdensome tax, and would remove his stock to some other country where he could either carry on his business or enjoy his fortune more at his ease" (*Wealth of Nations*, book 5, chap. 2, part 2, art. 2).

12. It is worth pointing out that a graph such as the one shown in Figure 2.4 presents a very succinct summary of the main features of an economy: it provides the plot of the second moment of the distribution of

personal incomes (if incomes are distributed lognormally, the Gini coefficient is uniquely determined by the variance) against the first moment of the distribution (mean per capita income).

13. In this chapter, where we deal with historical long-time series, all income (GDP per capita) data come from the Maddison Project, which is a continuation of Angus Maddison's pioneering work. I use the 2013 update of the Maddison data, available at http://www.ggdc.net/maddison /maddison-project/data.htm. The estimates are discussed in Bolt and van Zanden (2014). GDP per capita is expressed in 1990 international dollars.

14. This borderline will occur at a different time for societies that experienced the Industrial Revolution much later, some not until the second half of the twentieth century.

15. Between 1400 and 1800, output per capita increased by less than 20 percent (see Álvarez-Nogal and Prados de la Escosura 2007, table 4).

16. Alfani (2014, 25) is skeptical of Herlihy's (1978) "fascinating" thesis, based on meager evidence from one town (Pistoia) in Tuscany, that the Florentine plague of 1348 led to an increase in inequality. Herlihy argues that many estates lost their owners as a result of the plague; these estates were then bought for a low price by those who survived, thus concentrating wealth. Even if this might have happened in the fourteenth century, Alfani writes, by the mid-seventeenth century, when the last of the big plagues occurred, new institutional arrangements were in place, making it more difficult for small parcels of land that had lost their owners to be bought up and concentrated in larger estates. Herlihy's mistake, according to Alfani and Ammannati (2014, 23), seems to have been in not making adequate allowance for the differences in wealth and income coverage in the two sources he used, the *quota d'estimo* (the earlier taxation mechanism used by the Florentine state) and the more well-known *catasto* of 1427.

17. This decline corresponds to the crisis or state breakdown stage in a four-part classification (expansion, stagflation, breakdown, depression) introduced by Turchin and Nefedov (2009, chap. 1). In the crisis stage, when social disintegration is at its peak, real wages are increasing and land rent is decreasing, with inequality thus becoming less. The evolution of inequality in the Roman Empire from the third century onward, discussed in Excursus 2.1, illustrates the Turchin-Nefedov thesis rather well.

18. Interestingly, Fochesato (2014) claims that this difference in reaction to the effects of the plague in the fourteenth century had long-term

consequences: higher wages in the north made labor-substituting machinery much more attractive and eventually led to the Industrial Revolution. Robert Allen (2003, 2011) also makes this point.

19. See Milanovic (2010b, table 1). The sources are Ward-Perkins (2005), Allen (2007), Maddison (2007, 2008), and Scheidel and Friesen (2009).

20. Social tables, invented by Gregory King in seventeenth-century England, provide a shorthand description of the social structure of a society by listing key social classes (landless peasants, peasants with small holdings, etc., all the way to the richest nobility and the court) and giving their estimated mean incomes and population. In the absence of household surveys or fiscal data, social tables are our best source of information about income distribution prior to the twentieth century.

21. The story as told here is somewhat of a simplification, because the eastern portion of the Roman Empire continued more or less as before. Thus, the average income in the Aegean world and the Levant was about the same during the whole period (excluding short-term fluctuations) as it was at the time of Octavian.

22. Mendershausen (1946) also claims that peak inequality occurred in 1933.

23. There are also social and demographic forces that can influence inequality but which we, in this very broad approach, have to leave out. For example, the aging of the population and the greater prevalence of one-person households (encouraged by the increase in wealth of a country) exert an inequality-increasing effect on all our statistics, especially if we use per capita measurement, as we do here. Another demographic force is marriage or partnership of individuals who have similar incomes. This has also become more common in rich countries, and likewise exerts an upward effect on measured inequality. I do not believe, however, that over the long run these factors are as important as economic and political factors.

24. One case where it did happen is in socialist societies; see Excursus 2.2.

25. The upswing of inequality in the United Kingdom has been the subject of controversy. Our data here, based on Gini values calculated from the social tables (see Milanovic, Lindert, and Williamson 2011), are practically identical to the results given by Lindert and Williamson (1982, 1983). Feinstein (1988), however, has argued that English inequality was very high, but stable, for at least a century before the Industrial Revolution.

Hence, Feinstein's data do not show the upswing in the Kuznets curve that should in principle be coincidental with the Industrial Revolution.

26. Clark (2005) shows a doubling of English real wages between the time of publication of David Ricardo's *On the Principles of Political Economy and Taxation* (1817) and Karl Marx's *Das Kapital* (1867), with real wage growth continuing and accelerating into the latter part of the nineteenth century. Feinstein (1988) finds a slower but nevertheless perceptible increase.

27. The income level at which the Spanish peak occurred is similar to the British and American level of about $2,500 (in the same PPPs). The only difference is that this income level was achieved almost a century later in Spain.

28. The data for Italy are from the painstaking and innovative work of Brandolini and Vecchi (2011).

29. The Williamson ratio is the ratio of the mean income to the unskilled wage rate. An increase in the ratio implies greater inequality.

30. Frontier expansion led to a reduction in inequality in Chile because there was no migration. Hence unskilled laborers became scarcer and their wages went up. In contrast, in New Zealand and Argentina, where there was migration, expansion led to increased inequality.

31. These Kuznets waves, which are well-delineated when plotted against time, are much more difficult to find, or rather vanish, when we plot them against income per capita. It is, however, only in the first period identified by Rodríguez Weber (1850–1903) that we can treat the evolution in Chile as that of the evolution in a country with no increase in mean income—where, indeed, we do not expect to see a relationship between Gini value and income level. During that half century, per capita income growth was around 1 percent per annum; afterward, that is, for the entire twentieth century, it exceeded 2 percent per annum.

32. The World Top Incomes Database shows that the decline in the share of the top 1 percent happened entirely during the war. Since we have no distributional data between 1937 and 1962, it is impossible to say whether the decline was entirely due to the war or if it continued afterward. To make matters worse, the quality of Japanese income distribution data is not very good (Tachibanaki and Yagi 1997), and the Japanese Statistical Office does not allow access to the microdata.

33. In an innovative paper, Albaquerque Sant'Anna (2015) showed a statistically significant negative correlation (controlled for relevant factors

like marginal tax rates and financial openness) between the income share of the top 1 percent and both trade union density and the relative (vis-à-vis that country) military power of the USSR. The relative military power of the USSR is approximated by the ratio of Soviet military expenditures to those of each relevant country, adjusted by the distance from Moscow (the relative power of the USSR declines with distance).

34. The change in Gini points per decade is, for simplicity, calculated as an arithmetic average: the number of Gini points lost during the downward portion of the Kuznets curve is divided by the number of decades (both as given in Table 2.2).

35. There may be hysteresis or path dependency in the movement of taxes. Once higher taxes are introduced at the time of war, and large bureaucracies are created to run various new programs, neither taxes nor bureaucracies can be easily brought back to earlier levels after the war is over. Thus, wars, usually considered a malign force, can be important catalysts of social change.

36. Piketty writes: "The decline of high incomes is closely linked to the two world wars, and the fact that high incomes have never fully recovered seems likely to be explained by an eminently political factor (progressive taxation of income and inheritance), and certainly not by variable developments in the agricultural and industrial sectors. It can thus be seen that Kuznets's theory, and more generally any theory based on the idea of an inevitable decrease of income inequality in the advanced stages of capitalist development, seems incapable of fitting the facts that characterize the history of income inequality in the twentieth century, at least as far as France is concerned" (Piketty 2001a, 147–148; my translation).

37. In the 1990s, the estates left by the richest 1 percent of the top 1 percent (among those who left estates) were worth only one-fourth of what they had been in 1900–1910 (Piketty 2001a, 139; 2001b, 24).

38. Exploitation was taken as a given even by the most free-market-oriented economists. Here is Vilfredo Pareto, not exactly a thirdworldist wont to complain about capitalist exploitation, writing in 1921: "We have . . . to take account of the exploitation of vast regions of Africa and Asia [as a way to increase colonizers' income]. This will very likely prove to be of special benefit to England, the United States and France; but it can be of little or no benefit to Italy which has picked up merely the scraps which these

voracious gourmands have let fall from their festive boards" (Pareto 1966, 325; originally from "Trasformazione della democratia," 1921).

39. On maldistribution of income: "The ultimate reason for all real crises always remains the poverty and restricted consumption of the masses, in the face of the drive of capitalist production to develop the productive forces as if only the absolute consumption capacity of society sets a limit to them" (Marx [1894] 1991, 615). On the crisis being "exported": "The internal contradictions seek resolution by extending the external field of production" (p. 353).

40. The most important feature of these theories of imperialism is that the roots of every foreign policy have to be sought in domestic social and economic relations, and not, as for example in David Landes's (1961) theory of imperialism, in the disproportion of economic and military power between the states.

41. The outbreak of World War I has always been an extremely unpleasant problem for those who believe in the fundamentally benign character of globalization and are not concerned with income inequality. In 2004, before he became more skeptical about the benefits of globalization, Martin Wolf published *Why Globalization Works*, in which he attributed the war to German militarism and nationalism (p. 125). But militarism was not specific to Germany. What was specific was that German capitalists, being latecomers to the game, wanted to have the same advantages as the French and English, but most of the world had already been parceled out.

42. See my blog post "The economics of Niall Ferguson in the 'Pity of War': unwittingly back to Marx?" available at http://glineq.blogspot.com /2014/09/the-economics-of-niall-ferguson-in-pity.html.

43. Although Ferguson (1999, 140) writes that it is "no longer fashionable" to speak of the domestic origins of the war, he ultimately does so himself.

44. See Lydall (1968), Atkinson and Micklewright (1992), and Redor (1992). See also the first chapter of Milanovic (1998).

45. I use the terms Industrial Revolution and first technological revolution interchangeably.

46. OECD data, available at https://stats.oecd.org/Index.aspx ?DataSetCode=UN_DEN.

47. For example, in 1995, trade union membership in public and private sectors in the United Kingdom was about the same (some 3.5 million

each). Twenty years later, membership in the public sector was almost 4 million and in the private sector just 2.5 million (see chart 2.1 in https://www .gov.uk/government/uploads/system/uploads/attachment_data/file/313768 /bis-14-p77-trade-union-membership-statistical-bulletin-2013.pdf).

48. Based on Robert Solow's presentation at the Graduate Center, City University of New York, April 30, 2015. There was no written paper as of May 2015.

49. For a discussion of the technology versus globalization "contest," see Krugman (1995), Slaughter and Swagel (1997), and Slaughter (1999). The technological change literature argues that wage inequality increased mostly as a result of the race between technology and skills (with periods of greater demand for skills unmatched by a sufficient increase in their supply). This idea is discussed at length in Autor, Katz, and Kearney (2008) and Goldin and Katz (2010). The literature on technological change as the main force behind rising wage inequality comes in two forms. The first, which was dominant in the 1980s, sees skill-biased technological change increasing the wage premium throughout the wage distribution, leading to rising wage gaps between all skill types. The second, which dominated in the 1990s, sees technological change as working through computerization and robots, which replace human labor in routine tasks but not in either sophisticated and highly skilled tasks at the high end of the wage spectrum or in low-skill but non-routinized service jobs. According to the latter hypothesis, championed by David Autor (see, e.g., Autor and Dorn 2010), increase in wage inequality is associated with wage polarization. Recent OECD findings (OECD 2015) provide some support for this hypothesis. (Note that according to the latter hypothesis the wage gap between medium- and low-skilled labor should decrease, while according to the first, it should increase.) For the emphasis on globalization's role on wages, see Ebenstein et al. (2014). Feenstra and Hanson (1999) find that globalization explains 15–33 percent of the widening of US wage distribution between the late 1970s and the early 1990s. For a nice theoretical approach to the effect of globalization on labor inequality in both developed and emerging econo-mies, see an unpublished paper by Kremer and Maskin (2003).

50. This point was made by Ann Harrison in a private communication.

51. Barro-Lee Educational Attainment data set, available at http://www .barrolee.com/.

52. Reshef (2013) argues that there is a low-skill-biased technological change in the US service sector, where apparently the productivity of lower-skilled workers increases faster than that of college-educated workers.

3. Inequality among Countries

Epigraph: Jan Pieterszoon Coen, Dutch East India Company proconsul in Batavia, to the board of directors of the company, December 27, 1614, quoted in Landes (1988, 43).

1. A less positive way to state this is to say that global inequality today is at almost the highest point ever in history.

2. In this type of calculation, global inequality is estimated as follows: a mean income, which is a more or less reliable statistic, is taken from Maddison's long-term economic series (Maddison Project 2013); then a lognormal distribution is generated around the mean for each country, with a standard deviation that is more or less guessed on the basis of historical sources. Once a distribution for each country is derived, these national distributions are combined to obtain a global distribution. Bourguignon and Morrisson (2002) provide additional information by estimating income deciles, not of individual countries but of broad geographical areas (33 in total). They assume that all countries within each geographical area have the same income distribution.

3. Other studies undertaken after the pioneering work of Bourguignon and Morrisson (2002), using slightly different methodologies, have found exactly the same pattern of a long-run nineteenth-century increase in global inequality (Milanovic 2011b; van Zanden et al. 2014). All three studies rely, crucially, on Maddison's estimates of GDP per capita, which essentially drive the changes in global inequality. Van Zanden et al. (2014) used all sorts of additional evidence, including wage/GDP ratios and distribution of people by height (both as estimates of within-national inequalities), while Milanovic (2011b) used data from social tables for the early nineteenth century.

4. My previous work (Milanovic 2002a) showed an increase in global inequality between 1988 and 1993.

5. In theory, of course, a different assessment of Chinese incomes, for example, could affect our estimates of changes over time in the Gini value,

and not solely its level. However, in practice, the revisions in the pattern of Gini change are minimal.

6. Author's unpublished data.

7. As discussed in Chapter 2, there were, strangely, no data for the United States as a whole (or for the thirteen colonies that constituted the original United States) for the period before 1929. There were plentiful data on wealth from probates, for example, but they were fragmentary and covered either individual states or cities. There were no contemporaneous social tables, which was odd given that such tables were produced in Great Britain with some frequency. Lindert and Williamson (2016), however, have recently constructed detailed social tables for the United States for 1774, 1850, 1860, and 1870. These data were used in Chapter 2 to estimate long-run US inequality.

8. The EU15 are Austria, Belgium, Denmark, Finland, France, Germany, Greece, Ireland, Italy, Luxembourg, Netherlands, Portugal, Spain, Sweden, and the United Kingdom.

9. The additional 13 countries are Bulgaria, Croatia, Cyprus, Czech Republic, Estonia, Hungary, Latvia, Lithuania, Malta, Poland, Romania, Slovakia, and Slovenia.

10. Another advantage of Theil (0), as pointed out by Anand and Segal (2008), is somewhat technical but nonetheless important. Theil (0), also known as the entropy index, is the only one of the popular measures of inequality in which the absolute values of inequality calculated for class (or location) do not change when the other component (location or class) is fully equalized. As a result, if the class component of Theil is calculated to be x with the actual data, then the hypothetical elimination of all locational inequalities will leave the class component (and thus the total Theil) at x.

11. It is worth mentioning here the increased spread of European colonialism, which achieved one of its high points in 1914. In 1914, almost 42 percent of the world population lived in colonies. The most important powers were Great Britain, which controlled 24 percent of the world population, and France, with about 6 percent.

12. In some individual cases, however, Europeans might have fared better by going to colonies than by staying at home.

13. "Marxist analysis should be always slightly stretched when we deal with the colonial rule. . . . It is neither the act of owning factories, nor [landed] estates, nor a bank balance which distinguishes the governing

classes. The governing class is first and foremost those who come from elsewhere, those who are unlike the original inhabitants, 'the others'" (Fanon 2005, 5).

14. Karl Marx and Friedrich Engels, *Sochineniya*, xxii, 360 (quoted in Carr [1952] 1973, 187). As Carr writes, the idea was first voiced by Engels in a letter to Marx in 1858.

15. The stock of migrants estimated from censuses around the year 2000 was 165 million (Özden et al. 2011). Less detailed but more current UN data put the stock at 230 million in 2013.

16. In the original paper from which these numbers come (Milanovic 2015), the income premiums were calculated from the income log ratios; that is, the premium for the United States was expressed as so many percent of US (natural) log income over the (natural) log income of Congo. The premiums expressed using logs are, of course, much smaller than what is reported here. I am grateful to Simone Bertoli and Jesús Fernández-Huertas Moraga for pointing this out.

17. I abstract here from other, often important, elements that may influence migration patterns: geographical proximity, language, religion, the already existing diasporas, and so on.

18. Borrowing rather than relying on aid applies only to what Rawls calls "well-ordered" societies, that is, societies that are not prevented by poverty from developing somewhat, if not fully, democratic and liberal institutions. Aid is reserved only for "burdened" societies whose very poverty prevents them from becoming liberal. In Rawls's terminology, the Society of Peoples is a United Nations cum World Bank.

19. David Miller (2005, 71) writes: "To preserve equality we would have continually to transfer resources from nations that had become relatively better-off to those who had become worse-off, undermining political responsibility, and in a sense undermining self-determination too." It is striking how the arguments against cross-nation transfers parallel the arguments made by those who oppose Rawls in regard to within-nation transfers. It almost seems as though all the arguments that Rawls has rejected at the level of the nation-state are now accepted at the level of the world as a whole.

20. Using comparable data provided by the OECD, the only three countries showing more than 2,000 hours of work per person per year in 2013 were Greece, Chile, and Mexico. Workers in rich countries (France,

Denmark, Germany, and the Netherlands) worked less than 1,500 hours. See https://stats.oecd.org/Index.aspx?DataSetCode=ANHRS. We do not have as reliable data for the hours worked in poor countries (outside of the OECD), but we find in time-use surveys that poor people tend to work more hours than rich people (Lee, McCann, and Messenger 2007, 27–33).

21. Rosenzweig (2010) shows that cross-country variability in skill prices (wage per unit of skill) vastly exceeds cross-country variability in average levels of education or returns to education. Rosenzweig concludes that increased levels of education alone in poor countries will not contribute to the equalization of wages globally (so long, of course, as these increased levels of education are not translated into higher GDP per capita and thus higher average wages).

22. Cannan's question is quoted from Frenkel (1942, 177). I am grateful to Anthony Atkinson for bringing to my attention this undeservedly obscure reference.

23. One might ask if Shachar's approach could be even broader. For example, her proposal would exclude those who do not have any social connectedness (e.g., family and friends) in a country to which they would like to emigrate for social or economic reasons.

24. Household surveys taken in 2008 show the mean annual per capita PPP-adjusted income in Israel to be a bit over $11,000, as compared with $1,100 in the West Bank and Gaza.

25. An article in the *International New York Times* (April 7, 2015) on the Bulgarian fence notes that "one reason Bulgarian officials are eager to complete the wall is to demonstrate to European leaders that the country deserves to be admitted into the Schengen group of nations whose members do not require . . . passports to travel among them." The statement is thick with irony because under communism, Bulgaria built a similar wall to demonstrate to the Soviet leaders that other East European tourists would not be able to flee to Turkey or Greece.

26. In an interesting twist, Tan (2006) writes that "accepting the legitimacy of the restrictive laws of immigration . . . must be conditional on there being some global distributive commitment." In other words, a human right can be traded for income.

27. Perhaps the earliest statement on the incompatibility between limits to migration and maximization of output comes from Jean-Baptiste Say,

who in his *Treatise on Political Economy or the Production, Consumption and Distribution of Wealth,* first published in 1804, writes: "Europe had . . . gained by the partial removal of the internal barriers between its different political states; and the world at large would derive similar benefit from the demolition of those, which insulate . . . the various communities, into which the human race is divided" ([1821] 1971, 167).

28. See United Nations Department of Social and Economic Affairs (available at http://www.un.org/en/development/desa/population/migration/data/index.shtml).

29. See Gallup's 2010–2012 results at http://www.gallup.com/poll/161435/100-million-worldwide-dream-life.aspx. See also Minter (2011, 40).

30. Hanson (2010) calculates that the current migration from Mexico to the United States has increased global income by an amount equivalent to about 1 percent of US GDP.

31. Note that technically there are no equivalent requirements in policy change for the sending countries because the principle of freedom to leave one's own country is observed by the vast majority of countries. Only a few exceptions, like North Korea and Cuba, remain.

4. Global Inequality in This Century and the Next

Epigraph: Letter from Alfred Marshall to A. L. Bowley, March 3, 1901, in Marshall (1961, 2:774).

1. Dismal forecasting of the 2008 global financial crisis, even once it had started, is documented in Wieland and Wolters (2012).

2. It is also remarkable that the writers of this period were unable to define the "new society" except negatively, that is, by what it no longer was. Hence, the proliferation of "post" prefixes in Bell's *Coming of Post-Industrial Society* (1973): a cursory review reveals "post-industrial," "post-bourgeois," "post-Marxist," "post-capitalist," and "post-scarcity."

3. *Limits to Growth* (1972) was also the first report of the Club of Rome. The second report, *Mankind at the Turning Point* (1974), by Mihailo Mesarovic and Eduard Pestel, was even more quantitative and ostensibly scientific.

4. Sicco Mansholt, then the president of the European Commission, was a strong proponent of zero growth. See also Kahn and Wiener (1968). A much more realistic, and in some areas like migration, strikingly prescient,

picture was painted by Alfred Sauvy in his excellent *Zero Growth?* (1976) (the French original was published in 1973).

5. See Francis Fukuyama's interview with *Spiegel International*, "A Model Democracy Is Not Emerging in Iraq" (March 22, 2006), available at http://www.spiegel.de/international/interview-with-ex-neocon-francis -fukuyama-a-model-democracy-is-not-emerging-in-iraq-a-407315.html.

6. It could be that Chinese weapons producers, which are all state-owned, are less belligerent than their American counterparts because there is nothing for them to gain in case of a war.

7. Steamship technology took almost one hundred years to spread from rich to poor countries, while today's technological developments are almost instantly available to poor countries (see Comin 2014). Expensive patent rights and licensing are a problem though.

8. Special effort is made not to allow the increase in the sample size (the number of countries), brought about by the breakups of the USSR, Czechoslovakia, Yugoslavia, Pakistan, Ethiopia, Sudan, and so on, to drive the results. Thus for all the years for which we have such data, we treat what were then provincial or republican GDPs per capita (e.g., of Ukraine, Croatia, South Sudan) as if they were GDPs per capita of independent countries. Still, in 1980 there is a large increase in the number of countries in the World Bank database (World Development Indicators) because of the inclusion of many small economies, especially island states. The sample is practically fixed, that is, there are almost no countries added or dropped, after 1980.

9. These figures are weighted by population; weighting by total GDP gives very similar results.

10. The slowdown of China is still compatible with this rosy scenario, but a reversal in China's development may not be.

11. The negative slope remains even if we drop China.

12. In order for the region to have a value of 1, all countries need to be at their historical peak incomes.

13. Only marginally better are the situations of Zambia, which first achieved its current level of GDP per capita in 1953, and Zimbabwe, which probably did so in the mid-1950s. They could be said to have wasted some sixty years.

14. The exact condition at which China begins to add to global inequality is however a bit more complicated (see the following discussion and notes).

15. The results are almost identical in terms of GDP per capita in international dollars. In 2013, China's GDP per capita was 18 percent below the world average and was higher than the GDPs per capita of 48.5 percent of world population (assuming, as before, that each person has the GDP per capita of her country).

16. In the case of the Gini coefficient (with which we work here), the point at which a unit begins to add to inequality depends on its rank (let's call it the "turning point rank"), that is, the number of units from which it has a higher income, but also on the initial Gini. The turning point rank formula is $i > \frac{1}{2}(G+1)(n+1)$ which for a large n simplifies to $i > \frac{1}{2}(G+1)n$, where $i =$ the turning point rank (the rank i runs from 1 to n), $n =$ total number of units, $G =$ Gini coefficient. Note that the turning point is $n/2$ (i.e., the median) only when the Gini is zero. For the derivation of the formula, see Milanovic (1994).

With the current level of population-weighted global Gini being around 0.54, the turning point rank is $0.77n$. That means that China's mean income has to be such that, when all individuals in the world are ranked by the mean incomes of their countries, 77 percent of the world population is left behind China. But because China's population is 20 percent of world population, for a Chinese person to be at that ("turning") point, he or she needs to leave behind only 57 percent (77 − 20) of the world population. Currently, as we have seen, China's mean income exceeds the mean income of 49 percent of world population. This means that China needs to leave behind just an additional 8 percent of people in the world to begin adding to global population-weighted inequality. This could already be happening by the time this text is being read.

17. Zhang (2014, 3) calculates inequality among mean wages across different industrial sectors which, however, do not include workers in privately owned enterprises and the self-employed. There are thus two important caveats: intersectoral inequality is simply inequality calculated across the sectoral wage means (wages of individuals workers within each sector are ignored), and the data omit wages in the private sector (a sector whose importance in the economy is rising), which are likely to be more unequally distributed.

18. Also, the increased share of capital income in China may make conclusions based on the evolution of wage inequality less relevant (see Chi 2012).

19. To be exact, large capital returns make capitalists rich.

20. For the middle class, housing is by far the dominant type of wealth.

21. The large share of financial assets held by the wealthy is the reason why investment companies and hedge funds are interested in "high financial net worth individuals," that is in the rich who have potentially investible resources. Those with most of their wealth in housing do not have many resources available to invest.

22. For the people in the lower one-half of the top 1 percent, labor income in 1998 was 70 percent of total income; in 1929, labor income among the same group was just 40 percent of total income (Piketty and Saez 2003, 16).

23. In the other polar case (socialism), the correlation between capital and labor income would be zero: everybody (regardless of his or her labor income) would receive the same capital income. Arthur Pigou's concept of a "social dividend," which is equally distributed among citizens, is not far from that situation.

24. The Pell Institute report on higher education equity in the United States finds a steadily rising gap in achievement between students from rich families and students from poor families. The percentage of those from the wealthiest income quartile (25 percent) receiving bachelor's degrees went up from 40 to 77 percent between 1970 and 2013. For those from the poorest quartile, the percentage barely edged up from 6 percent to 9 percent. Thus, the gap increased from 34 percentage points to an astonishing 68 points. Available at http://www.pellinstitute.org/downloads/publications-Indicators _of_Higher_Education_Equity_in_the_US_45_Year_Trend_Report.pdf (accessed February 3, 2015).

25. Based on US decennial microcensus; results reported in van der Weide and Milanovic (2014, table 2).

26. One has to be careful, however, to distinguish between two effects which, even if they affect inequality equally, are substantively different. The first is the composition effect: the simple fact that even if pairing were thoroughly random, an increase in the proportion of highly educated and high-earning women would lead to an observed increase in marriages between highly educated individuals. The second has to do with preferences: Has assortative mating increased beyond the level resulting from the first effect only, or, in other words, do individuals now have a greater preference for marrying people who are like themselves?

27. Data from Open Secrets: Center for Responsive Politics, available at https://www.opensecrets.org/bigpicture/index.php?cycle=2012.

28. A policy *not* supported by the rich has only an 18 percent chance of being adopted, versus 45 percent for a policy not favored by the non-rich (Gilens and Page 2014). Gilens's (2012) results are especially striking in cases where the preferences of the rich, the middle class, and the poor diverge. In these cases, only the views of the rich matter. If the preferences of the three groups are the same, politicians do respond to the preferences of the poor and the middle class, but only because the poor and the middle class "free ride" on the influence of the rich.

29. Quoted in Hacker and Pierson (2010, 222).

30. There is possibly a sixth factor, the finding by van der Weide and Milanovic (2014) that greater inequality now tends to imply a higher growth rate of the rich in the future. They argue that this effect of inequality works through "social separatism," whereby the rich opt out of funding of social services (because they provide better ones for themselves privately). Lack of quality social services such as health and education has an especially negative effect on the poor and hampers the growth rate of their income. The implication of van der Weide and Milanovic's work is that the rich have no interest in reducing inequality because inequality is good for their income growth.

31. Islamic texts do not explicitly ban slavery (no more than Christian or Jewish texts do) but rather consider it reprehensible. However, in several majority-Muslim countries (Mauritania, the Sudan), slavery was tolerated until recently.

32. The share of those below the middle-class lower bound (median income minus 25 percent) increased from 32 to 35 percent of the US population. The share of those above the middle-class upper bound (median plus 25 percent) increased from 36 to 38 percent. These shifts do not necessarily involve the same actual people moving from one category to another, since we use cross-sectional data here (LIS data based on US Current Population Surveys for 1979 and 2010).

33. Everybody who visits New York City for the first time cannot but be impressed by the omnipresence of security guards in most large Manhattan stores. Just a simple glance at dozens of people standing around in fancy blazers wearing earpieces is a reminder that a significant chunk of labor is

wasted in protective activities (compared to what the same workers could contribute elsewhere).

34. Voting participation increases monotonically with income level. See Demos for the 2008 elections, available at http://www.demos.org/data-byte /voter-turnout-income-2008-us-presidential-election (data from US Census Bureau).

35. See also Kraus, Davidai, and Nussbaum (2015).

36. There are of course exceptions: had Ralph Nader not run as the third party candidate in 2000, it is unlikely that George W. Bush would have been elected.

37. It is remarkable that although Bartels finds that the responsiveness income gradient is steeper for Republican senators than for Democratic senators, the difference between the two is small. (A positive income gradient means that senators' responsiveness to the issues increases with income level of the constituents.) See Bartels (2010, 270, fig. 9.3).

38. Europe is also plagued by low population growth, the habitual dysfunction of the European Union, and a general malaise, but although these factors all influence European politics, their effects are secondary.

39. I am aware that "objectively" small differences may loom large in the view of the people concerned.

40. The situation in France is changing, as shown by the first detailed statistical analysis of immigrants, published in 2012 (INSEE 2012).

41. International Migration Outlook 2013 (OECD 2013), the most comprehensive study of the costs and benefits of migration in Europe, finds that, on average, an immigrant household contributed €2,000 more in taxes than it received in benefits.

42. The term "net" in this context comes from Sumarto, Suryahadi, and Pritchett (2003).

43. This attitude is not present only among populist and nativist movements. Todd (1998) takes a similar aim at globalization by emphasizing family values and national cultures.

5. What Next?

Epigraph: Machiavelli (1970, 502).

1. According to the US General Social Survey conducted in 2010, 46 percent of Americans think that knowing the right people is important for getting ahead. Survey respondents ranked it as the third most important

characteristic for personal success, after hard work and parents' education. (Based on Leslie McCall's presentation at the Graduate Center CUNY in New York, June 3, 2015.)

2. See http://www.bloomberg.com/news/articles/2015-04-23/finance -industry-tops-china-list-of-most-wanted-graft-fugitives.

3. However, this type of equalization is possible, although not desirable, in more state-directed and bureaucratic systems where wages are set as a function of the number of years of schooling regardless of its quality, and where not paying a worker according to that rule could be legally challenged.

4. Piketty (2014, 485–486) writes that the data on parental income of those who attend elite schools are closely guarded secrets. However, he estimates that the average income of parents of Harvard University students is in the second percentile from the top, while for students of the prestigious French university Sciences Po, it is in the top decile.

5. The discussion of scalability and top earnings goes back to Sherwin Rosen's paper (1981) on the economics of superstars. In a much earlier work, Kuznets and Friedman (1954) discussed the incomes of people in the "liberal professions": doctors, dentists, public accountants, lawyers, and consulting engineers.

6. It may be argued that the products sold remotely are only proxies of the "real" products, and that in order to eat a real meal made by a chef or to have real sex, you have to meet the provider of the service "physically." But judging from the popularity of the proxies, they must be pretty close to the original.

7. "Lunch with the FT," interview of Josh Ostrovsky by John Sunyer, *Financial Times* online, July 24, 2015. Available at http://www.ft.com/cms/s /2/15fe6c4a-3127-11e5-8873-775ba7c2ca3d.html#axzz3pgehPaFK.

8. The wage gap is measured as the ratio between men's and women's earnings at the medians of their respective distributions. The gap is not adjusted for some characteristics like education and experience; since these tend to favor men, the "true" wage gap may be less.

9. Chancel and Piketty (2015, 31) estimate the share of CO_2 emissions made by the top 10 percent of emitters (individuals) in the world at 45 percent. That assumes an income elasticity of 0.9.

10. See http://www.federalreserve.gov/faqs/currency_12773.htm. This amount is equal to almost a third of the US cash money supply in 2015.

11. In addition, these dollars provide a significant seigniorage revenue to the United States.

References

Acemoglu, Daron, and James Robinson. 2012. *Why Nations Fail: The Origins of Power, Prosperity, and Poverty.* New York: Crown.

Albaquerque Sant'Anna, André. 2015. "A Spectre Has Haunted the West: Did Socialism Discipline Income Inequality?" Unpublished ms. Available at https://mpra.ub.uni-muenchen.de/64756/1/MPRA_paper_64756.pdf.

Alfani, Guido. 2010. "The Effects of Plague on the Distribution of Property: Ivrea, Northern Italy 1630." *Population Studies* 64(1): 61–75.

Alfani, Guido. 2014. "Economic Inequality in Northwestern Italy: A Long-term View (Fourteenth to Eighteenth Century)." Dondena Working Paper No. 61, Bocconi University, Milan. Available at ftp://ftp.dondena.unibocconi.it/WorkingPapers/Dondena_WP061.pdf.

Alfani, Guido, and Francesco Ammannati. 2014. "Economic Inequality and Poverty in the Very Long Run: The Case of the Florentine State (Late Thirteenth–Early Nineteenth Centuries)." Dondena Working Paper No. 70, Bocconi University, Milan. Available at ftp://ftp.dondena.unibocconi.it/WorkingPapers/Dondena_WP070.pdf.

Allen, Robert C. 2003. "Poverty and Progress in Early Modern Europe." *Economic History Review* 56(3): 403–433.

Allen, Robert C. 2005. "Capital Accumulation, Technological Change, and the Distribution of Income during the British Industrial Revolution." University of Oxford, Department of Economics Discussion Paper Series, no. 239. Available at http://www.economics.ox.ac.uk/materials /working_papers/paper239.pdf.

Allen, Robert C. 2007. "How Prosperous Were the Romans? Evidence from Diocletian's Price Edict (301 AD)." University of Oxford, Department of Economics Discussion Paper Series, no. 363. Available at http://www .economics.ox.ac.uk/materials/working_papers/paper363.pdf.

Allen, Robert C. 2011. *Global Economic History: A Very Short Introduction.* Oxford: Oxford University Press.

Alvaredo, Facundo, Anthony B. Atkinson, Thomas Piketty, and Emmanuel Saez. 2013. "The Top 1 Percent in International and Historical Perspective." *Journal of Economic Perspectives* 27(3): 3–20.

Álvarez-Nogal, Carlos, and Leandro Prados de la Escosura. 2007. "The Decline of Spain, 1500–1850: Conjectural Estimates." *European Review of Economic History* 11: 319–366.

Álvarez-Nogal, Carlos, and Leandro Prados de la Escosura. 2009. "The Rise and Decline of Spain (800–1850)." Paper presented at the 15th World Economic History Congress, Utrecht, Netherlands.

Álvarez-Nogal, Carlos, and Leandro Prados de la Escosura. 2013. "The Rise and Fall of Spain (1270–1850)." *Economic History Review* 66(1): 1–37.

Anand, Sudhir, and Paul Segal. 2008. "What Do We Know about Global Income Inequality?" *Journal of Economic Literature* 46(1): 57–94.

Atkinson, Anthony B., and John Micklewright. 1992. *Economic Transformation in Eastern Europe and the Distribution of Income.* Cambridge: Cambridge University Press.

Autor, David, and David Dorn. 2010. "The Growth of Low-skill Service Jobs and the Polarization of the US Labor Market." *American Economic Review* 103(5): 1553–1597.

Autor, David H., Lawrence F. Katz, and Melissa S. Kearney. 2008. "Trends in US Wage Inequality: Revising the Revisionists." *Review of Economics and Statistics* 80(2): 300–323.

Bairoch, Paul. 1997. *Victoires et déboires: Histoire économique et sociale du monde du XVIe siècle à nos jours,* vol. 2. Paris: Gallimard.

Bartels, Larry M. 2005. "Economic Inequality and Political Representation." Unpublished ms. Available at http://www.princeton.edu/~bartels /economic.pdf .

Bartels, Larry M. 2010. *Unequal Democracy: The Political Economy of the New Gilded Age.* Princeton: Princeton University Press.

Beitz, Charles. 1999. "International Liberalism and Distributive Justice: A Survey of Recent Thought." *World Politics* 51: 269–296.

Bell, Daniel. 1973. *The Coming of Post-Industrial Society: A Venture in Social Forecasting.* New York: Basic Books.

Beloff, Max. 1984. *Wars and Welfare: Britain, 1914–1945.* Baltimore: E. Arnold.

Bértola, Luis, Cecilia Castelnovo, Javier Rodríguez, and Henry Willebald. 2009. "Income Distribution in the Latin American Southern Cone during the First Globalization Boom and Beyond." *International Journal of Comparative Sociology* 50: 452–485.

Bilmes, Linda, and Joseph Stiglitz. 2008. *The Three-Trillion Dollar War: The True Cost of the Iraq Conflict.* New York: W. W. Norton.

Bolt, Jutta, and Jan Luiten van Zanden. 2014. "The Maddison Project: Collaborative Research on Historical National Accounts." *Economic History Review* 67(3): 627–651.

Bourguignon, François, and Christian Morrisson. 2002. "Inequality among World Citizens: 1820–1992." *American Economic Review* 92(4): 727–744.

Bowles, Samuel, and Arjun Jayadev. 2005. "Guard Labor." Santa Fe Institute Working Paper, 2005-07-30. Available at http://www.santafe.edu/media /workingpapers/05-07-030.pdf.

Brandolini, Andrea, and Giovanni Vecchi. 2011. "The Well-Being of Italians: A Comparative Historical Approach." Bank of Italy, Economic History Working Papers, no. 19. Available at https://www.bancaditalia.it /pubblicazioni/quaderni-storia/2011-0019/index.html?com .dotmarketing.htmlpage.language=1.

Bukharin, Nikolai. 1929. *Imperialism and World Economy.* With an introduction by V. I. Lenin. New York: Monthly Review Press; reprint of the 1929 Progress Publishers edition. (Orig. Russian ed. pub. 1917.)

Canbakal, Hülya. 2012. "Wealth and Inequality in Ottoman Bursa, 1500–1840." Unpublished ms. Available at http://www.econ.yale.edu.

/~egcenter/Wealth%20and%20Inequality%20in%20Ottoman%20Bursa
-Canbakal.pdf.

Caney, Simon. 2002. "Cosmopolitanism and the Law of Peoples." *Journal of Political Philosophy* 10(1): 95–123.

Carr, E. H. (1952) 1973. *The Bolshevik Revolution, 1917–1923*, vol. 3. Harmondsworth: Penguin Books.

Chancel, Lucas, and Thomas Piketty. 2015. "Carbon and Inequality: From Kyoto to Paris." Paris School of Economics, November. Available at http://piketty.pse.ens.fr/files/ChancelPiketty2015.pdf.

Chau, Nancy H., and Ravi Kanbur. 2013. "On Footloose Industries and Labor Disputes with Endogenous Labor Asymmetry." *Review of Development Economics* 17(2): 319–341.

Chi, Wei. 2012. "Capital Income and Income Inequality." *Journal of Comparative Economics* 40: 228–239.

Clark, Gregory. 2005. "The Condition of the Working Class in England, 1209–2004." *Journal of Political Economy* 113(6): 1307–1340.

Clemens, Michael, and Lant Pritchett. 2008. "Income per Natural: Measuring Development for People Rather Than Places." *Population and Development Review* 34(3): 395–434.

Comin, Diego. 2014. "The Evolution of Technology Diffusion and the Great Divergence." Policy Brief for the Brookings Blum Roundtable on Global Poverty, August. Available at http://www.brookings.edu/~/media /Programs/global/bbr-final-briefs-2014/Session-3—Leapfrogging— Comin_POST-FINAL.pdf?la=en.

Corak, Miles. 2013. "Income Inequality, Equality of Opportunity, and Intergenerational Mobility." *Journal of Economic Perspectives* 27(3): 79–102.

Crafts, Nicholas. 2000. "Globalization and Growth in the Twentieth Century." IMF Working Paper 00/44. Available at https://www.imf.org /external/pubs/ft/wp/2000/wp0044.pdf.

Credit Suisse Research Institute. 2013. *Global Wealth Databook 2013*. Zurich: Credit Suisse. Available at https://publications.credit-suisse .com/tasks/render/file/?fileID=1949208D-E59A-F2D9 -6D0361266E44A2F8.

Credit Suisse Research Institute. 2014. *Global Wealth Databook 2014*. Zurich: Credit Suisse. Available at https://publications.credit-suisse

.com/tasks/render/file/?fileID=5521F296-D460-2B88
-081889DB12817E02.

Davies, James B., Susanna Sandström, Anthony B. Shorrocks, and
Edward N. Wolff. 2011. "The Level and Distribution of Global Household
Wealth." *Economic Journal* 121: 223–254.

Deaton, Angus. 2005. "Measuring Poverty in a Growing World (or Measuring Growth in a Poor World)." *Review of Economics and Statistics*
87: 353–378.

Deaton, Angus. 2013. *The Great Escape and the Origins of Inequality.*
Princeton: Princeton University Press.

Deaton, Angus, and Bettina Aten. 2014. "Trying to Understand the PPPs in
ICP 2011: Why Are the Results So Different?" National Bureau of
Economic Research Working Paper, no. 20244, June. Available at
http://www.nber.org/papers/w20244.

de Soto, Hernando. 1989. *The Other Path: The Invisible Revolution in the
Third World.* New York: Basic Books.

Ebenstein, Avraham, Ann Harrison, and Margaret McMillan. 2015. "Why
Are American Workers Getting Poorer? China, Trade and Offshoring."
National Bureau of Economic Research Working Paper, no. 21027,
March. Available at http://www.nber.org/papers/w21027.

Ebenstein, Avraham, Ann Harrison, Margaret McMillan, and Shannon
Phillips. 2014. "Estimating the Impact of Trade and Offshoring on
American Workers Using the Current Population Surveys." *Review of
Economics and Statistics* 96(4): 581–595.

Ehrlich, Paul R. 1968. *The Population Bomb.* New York: Ballantine.

Elsby, Michael W. L., Bart Hobijn, and Ayşegül Şahin. 2013. "The Decline of
US Labor Share." Paper prepared for the Brookings Panel on Economic
Activity (September 2013), October 18, 2013, version. Available at
http://www.newyorkfed.org/research/economists/sahin/LaborShare
.pdf.

Esping-Andersen, Gøsta. 1990. *The Three Worlds of Welfare Capitalism.*
Princeton: Princeton University Press.

Fanon, Frantz. 2005. *The Wretched of the Earth.* Translated by Richard
Philcox. New York: Grove Press. (Orig. French ed. 1961.)

Feenstra, Robert, and Gordon H. Hanson. 1999. "The Impact of
Outsourcing and High-Technology Capital on Wages: Estimate for

the United States, 1979–90." *Quarterly Journal of Economics* 114: 907–940.

Feinstein, Charles H. 1988. "The Rise and Fall of the Williamson Curve." *Journal of Economic History* 48: 699–729.

Feinstein, Charles H. 1998. "Pessimism Perpetuated: Real Wages and the Standard of Living in Britain During and After the Industrial Revolution." *Journal of Economic History* 58(3): 625–658.

Ferguson, Niall. 1999. *The Pity of War: Explaining World War I.* New York: Basic Books.

Ferreira, Francisco H. G., Phillippe G. Leite, and Julie A. Litchfield. 2008. "The Rise and Fall of Brazilian Inequality, 1981–2004." *Macroeconomic Dynamics* 12(S2): 199–230.

Fochesato, Mattia. 2014. "Demographic Shocks, Labor Institutions and Wage Divergence in Early Modern Europe." Unpublished ms. Available at http://econ.sciences-po.fr/sites/default/files/file/mattia-fochesato .pdf.

Freeman, Richard. 2006. "People Flows in Globalization." National Bureau of Economic Research Working Paper, no. 12315, July. Available at http://www.nber.org/papers/w12315.pdf.

Frenkel, Herbert. 1942. "Presidential Address: World Economic Solidarity." *South African Journal of Economics* 10(3): 169–192.

Frick, Joachim, and Markus Grabka. 2009. "Wealth Inequality on the Rise in Germany." DIW Berlin, German Institute for Economic Research, Weekly Report, vol. 5, no. 10. Available at http://www.diw.de /documents/publikationen/73/diw_01.c.98509.de/diw_wr_2009-10.pdf.

Galbraith, James K. 2012. *Inequality and Instability: A Study of the World Economy Just Before the Great Crisis.* Oxford: Oxford University Press.

Gasparini, Leonardo, Guillermo Cruces, and Leopoldo Tornarolli. 2011. "A Turning Point? Recent Trends in Income Inequality in Latin America." *Economía* 11(2): 147–190.

Gibbon, Edward. 1996. *The History of the Decline and Fall of the Roman Empire.* 3 vols. London: Penguin Classics.

Gilens, Martin. 2012. *Affluence and Influence.* Princeton: Princeton University Press.

Gilens, Martin, and Benjamin I. Page. 2014. "Testing Theories of American Politics: Elites, Interest Groups, and Average Citizens." *Perspectives on Politics* 12(3): 564–581.

Goldin, Claudia, and Lawrence F. Katz. 2010. *The Race between Education and Technology.* Cambridge, MA: Belknap Press of Harvard University Press.

Goldsmith, Selma, George Jaszi, Hyman Kaitz, and Maurice Liebenberg. 1954. "Size Distribution of Income since the Mid-Thirties." *Review of Economics and Statistics* 36(1): 1–32.

Goldsworthy, Adrian Keith. 2009. *How Rome Fell: Death of a Superpower.* New Haven, CT: Yale University Press.

Grant, Oliver Wavell. 2002. "Does Industrialization Push Up Inequality? New Evidence on the Kuznets Curve from Nineteenth Century Prussian Tax Statistics." University of Oxford, Oxford Economic and Social History Working Papers, no. 48, September. Available at http://www.economics.ox.ac.uk/materials/papers/2284/48grant.pdf.

Greenwood, Jeremy, Nezih Guner, Georgi Kocharkov, and Cezar Santos, 2014. "Marry Your Like: Assortative Mating and Income Inequality." *American Economic Review* 104(5): 348–353.

Hacker, Jacob S., and Paul Pierson. 2010. *Winner-Take-All Politics: How Washington Made the Rich Richer—and Turned Its Back on the Middle Class.* New York: Simon and Schuster.

Hanson, Gordon H. 2010. "International Migration and Human Rights." National Bureau of Economic Research Working Paper, no. 16472, October. Available at http://www.nber.org/papers/w16472.

Hellebrandt, Tomáš, and Paolo Mauro. 2015. "The Future of Worldwide Income Distribution." Peterson Institute for International Economics Working Paper, no. 15-7, April. Available at https://www.piie.com/publications/wp/wp15-7.pdf.

Herlihy, David. 1978. "The Distribution of Wealth in a Renaissance Community: Florence 1427." In *Towns in Societies: Essays in Economic History and Historical Sociology,* edited by Philip Abrams and E. A. Wrigley, 131–157. Cambridge: Cambridge University Press.

Hobson, John A. (1902) 1965. *Imperialism: A Study.* Introduction by Philip Siegelman. Ann Arbor: University of Michigan Press.

INSEE. 2012. Immigrés et descendants d'immigrés en France: Édition 2012. INSEE (Institut national de la statistique et des études économiques), Paris. Press release (including figures and tables) available at http://www.insee.fr/fr/ppp/comm_presse/comm/dossier_presse_complet_web.pdf.

Jongman, Willem M. 2014. "Re-constructing the Roman Economy." In *The Cambridge History of Capitalism*, vol. 1: *The Rise of Capitalism: From Ancient Origins to 1848*, edited by Larry Neal and Jeffrey G. Williamson, 75–100. Cambridge: Cambridge University Press.

Kahn, Herman, and Anthony J. Wiener. 1968. *The Year 2000: A Framework for Speculation on the Next Thirty-Three Years*. New York: Collier McMillan.

Karabarbounis, Loukas, and Brent Neiman. 2013. "The Global Decline of the Labor Share." *Quarterly Journal of Economics* 129(1): 61–103.

Keynes, John Maynard. (1936) 1964. *The General Theory of Employment, Interest and Money*. New York: Harcourt, Brace and World.

Kraus, Michael W., Shai Davidai, and A. David Nussbaum. 2015. "American Dream? Or Mirage?" *New York Times*, May 3, 2015, p. SR9.

Kraus, Michael W., and Jacinth J. X. Tan. 2015. "Americans Overestimate Social Class Mobility." *Journal of Experimental Social Psychology* 58: 101–111.

Kremer, Mark, and Eric Maskin. 2003. "Globalization and Inequality." Unpublished ms. Available at http://219.223.223.125/userfiles/2008-12 -17/20081217100448217.pdf.

Kristov, Lorenzo, Peter Lindert, and Robert McClelland. 1992. "Pressure Groups and Redistribution." *Journal of Public Economics* 48(2): 135–163.

Krugman, Paul R. 1995. "Growing World Trade: Causes and Consequences." Brookings Papers on Economic Activity, 1:1995, pp. 327–377. Available at http://www.brookings.edu/~/media/Projects/BPEA/1995-1 /1995a_bpea_krugman_cooper_srinivasan.PDF.

Kuznets, Simon. 1955. "Economic Growth and Income Inequality." *American Economic Review* 45: 1–28.

Kuznets, Simon. (1958) 1965. "Regional Economic Trends and Levels of Living." In *Economic Growth and Structure: Selected Essays*. New York: W. W. Norton. Originally published in Philip M. Hauser (ed.), *Population and World Politics:* New York: Free Press, 1958. The paper was presented at the 30th Institute of the Norman Wait Harris Foundation at the University of Chicago, November 24–28, 1954.

Kuznets, Simon. 1966. *Modern Economic Growth*. New Haven, CT: Yale University Press.

Kuznets, Simon, and Milton Friedman. 1954. "Income from Independent Professional Practice." National Bureau of Economic Analysis. Available at http://papers.nber.org/books/frie54-1.

Lakner, Christoph, and Anthony Atkinson. 2014. "Wages, Capital and Top Incomes: The Factor Income Composition of Top Incomes in the USA, 1960–2005." Unpublished ms., November version.

Lakner, Christoph, and Branko Milanovic. 2013. "Global Income Distribution: From the Fall of the Berlin Wall to the Great Recession." World Bank, Policy Research Working Paper, no. 6719, December. Available at http://elibrary.worldbank.org/doi/pdf/10.1596/1813-9450-6719.

Lakner, Christoph, and Branko Milanovic. 2015. "Global Income Distribution: From the Fall of the Berlin Wall to the Great Recession." *World Bank Economic Review,* Advance Access published August 12, 2015, doi: 10.1093/wber/lhv039.

Landes, David. 1961. "Some Thoughts on the Nature of Economic Imperialism." *Journal of Economic History* 21(4): 496–512.

Landes, David. 1988. *The Wealth and Poverty of Nations.* New York: W. W. Norton.

Lee, Sangheon, Deirdre McCann, and Jon C. Messenger. 2007. *Working Time around the World: Trends in Working Hours, Laws and Policies in a Global Comparative Perspective.* Routledge Studies in the Modern World Economy. London: Routledge; Geneva: International Labour Office.

Levy, Frank, and Peter Temin. 2007. "Inequality and Institutions in the 20th Century America." MIT, Industrial Performance Center Working Paper 07-002, June 27. Available at https://ipc.mit.edu/sites/default/files/documents/07-002.pdf.

Lindbeck, Assar. 1994. "Welfare State Disincentives with Endogenous Habits and Norms." University of Stockholm, Institute for International Economic Studies Seminar Paper, no. 589. Available at http://www.diva-portal.org/smash/get/diva2:342937/FULLTEXT01.pdf.

Lindert, Peter H. 2014. "Private Welfare and the Welfare State." In *The Cambridge History of Capitalism,* vol. 2: *The Spread of Capitalism: From 1848 to the Present,* edited by Larry Neal and Jeffrey G. Williamson, 464–500. Cambridge: Cambridge University Press.

Lindert, Peter H., and Jeffrey G. Williamson. 1982. "Revising England's Social Tables, 1688–1812." *Explorations in Economic History* 19: 385–408.

Lindert, Peter H., and Jeffrey G. Williamson. 1983. "Reinterpreting Britain's Social Tables, 1688–1913." *Explorations in Economic History* 20: 94–109.

Lindert, Peter H., and Jeffrey G. Williamson. 1985. "Essays in Exploration: Growth, Equality, and History." *Explorations in Economic History* 22: 341–377.

Lindert, Peter H., and Jeffrey G. Williamson. 2012. "American Incomes 1774–1860." National Bureau of Economic Research Working Paper, no. 18396, September. Available at http://www.nber.org/papers /w18396.

Lindert, Peter H., and Jeffrey G. Williamson. 2016. *Unequal Gains: American Growth and Inequality since 1700*. Princeton: Princeton University Press.

Lydall, Harold. 1968. *The Structure of Earnings*. Oxford: Clarendon Press.

Ma, Debin. 2011. "Rock, Scissors, Paper: The Problem of Incentives and Information in Traditional Chinese State and the Origin of Great Divergence." London School of Economics, Economic History Working Papers No. 152/11, July. Available at http://eprints.lse.ac.uk /37569/1/Rock%2C_Scissors%2C_Paper_the_Problemof_Incentives _and_Information_in_Traditional_Chinese_State_and_the_Origin _of_Great_Divergence%28lsero%29.pdf.

Machiavelli, Niccolò. 1970. *The Discourses [on Livy]*. Translated by Leslie J. Walker and Brian Richardson. Edited by Bernard Crick. Harmondsworth: Penguin Books.

Maddison, Angus. 2007. *Contours of the World Economy, 1–2030 AD: Essays in Macro-Economic History*. Oxford: Oxford University Press.

Maddison, Angus. 2008. "World Population, GDP and Per Capita GDP, 1–2008 AD." Available at http://www.ggdc.net/MADDISON/oriindex .htm.

Maddison Project. 2013. Available at http://www.ggdc.net/maddison /maddison-project/home.htm.

Mankiw, N. Gregory. 2015. "Yes, r > g. So What?" *American Economic Review* 105(5): 43–47.

Marshall, Alfred. 1961. *Principles of Economics,* 9th (variorum) ed., with annotations by C. W. Guillebaud. London and New York: Macmillan, for the Royal Economic Society.

Marx, Karl. (1894) 1991. *Capital: A Critique of Political Economy,* vol. 3. Penguin Classics.

Marx, Karl. 1965. *Pre-capitalist Economic Formations.* Translated by Jack Cohen. Edited and with an introduction by E. J. Hobsbawm. New York: International Publishers. Originally published as *Grundrisse der Kritik der politischen Ökonomie (Rohentwurf).* Moscow: Verlag für Fremdsprachige Literatur, 1939.

Marx, Karl. 1973. *Grundrisse: Foundations of the Critique of Political Economy.* Translated and with an introduction by Martin Nicolaus. London: Penguin Classics.

McGuire, Martin C., and Mancur Olson. 1996. "The Economics of Autocracy and Majority Rule: The Invisible Hand and the Use of Force." *Journal of Economic Literature* 34(1): 72–96.

Meadows, Donella H., Dennis L. Meadows, Jørgen Randers, and William W. Behrens III. 1972. *The Limits to Growth: A Report for the Club of Rome's Project on the Predicament of Mankind.* New York: Universe Books.

Mendershausen, Horst. 1946. *Changes in Income Distribution during the Great Depression.* Studies in Income and Wealth, vol. 7. New York: National Bureau of Economic Research.

Mesarovic, Mihailo, and Eduard Pestel. 1974. *Mankind at the Turning Point: The Second Report to the Club of Rome.* New York: Dutton.

Milanovic, Branko. 1994. "The Gini-type Functions: An Alternative Derivation." *Bulletin of Economic Research* 46(1): 81–90.

Milanovic, Branko. 1998. *Income, Inequality, and Poverty during the Transition from Planned to Market Economy.* Washington, DC: World Bank.

Milanovic, Branko. 2000. "The Median Voter Hypothesis, Income Inequality and Income Redistribution: An Empirical Test with the Required Data." *European Journal of Political Economy* 16(3): 367–410.

Milanovic, Branko. 2002a. "True World Income Distribution, 1988 and 1993: First Calculations Based on Household Surveys Alone." *Economic Journal* 112(476): 51–92.

Milanovic, Branko. 2002b. "The Two Faces of Globalization: Against Globalization as We Know It." *World Development* 31(4): 667–683.

Milanovic, Branko. 2005. "Globalization and Goals: Does Soccer Show the Way?" *Review of International Political Economy* 12(5): 829–850.

Milanovic, Branko. 2010a. "Four Critiques of the Redistribution Hypothesis: An Assessment." *European Journal of Political Economy* 26(1): 147–154.

Milanovic, Branko. 2010b. "Income Level and Income Inequality in the Euro-Mediterranean Region: From the Principate to the Islamic Conquest." Unpublished ms. Available at https://www.gc.cuny.edu/CUNY_GC/media/CUNY-Graduate-Center/PDF/Centers/LIS/Milanovic/papers/2010/Euro_mediterranean4.pdf.

Milanovic, Branko. 2011a. *The Haves and the Have-nots: A Short and Idiosyncratic History of Global Inequality.* New York: Basic Books.

Milanovic, Branko. 2011b. "A Short History of Global Inequality: The Past Two Centuries." *Explorations in Economic History* 48: 494–506.

Milanovic, Branko. 2012a. "Evolution of Global Inequality: From Class to Location, from Proletarians to Migrants." *Global Policy* 3(2): 124–133.

Milanovic, Branko. 2012b. "Global Inequality Recalculated and Updated: The Effect of New PPP Estimates on Global Inequality and 2005 Estimates." *Journal of Economic Inequality* 10(1): 1–18.

Milanovic, Branko. 2015. "Global Inequality of Opportunity: How Much of Our Income Is Determined by Where We Live." *Review of Economics and Statistics* 97(2): 452–460.

Milanovic, Branko, Peter H. Lindert, and Jeffrey G. Williamson. 2007. "Measuring Ancient Inequality." National Bureau of Economic Research Working Paper, no. 13550, October. Available at http://www.nber.org/papers/w13550.

Milanovic, Branko, Peter H. Lindert, and Jeffrey G. Williamson. 2011. "Pre-Industrial Inequality." *Economic Journal* 121(551): 255–272.

Miller, David. 2005. "Against Global Egalitarianism." *Journal of Ethics* 9: 55–79.

Minami, Ryoshin. 1998. "Economic Development and Income Distribution in Japan: An Assessment of the Kuznets Hypothesis." *Cambridge Journal of Economics* 22: 39–58.

Minami, Ryoshin. 2008. "Income Distribution in Japan: Historical Perspective and Its Implications." *Japan Labor Review* 5(4): 5–20.

Minter, William. 2011. "Africa Migrations, Global Inequalities and Human Rights: Connecting the Dots." Nordiska Afrikainstitutet, Uppsala, Current African Issues, no. 48.

Mistiaen, Johan, and Martin Ravallion. 2006. "Survey Nonresponse and the Distribution of Income." *Journal of Economic Inequality* 4: 33–55.

Moellendorf, Darrel. 2009. *Global Inequality Matters.* London: Palgrave Macmillan.

Myrdal, Gunnar. 1968. *Asian Drama: An Inquiry into the Poverty of Nations.* New York: Pantheon.

National Bureau of Statistics of China. 2014. *China Statistical Yearbook 2013.* Available at http://www.stats.gov.cn/tjsj/ndsj/2014/indexeh.htm.

OECD. 2008. *Growing Unequal? Income Distribution and Poverty in OECD Countries.* Paris: OECD. Available at http://dx.doi.org/10.1787/9789264044197-en.

OECD. 2011. *Divided We Stand. Why Inequality Keeps Rising.* Paris: OECD. Available at http://dx.doi.org/10.1787/9789264119536-en.

OECD. 2012. *Closing the Gender Gap: Act Now.* Paris: OECD. Available at http://dx.doi.org/10.1787/9789264179370-en.

OECD. 2013. International Migration Outlook 2013. Paris: OECD. Available at http://www.oecd-ilibrary.org/social-issues-migration-health/international-migration-outlook-2013_migr_outlook-2013-en.

OECD. 2015. *In It Together: Why Less Inequality Benefits All.* Paris: OECD, 2015. Available at http://dx.doi.org/10.1787/9789264235120-en.

Özden, Çağlar, Christopher R. Parsons, Maurice Schiff, and Terrie L. Walmsley. 2011. "Where on Earth Is Everybody? The Evolution of Global Bilateral Migration, 1960–2000." *World Bank Economic Review* 25(1): 12–56.

Page, Benjamin I., Larry M. Bartels, and Jason Seawright. 2013. "Democracy and the Policy Preferences of Wealthy Americans." *Perspectives on Politics* 11(1): 51–73.

Pamuk, Şevket. 2007. "The Black Death and the Origins of the 'Great Divergence' across Europe, 1300–1600." *European Review of Economic History* 11(3): 289–317.

Pareto, Vilfredo. 1966. *Vilfredo Pareto: Sociological Writings,* edited by S. E. Finer. New York: Praeger.

Piketty, Thomas. 2001a. *Les Hauts revenus en France au 20ᵉ siècle: inégalités et redistribution, 1901–1998.* Paris: B. Grasset.

Piketty, Thomas. 2001b. "Income Inequality in France 1901–98." Centre for Economic Policy Research Discussion Paper, no. 2876, July. Available at http://piketty.pse.ens.fr/fichiers/public/Piketty2001a.pdf.

Piketty, Thomas. 2003. "Income Inequality in France, 1901–1998." *Journal of Political Economy* 111(5): 1004–1042.

Piketty, Thomas. 2014. *Capital in the Twenty-First Century.* Translated by Arthur Goldhammer. Cambridge, MA: Harvard University Press.

Piketty, Thomas, and Emmanuel Saez. 2003. "Income Inequality in the United States, 1913–1998." *Quarterly Journal of Economics* 118(1): 1–39.

Pogge, Thomas. 1994. "An Egalitarian Law of Peoples." *Philosophy and Public Affairs* 23: 193–224.

Polak, Ben, and Jeffrey G. Williamson. 1993. "Poverty, Policy, and Industrialization in the Past." In *Including the Poor,* edited by Michael Lipton and Jacques van der Gaag. Washington, DC: World Bank.

Posner, Eric, and Glen Weyl. 2014. "A Radical Solution to Global Income Inequality: Make the US More Like Qatar." *New Republic,* November 6. Available at http://www.newrepublic.com/article/120179/how-reduce -global-income-inequality-open-immigration-policies.

Prados de la Escosura, Leandro. 2007. "Inequality, Poverty and the Kuznets Curve in Spain: 1850–2000," Working Papers in Economic History, Universidad Carlos III, WP 07-13.

Prados de la Escosura, Leandro. 2008. "Inequality, Poverty and the Kuznets Curve in Spain, 1850–2000." *European Review of Economic History* 12: 287–324.

Pritchett, Lant. 2006. *Let Their People Come: Breaking the Gridlock on International Labor Mobility.* Washington, DC: Center for Global Development. Available at http://www.cgdev.org/sites/default/files /9781933286105-Pritchett-let-their-people-come.pdf.

Prokopovitch, Sergey N. 1926. "The Distribution of National Income." *Economic Journal* 36: 69–82.

Quah, Danny. 2011. "The Global Economy's Shifting Centre of Gravity." *Global Policy* 2(1): 3–9.

Radner, Daniel B., and John C. Hinrichs. 1974. "Size Distribution of Income in 1964, 1970, and 1971." *Survey of Current Business* 54(10): 19–30.

Rawls, John. 1971. *A Theory of Justice.* Cambridge, MA: Belknap Press of Harvard University Press.

Rawls, John. 1999. *The Law of Peoples*. Cambridge, MA: Harvard University Press.

Redor, Dominique. 1992. *Wage Inequalities in East and West*. Cambridge: Cambridge University Press.

Reshef, Ariell. 2013. "Is Technological Change Biased Towards the Unskilled in Services? An Empirical Investigation." *Review of Economic Dynamics* 16: 312–331.

Rodríguez Weber, Javier E. 2014. "La economic politica de la desigualdad en Chile, 1850–2009." Ph.D. diss., Universidad de la República, Montevideo.

Roemer, John. 2000. *Equality of Opportunity*. Cambridge, MA: Harvard University Press.

Rosen, Sherwin. 1981. "The Economics of Superstars." *American Economic Review* 71(5): 845–858.

Rosenzweig, Mark R. 2010. "Global Wage Inequality and the International Flow of Migrants." Yale University, Economic Growth Center Discussion Paper, no. 983, January. Available at http://www.econ.yale.edu /growth_pdf/cdp983.pdf.

Ryckbosch, Wouter. 2014. "Economic Inequality and Growth before the Industrial Revolution: A Case Study of the Low Countries (14th–19th century)." Dondena Working Paper No. 67, Bocconi University, Milan, November. Available at ftp://ftp.dondena.unibocconi.it/WorkingPapers /Dondena WP067.pdf.

Sahota, Gian S. 1977. "Personal Income Distribution Theories of the Mid-1970s." *Kyklos* 30: 724–740.

Sakharov, Andrei. 1968. *Progress, Coexistence and Intellectual Freedom*. New York: W. W. Norton.

Sauvy, Alfred. 1976. *Zero Growth?* New York: Praeger.

Say, Jean-Baptiste. (1821) 1971. *A Treatise on Political Economy or the Production, Consumption and Distribution of Wealth*. New York: Augustus M. Kelly, 1971. (Orig. French ed. pub. 1804.)

Scheidel, Walter, and Steven J. Friesen. 2009. "The Size of the Economy and the Distribution of Income in the Roman Empire." *Journal of Roman Studies* 99: 61–91.

Schiavone, Aldo. 2002. *The End of the Past: Ancient Rome and the Modern West*. Translated by Margaret J. Schneider. Cambridge, MA: Harvard University Press. (Orig. Italian ed. pub. 1996.)

Shachar, Ayelet. 2009. *The Birthright Lottery: Citizenship and Global Inequality.* Cambridge, MA: Harvard University Press.

Singer, Peter. 2004. *One World: The Ethics of Globalization.* New Haven, CT: Yale University Press.

Slaughter, Matthew J. 1999. "Globalisation and Wages: A Tale of Two Perspectives." *World Economy* 22(5): 609–629.

Slaughter, Matthew J., and Phillip Swagel. 1997. "The Effect of Globalization on Wages in the Advanced Economies." International Monetary Fund Staff Studies for the World Economic Outlook, December.

Smolensky, Eugene, and Robert Plotnick. 1992. "Inequality and Poverty in the United States: 1900 to 1990." University of Wisconsin–Madison, Institute for Research on Poverty, Discussion Paper no. 998-93. Available at http://www.irp.wisc.edu/publications/dps/pdfs/dp99893 .pdf.

Soltow, Lee, and Jan Luiten van Zanden. 1998. *Income and Wealth Inequality in the Netherlands 16th–20th Century.* Amsterdam: Het Spinhuis.

Sumarto, Sudarno, Asep Suryahadi, and Lant Pritchett. 2003. "Safety Nets or Safety Ropes? Dynamic Benefit Incidence of Two Crisis Programs in Indonesia." *World Development* 31(7): 1257–1277.

Tachibanaki, Toshiyaki, and Tadashi Yagi. 1997. "Distribution of Economic Well-Being in Japan: Towards a More Unequal Society." In *Changing Patterns in the Distribution of Economic Welfare: An International Perspective,* edited by Peter Gottschalk, Björn Gustaffson, and Edward Palmer, 108–131. Cambridge: Cambridge University Press.

Taleb, Nassim N. 2007. *The Black Swan: The Impact of the Highly Improbable.* New York: Random House.

Tan, Kok-Chor. 2006. "The Boundary of Justice and the Justice of Boundaries: Defending Global Egalitarianism." *Canadian Journal of Law and Jurisprudence* 19(2): 319–344.

Tinbergen, Jan. 1961. "Do Communist and Free Economies Show a Converging Pattern?" *Soviet Studies* 12(4): 333–341.

Tinbergen, Jan. 1975. *Income Distribution: Analysis and Policies.* Amsterdam: North Holland.

Todd, Emmanuel. 1998. *L'Illusion économique: Essai sur la stagnation des sociétés developpées.* Paris: Gallimard.

Turchin, Peter, and Sergey Nefedov. 2009. *Secular Cycles.* Princeton: Princeton University Press.

UBS. 2009. *Prices and Earnings: A Comparison of Purchasing Power around the Globe.* Zurich: UBS AG.

van der Weide, Roy, and Branko Milanovic. 2014. "Inequality Is Bad for the Growth of the Poor (But Not for That of the Rich)." World Bank Working Paper, no. 6963, July. Available at http://elibrary.worldbank.org/doi/pdf/10.1596/1813-9450-6963.

van Zanden, Jan Luiten. 1995. "Tracing the Beginning of the Kuznets Curve: Western Europe during the Early Modern Period." *Economic History Review* 48(4): 1–23.

van Zanden, Jan Luiten, Joerg Baten, Peter Foldvari, and Bas van Leeuwen. 2014. "The Changing Shape of Global Inequality, 1820–2000." *Review of Income and Wealth* 60(2): 279–297.

Varoufakis, Yanis. 2014. "Egalitarianism's Latest Foe: A Critical Review of Thomas Piketty's *Capital in the 21st Century.*" *Real-World Economics Review* 69: 18–35.

Večernik, Jiři. 1994. "Changing Earnings Inequality under the Economic Transformation. The Czech and Slovak Republics in 1984–92." Unpublished ms. Institute of Sociology, Prague.

Vries, Peer. 2013. *Escaping Poverty: The Origins of Modern Economic Growth.* Gottingen: Vandenhoeck and Ruprecht.

Ward-Perkins, Bryan. 2005. *The Fall of Rome and the End of Civilization.* Oxford: Oxford University Press.

Wesseling, H. L. 1996. *Divide and Rule: The Partition of Africa, 1880–1914.* Translated by Arnold J. Pomerans. Westport, CT: Praeger.

Wieland, Volker, and Maik Wolters. 2012. "Macroeconomic Model Comparisons and Forecast Competition." EU Vox, February 13. Available at http://www.voxeu.org/article/failed-forecasts-and-financial-crisis-how-resurrect-economic-modelling.

Williamson, Jeffrey G. 2011. *Trade and Poverty.* Cambridge, MA: MIT Press.

Williamson, Jeffrey G., and Peter H. Lindert. 1980. *American Inequality: A Macroeconomic History.* Institute for Research on Poverty monograph series. New York: Academic Press.

Wolf, Martin. 2004. *Why Globalization Works.* New Haven, CT: Yale University Press.

Wolff, Edward. 2010. "Recent Trends in Household Wealth in the United States: Rising Debt and the Middle-Class Squeeze—an Update to 2007." Levy Economics Institute of Bard College, Working Paper no. 589, March. Available at http://www.levyinstitute.org/publications /recent-trends-in-household-wealth-in-the-united-states-rising-debt -and-the-middle-class-squeezean-update-to-2007.

World Bank. 2006. *Global Economic Prospects: Economic Implications of Migration and Remittances.* Washington, DC: World Bank. Available at https://openknowledge.worldbank.org/bitstream/handle/10986/7306 /343200GEP02006.pdf?sequence=1.

Xu, Chenggang. 2015. "China's Political-Economic Institutions and Development." *Cato Journal* 35(3): 525–545.

Zhang, Wenjie. 2014. "Has China Crossed the Threshold of the Kuznets Curve? New Measures from 1987 to 2012 Show Declining Pay In-equality in China after 2008." University of Texas Inequality Project, Working Paper no. 67, April 21. Available at http://utip.gov.utexas.edu /papers/UTIP_67.pdf.

Zucman, Gabriel. 2013. "The Missing Wealth of Nations: Are Europe and the U.S. Net Debtors or Net Creditors?" *Quarterly Journal of Economics* 128(3): 1321–1364.

Zucman, Gabriel. 2015. *The Hidden Wealth of Nations: The Scourge of Tax Havens.* Chicago: University of Chicago Press.

Index

billionaires (*continued*)
and, 244n24. *See also* plutocracy; rich people and money (including one-percenters); wealth
Bolt, Jutta, 247n13
Bourguignon, François, 119, 121, 253n2
Bowles, Samuel, 197
Brandolini, Andrea, 249n28
Brown, Lester, 156
Bukharin, Nikolai, 130

Canbakal, Hülya, 63–64
Caney, Simon, 141
Cannan, Edwin, 141–142
capital: inequality within countries and, 7, 183, 190; 1980s and, 54–55; mobility of, 55, 113–114, 138–139, 218, 246n11; world wars and, 64, 87, 94, 98; rate of return to, 69, 70; income from, 74, 107, 179, 181, 186–187, 190, 216–217, 259nn18,19; technological change and, 75; labor substitution by, 93, 109–110, 181–182; nationalization of, 99; socialism and, 101, 260n23; globalization and, 106, 138–139, 165, 204; power versus labor, 106, 182; right of movement and, 147; one-percenters and, 183–184, 260n19; education and, 186–187, 216, 221–222. *See also* property; rents; rich people and money
capitalism: twentieth-century Kuznets curve and, 47–50; world wars and, 48, 95, 125, 156–157, 251n41; wages and, 51, 186; globalization and, 55; preindustrial period and, 69; nineteenth century, 95–96; skill-biased technological change and, 116; socialism conver-

gence with, 156–157; China and, 178, 192; financial assets and, 184; rich people's labor income and, 184–185; "new," 186–188, 193, 214, 216; global, 192; Russia and, 192; Islam and, 192–193; democracy and, 193–194; welfare state and, 207; United States and, 214; political power and, 218; education and, 221; existential inequality and, 229; Piketty on, 245n4; Asia and, 250n38; crises and, 251n39. *See also* capital; colonialism; labor
Cardoso, Fernando Henrique, 81
Carr, E. H., 255n14
catastrophic events, 21, 56, 57, 62–65, 69, 98. *See also* epidemics; wars
Chancel, Lucas, 263n9
Chau, Nancy H., 106
Chaudhuri, Nirad, 6
Chi, Wei, 179
citizenship: equality of opportunity and, 139–143; migration and, 147, 210; discrimination and, 150–152, 154; rights, 151–152; France and, 205; globalization and, 210, 231; methodological nationalism and, 237–238
citizenship premium (location- versus class-based inequality), 5, 125–137, 143, 254n10. *See also* migration
Clark, Gregory, 249n26
classical explanation, 74, 80
Clemens, Michael, 237–238
Coase theorem, 137–139
Cold War, 94
colonialism, 95–96, 129–130, 250n38, 254nn11,13, 254nn11–13. *See also* imperialism; *individual colonial powers*
Commercial Revolution, 65, 69

communism: end of, 3, 6, 123; Piketty on, 94; capital and, 99; mistaken predictions and, 157, 159; Chinese, 179, 180; globalization and, 214

consumption: data sources, 12–13, 16; discrepancies in data and, 16; rich countries and, 39, 197; labor demand and, 64; "mal-distribution of consuming power" and, 96; middle class and, 195, 197; climate change and, 233; as metric, 244n21; Marx on, 251n39. See also scalable jobs

convergence. See economic convergence; income convergence, global

cosmopolitanism, 141

currencies, 14–15, 236, 239, 244n24, 263n9, 263n11

decolonization, 100

deglobalization, 192

democracy, 7, 164, 189–90, 193–194, 199–203, 210, 255n18. See also global governance

Democratic Republic of Congo, 173

demographic forces, 248n23. See also age and aging; marriages; migration; populations, global and national

de Soto, Hernando, 221

dictatorships, 99

discoveries, 69

distribution. See Coase theorem; welfare regimes

domain exclusion, 150

economic convergence, 5, 48, 132, 161–191, 212–213. See also income convergence, global

economic forces: preindustrial period and, 69; Kuznets cycles and, 72–73; political forces and, 73–74, 86–87;

Chile (1850–1970) and, 84–85; twentieth-century leveling and, 93–94; Kuznets on, 98; social frameworks and, 99, 102; 1950–1980, 102. See also capital; Industrial Revolution and industrialization; labor; skill-biased technological progress

economicism, naïve, 73

economic power, 102

economics, discipline of, 234–239

economies, main features of, 246n12

economies of scale, 13

education: twenty-first and twenty-second centuries and, 7, 181; skill-biased technological progress and, 47; twentieth century and, 53, 93–94; preindustrial period and, 70; Brazil and, 82; Chile and, 84; communist countries and, 99; Kuznets cycles and, 99, 117; socialist great leveling and, 100, 102; war and, 102; union density and, 106; race with skills and, 114; United States, 114, 188, 189, 260n24; migrant taxes and, 152; China and, 178; United States and, 181, 263n4; capital/labor income and, 186–187, 216; globalization and, 207–208, 215–217; equalizing, 218, 219–222; capital income and, 221–222; wages and, 256n21, 263n3; assortative mating and, 260n26; families and, 263n4. See also benign/malign forces; social services

effort, work, 140

Ehrlich, Paul, 21

1820–2011, 119–125, 127–132. See also Industrial Revolution; preindustrial period; twentieth century

elephant curve, 242n8

Elsby, Michael W. L., 182

income (*continued*)
249n32, 249nn28,32, 255n16, 258n8;
median, 19, 36, 242n4; caps, 24–25;
disposable, 25–26, 38–39, 107–109,
197, 219–221; market (pre-tax and
pre-transfer) (pre-fisc), 38–39,
107–109, 218, 219–221; global GDP,
44, 244n26; subsistence, 50–53,
69–70; stagnant mean, 55, 58, 59–65,
59–70, 70; rising mean, 70–91, 91–92;
maximization principle of, 147,
148–149; existential equality versus,
226–230; GNP and, 237; as metric,
244n1; premium, 255n16; voting
participation and, 262n34. *See
also* capital, income from; high
globalization period *and other
periods;* income convergence
(global); inequality among countries;
"inequality possibility frontier";
inequality within countries; Kuznets
cycles (waves); *specific countries*
income convergence: Indonesia and,
162, 167–168, 169, 213
income convergence, global: China
and, 33–36, 115, 162, 167, 176–191,
243n13; middle class, global, and,
115; within nation inequality and,
115, 175; middle classes, national,
compared, 123; globalization and,
161–162; twenty-first and twenty-
second centuries and, 161–191;
Kuznets cycles and, 162–163;
benign/malign forces and, 163–164;
ideology and, 164; high globalization period and, 165; poor/rich
countries (1950–2013) and, 165–169;
Asia and, 169–176, 174–175; gender
and, 228–229. *See also* economic
convergence; inequality among
countries (global inequality)

Industrial Revolution and industrialization: inequality among countries and, 2, 119, 130; England
and, 3; Kuznets cycles and, 4,
72–73, 247n14; maximum feasible
inequality and, 51–53; benign/
malign influences and, 55–57;
Kuznets curves and, 65, 248n25;
latecomers to, 65; labor transfers
and, 70; consuming power versus,
96; preindustrial plague and,
248n18; defined, 251n45. *See also*
nineteenth century; technological
change
industrial sector wages, 178, 259n17
inequality among countries (global
inequality), 1–9. *See also* 1820–2011
and other periods; globalization;
income; inequality within countries;
Kuznets cycles (waves)
inequality of opportunity, 137,
139–143, 203
"inequality possibility frontier,"
51–53, 69–70
inequality within countries:
inequality among countries and,
2–5, 45, 125–132, 238; Kuznets
hypothesis and, 4, 46–50, 250n36;
future of, 5; capital and, 7, 183, 190;
reducing, 7; Kuznets cycles and,
50–59, 91–117, 162–163; stagnant
mean income and, 59–70; rising
mean income and, 70–91; peak of,
71, 75, 248n22; World War I and,
93–97, 94–95; nineteenth century,
119–120; 2015–2035, 175; capital
ownership and, 183; horizontal,
226–230; studies of, 253n3. *See also*
methodological nationalism; rich
people and money (including
one-percenters)

inflation, 43, 64, 218
infrastructure spending, 181
inheritance, 186–187, 219, 221,
    250n36
institutions, 64, 73
intergenerational transfers, 141
international development policies,
    99
international dollars, 15
International Labor Day, 86
International Migration Outlook
    (2013) (OECD), 262n41
intersectoral inequality, 259n17
"invisible hand," 142
Iraq, 158, 163, 164
Islam, 192–193, 261n31
Islam, fundamentalist, 164, 203
Israel, 144–146, 158, 256n24

Jayadev, Arjun, 197
justice, 131, 137, 139–140, 141, 143

Kanbur, Ravi, 106
Karabarbounis, Loukas, 181
Katz, Lawrence, 47, 94, 252n49
Kearney, Melissa S., 252n49
Keynes, John Maynard, 95
King, Gregory, 248n19
Kraus, Michael W., 203
Krugman, Paul, 252n49
Kuznets, Simon: on Great Leveling,
    53, 246n7; on wars, 97, 98; on
    income gap reductions, 148; role
    of, 245n1; Gini points and, 250n34;
    on liberal profession incomes,
    263n5
Kuznets curves: technological changes
    (1980s) and, 54; super, 69; litera-
    ture on, 245n1; Prokopovitch and,
    245n1; Industrial Revolution and,
    248n25. See also Great Leveling

Kuznets cycles (waves): Brazil and
    Chile and, 4, 81–85, 249n30; 1980
    and after, 4, 72, 93; twenty-first and
    twenty-second centuries and, 6,
    161–164, 161–191; preindustrial
    period and, 50–51, 58, 76, 98; defined,
    50–59; inequality within countries
    and, 50–59, 91–117, 162–163; over-
    views, 50–59, 86–91; preindustrial
    through future, 57–62, 69; stagnant
    mean income and, 59–66, 69–70,
    249n31; England (Great Britain)
    and, 70, 74–76; rising mean income
    and, 70–86; rich countries and,
    71–76, 87, 113–117; United States
    and, 71–76, 87, 89, 90–91, 93, 113,
    162–163; globalization and, 72–73,
    214; United Kingdom and, 74–76,
    86, 87, 89, 91, 111, 248n25; Italy
    and, 76–78, 87, 89, 91; Spain and,
    76–77, 86, 87, 89, 91; Germany and
    the Netherlands and, 78–81, 87, 89,
    90, 91; second wave, downswing
    of, 84, 93, 113–114, 217, 222; Japan
    (1895–2011) and, 85–86, 91; first
    wave, downswing of, 87–88, 89,
    90, 91–103; second wave, upswing
    of, 87, 91, 93, 103–112; rising mean
    income and, 91–92; technological
    change and, 111; peaks of, 116–117;
    China and, 162–163, 176–180;
    income convergence and, 162–163.
    See also benign/malign forces;
    Great Leveling; S curves, reclining
Kuznets hypothesis: inequality within
    countries and, 4, 46–50, 250n36;
    1980 and after, 4, 71–72, 92–93;
    statement of, 4; United States and,
    4, 70, 72; redefinition of, 9; pre-
    industrial period and, 59–61, 70–73;
    Industrial Revolution and, 65;

173; China and, 178–180; globalization and, 217; European Union and, 262n38. *See also* communism; democracy; politics; socialism

political power, 102, 103, 179, 180, 181, 218. *See also* plutocracy; politics

political voluntarism, 74, 248n24

politics: trade and, 1; rich people and, 7, 87, 113, 114, 189–190, 194, 199; inequality within countries and, 45; Kuznets cycles and, 73; second Kuznets wave upswing and, 113; location-based inequality and, 125; income gap reductions and, 148; money and (United States), 163, 189–190, 199, 262n37; twenty-first and twenty-second centuries and, 163, 164; meritocracy and, 188–189; welfare-state protection and, 207; globalization and, 214, 217; wages and, 215–216; existential inequality and, 228, 229; US Republican versus Democratic senators' responsiveness, 262n37; European population and, 262n38. *See also* median voter hypothesis; political forces

poorer countries: twenty-first and twenty-second centuries and, 7, 232–234; consumption and, 12; annuals surveys and, 14; price levels and, 14–15; standard of living and, 15; Western incomes and, 21; absolute measures and, 27, 28; stagnant mean income and, 57; location-based inequality and, 127; just distribution and, 139–140; migration and, 147–148, 149, 151; economic convergence and, 162; Kuznets cycles and, 162; globalization and, 165; transfers and, 255n19; education and, 256n21;

work hours per person per year and, 256n21; technological change and, 258n7. *See also* income convergence; inequality among countries; inequality within countries; subsistence level

poorer people: omission from data and, 16; underestimation of, 16; high globalization period and, 20; absolute measures and, 28–29; poverty lines, 43; preindustrial period and, 50; technological progress and, 55; migration and, 152; equity and, 184; politics and, 189–190, 194; democracy and, 194, 200; false consciousness and, 201–202; social mobility and, 202; US student achievement and, 260n24. *See also* mobility, upward

population, global, 50–51, 63–64, 95. *See also* migration

populations, national, 21, 51, 55, 94, 248n23, 262n38. *See also* epidemics; Malthusian considerations

populism, 7, 204–211, 233. *See also* global governance

Posner, Eric, 152

PPP (purchasing power parity) exchange rates, 15–16, 17, 18, 33–34, 121, 244n24

Prados de la Escosura, Leandro, 59, 62, 63, 81

predictions, 5–6, 21, 28, 155–161, 257n1. *See also* twenty-first and twenty-second centuries

preindustrial period: Piketty and, 48–49; Kuznets cycles and, 50–51, 58, 76, 98; rich countries and, 53; benign/malign forces and, 55–57; catastrophic events and, 56, 57, 62–65, 69, 98; borderline of, 58;

preindustrial period (*continued*)
Kuznets hypothesis and, 59–61,
70–73; Spain (1326–1842), 60;
plague and, 62–64, 247n16, 247n18;
Italy and Low Countries, 62–63, 65,
247n16; inequality increases and,
65–66, 69–70; output per capita
and, 247n15

pre-transfer and pre-tax income. *See*
market income

price levels, 14–15, 17, 173, 242n11,
244n24. *See also* PPP (purchasing
power parity) exchange rates

Pritchett, Lant, 148, 149, 153, 237–238,
262n42

private sector, 259n17

privatization, rule of law and,
137–138

production, 112, 116, 181–182,
251n39

productivity: technological progress
and, 55; socialist great leveling and,
101; low-skill-biased technological
progress and, 115–116; scalable
jobs and, 223–226, 263nn5,7;
preindustrial, 247n15; US service
sector and, 253n52

Prokopovitch, Sergey N., 245n1

property: income from, 48, 64, 100;
socialist great leveling and, 101;
Kuznets cycles and, 111; rights to,
111, 138–139; broader ownership
of, 221. *See also* labor/land ratios

prostitution, 228–229

Proust, Marcel, 6

Prussia and Saxony, 245n1

purchasing power parity (PPP)
exchange rates, 15, 17, 18

race, 228

Rawls, John, 139–140, 141, 142, 230,
255n18

Reagan-Thatcher revolution, 20, 54,
87, 159

redistribution, government, 107, 114,
222. *See also* taxes; welfare regimes

reducing inequality, 7, 103

rents, 65–66, 69, 77, 103, 106, 114–115,
124, 140, 246n12

Reshef, Ariell, 252n50

Ricardo, David, 64, 239

rich countries (advanced economies):
middle classes and, 7, 132; annual
surveys and, 14; standard of living
and, 15; high globalization period
and, 19–20, 21; lower middle classes
and, 20; numbers of rich people and,
22; absolute measures and, 27, 28;
2008–2011, 31, 36; financial crisis
and, 32; one-percenters from, 37; net
wealth and, 39, 244n19; Kuznets
hypothesis and, 46–47; Piketty on,
48; wars and, 53; 1980s and, 54–55;
disease and, 57; 1995–2015, 78;
Kuznets cycles and, 87, 113–117,
162; union density, 104–106; Asian
middle classes compared, 123;
migration and, 150–151; 1980, 2000,
165; labor substitution by capital and,
181–182; globalization/middle class
and, 214–217; horizontal, 226–230;
globalized labor and, 230–231; future
of, 232–234; ecological balance and,
234; one-percenters, 242n10; social
forces and, 248n23; work hours per
person per year and, 255n20. *See
also* income convergence, global; inequality among countries; inequality
within countries; rich people and
money; wealth; welfare regimes

rich people and money (including one-
percenters): political regimes and,
7; 1988–2008, 10–11, 22, 23, 24, 26,
36–41; nonparticipation in surveys

and, 16; underestimation of, 16; high globalization period and, 21–22; absolute measures and, 28–29; 2008–2011, 36–41; national populations share of, 37–39; global income/wealth, share of (2000, 2010), 37–41; market versus disposable income and, 38–39; underestimation of incomes of, 40, 122–123, 243n18; global middle class shares versus, 40–41; war and, 64; economic forces and, 87; world wars and, 94, 97; nationalization and, 100–101; policy and, 103, 194, 261n28; US counties of, 115; inequality among countries and, 123; location-based inequality and, 125, 127; capital ownership and, 183–184, 260n19; labor income and, 184, 260n22; labor income (1979 and after), 184–188, 216, 260n22; marriages and, 188–189; democracy and, 194, 200–203; consumption and, 197; social services and, 197, 199, 261n30; US top 5 percent, 197; Western democracies, selected (1980–2010), 197; globalization and, 215; growth and, 232; climate change and, 233; rich countries and, 242n10; household surveys and, 243n15; WENAO countries and, 243n16; World War II and, 249n32; Soviet Union and, 250n33; US student achievement, 260n24; future growth rate and, 261n30; social services funding and, 261n30. *See also* billionaires; capital; capitalism; plutocracy; rich countries; rich people and money; wealth

Robinson, James, 102
robots, 181–182, 252n49
Rodríguez Weber, Javier, 82, 84, 249n31

Rosen, Sherwin, 263n5
Rosenzweig, Mark R., 256n21
rule of law, 137–139, 238
rural areas: Chinese, 19, 30–31, 35–36, 167, 176, 178, 241n3, 242n11; urban compared, 19, 57, 70, 93, 176, 241n3, 242n11; US immigrants and, 136. *See also* agriculture
Ryckbosch, Wouter, 65, 69

Sacz, Emmanuel, 184
Şahin, Ayşegül, 182
Sahota, Gian S., 245n2
Sakharov, Andrei, 157
Samuelson, Paul, 153
Sauvy, Alfred, 258n4
Say, Jean-Baptiste, 256n27
scalable jobs, 223–226, 263nn5,7
Scheidel, Walter, 67
Schiavone, Aldo, 111
Schumacher, Ernest F., 157
S curves, reclining, 23–24, 110, 118. *See also* Kuznets curves; Kuznets cycles (waves)
Seawright, Jason, 163
security services, 197, 261n33
Segal, Paul, 254n10
self-determination, 255n19
service sector, 54, 93, 103–105, 112, 215, 246n9, 252n49, 253n52
Shachar, Ayelet, 143, 256n23
Singer, Peter, 142
singular events, 159
skill-biased technological progress: education and, 47, 114, 256n21; wages and, 47, 54, 252n49, 256n21; 1980s and, 54; low skills and, 55, 115–116, 178, 253n52; marriages and, 109; globalization and, 109–112, 215; twenty-first and twenty-second centuries and, 163; China and, 178

wages (*continued*)
109, 181; skill-biased technological
progress and, 47, 252n49; the rich
and, 48, 115, 214, 216, 260n22;
capitalism and, 51, 186; 1980s and,
54; land rent and, 59–61; disease
and, 63; plague and, 64, 248n18;
wars and, 64; profit-wage ratios, 69;
rate of return to capital ratios, 69;
migration and, 74–75, 153; British
(nineteenth century), 75, 129–130,
249n26; twentieth-century leveling
and, 79; Brazil and, 82; Chile and,
82, 84; land/labor ratios and, 84;
nationalization and, 100; socialist
great leveling and, 101; upswings of
Kuznets cycles and, 103–104; ethical
pay norms, 109; globalization and,
109–110, 214, 215, 223–226, 252n49;
overdetermination of explanations,
109–110; global convergence of,
115; effort and, 140; undocumented
workers and, 153; twenty-first
and twenty-second centuries and,
163; industrial sector, 178, 259n17;
wealth and, 215; political dynasties
and, 215–216; existential inequality
and, 226–230; gender (OECD) and,
227, 263n8; technological change
and, 252n49; GDP ratios (nineteenth century), 253n3; education
and, 256n21, 263n3; intersectoral
inequality, 259n17; private sector
and, 259n17. *See also* capitalism; inequality of opportunity; labor; scalable jobs; skill-biased technological
progress; socialism
wars: causes/effects of, 4–5; data
access and, 14; forecasts and, 21;
rich countries (1918–1980) and, 48;
preindustrial period and, 50–51,
56, 62, 69; future and, 56; Piketty
on, 64, 97–98; Chile and, 84; Spain
and, 89; external investments and,
95; education and, 102; twenty-first
and twenty-second centuries and,
163–164; China/United States and,
163–164, 258n6; Africa and, 173;
modern era and, 246n5; taxes and,
250n35. *See also* World War I *and
other wars*
Washington Consensus, 157
wealth: income/consumption versus,
39, 40, 244n19; hidden, 40, 244n23;
2013 estimate of, 41; preindustrial
period and, 62–64, 65–66, 69; disease
and, 63; destruction of, 98; national
choices and, 139–142; capital income
and, 184; wages and, 215; inequality
interventions and, 218; US population share of, 244n19; negative
changes in rich peoples', 244n20;
as metric, 244n21; price levels and,
244n24; preindustrial plague and,
247n16; one-person households and,
248n23; pre-1929, 254n7; United
States and, 254n7; middle-class,
260n20; financial assets and,
260n21. *See also* billionaires; capital;
rich countries; rich people and
money (including one-percenters)
"wealth line," 43
welfare regimes: protectionism of, 20;
Great Leveling and, 53; 1980s and,
54–55; twentieth-century Britain
and, 75; Kuznets cycles and, 99; migrants and, 206–207; globalization
and, 207–208, 217–222; capitalism/
middle class and, 207; politics and,
208; twenty-first-century inequality
and, 217–222; benign/malign forces
and, 246n8. *See also* redistribution,

government; taxes; transfers, social
Weyl, Glen, 152
Wieland, Volker, 257n1
Williamson, Jeffrey G., 52, 71, 74, 254n7
Williamson ratio, 249n28
winner-take-all rule, 223–226
Wolf, Martin, 251n41
Wolff, Edward, 183–184
Wolters, Maik, 257n1
women, 112, 188–189. *See also* gender; marriages
World Bank data, 13, 123, 258n8

World Development Indicators, 258n8
World War I: causes/effects of, 48–50, 93–97, 130, 251nn41,43; capital/inflation and, 64; Great Leveling and, 97–99; lessons of, 102–103
World War II: US Gini points and, 71; Japan and, 85; capitalism and, 87, 125; Italy and, 89; one-percenters, 249n32
world wars: taxes and, 72; Britain and, 75; Piketty on, 94, 250n36

Zhang, Wenjie, 177–178, 259n17
Zucman, Gabriel, 237, 244nn22–23